SPIES LIKE US

Hugh Lunn's first memoir *Vietnam: A Reporter's War* was an *Age* Book of the Year and was subsequently published in New York. His next memoir *Over the Top with Jim* was the year's biggest selling Australian nonfiction book and has been serialised nationally on Macca's *Australia All Over* wireless show. Extra episodes for Macca were subsequently published as *More Over the Top with Jim Stories: The Fred & Olive's Blessed Lino Collection*. The popular *Head Over Heels* — sequel to *Over the Top with Jim* — followed.

Hugh Lunn was born in wartime Brisbane just months before Pearl Harbour and began his newspaper career on the *Courier-Mail* in 1960 before heading for Fleet Street via China and Russia. He worked on the London *Daily Mirror* and was a Reuters correspondent in Vietnam, Singapore and Indonesia. He has won five national awards for feature writing, including three Walkley Awards.

Spies Like Us

HUGH LUNN

University of Queensland Press

First published 1995 by University of Queensland Press
Box 42, St Lucia, Queensland 4067 Australia

Printed in Australia by McPherson's Printing Group, Victoria

ARTS QUEENSLAND

This work was assisted by a writers
fellowship from the Queensland Office of
Arts and Cultural Development.

Cataloguing in Publication Data
National Library of Australia

Lunn, Hugh, 1941–   .
  Spies like us.

  1. Lunn, Hugh, 1941–   . 2. Journalists — Biography.
  3. China — Social life and customs — 1949–   . 4. Soviet
  Union — Social life and customs — 1917–   . 5. Hong Kong —
  Social life and customs. I. Title.

070.92

ISBN 0 7022 2757 9

Contents

1 An Aussie Firecracker

For three weeks I'd been out walking the crowded streets of Hong Kong looking for my dream job as a foreign correspondent in the Orient. But, despite the large sky-blue scrapbook tucked under my arm, nothing.

Zilch.

It was reaching the stage where I was certain most of the four million Chinese in the British Colony recognised me as I lugged the awkward scrapbook, my stories pasted on its brown paper pages, up and down Nathan Road and across and back on the ferry from Kowloon to Hong Kong Island. I remembered how I laughed at my Russian classmate Jim Egoroff's difficulties with English when he arrived in Brisbane in 1950. Fourteen years later, October 1964, I couldn't pronounce even one local word right. Not even the suburb I was living in: "Tsim Sha Tsui".

I was a foreigner myself now.

In Australia I had never doubted that once in Hong Kong I'd get a job, perhaps even as a foreign correspondent. But my confidence in myself had evaporated. Not only couldn't I understand the Chinese language, but I could barely make sense of the English they spoke up here. English was taught at all the schools, but the Chinese had tremendous difficulty pronouncing the words: so that most of the time I couldn't understand what they were saying: even when they spoke English. And they seemed unable to understand me.

Hong Kong, I soon worked out, was a place where everybody spoke English but nobody understood it.

1

How could I work here when I couldn't interview most of the people? This weird city where even the smallest sign incongruously mixed English and Chinese: "Sow Mow Ping Central"; "Kai Tak Air Port"; "Kowloon Side". This Colony of neon signs which lit up like a Christmas tree every night: neon Chinese letters from the top of almost every building reflecting off the mile-wide harbour from both Hong Kong and Kowloon sides so that it was difficult to tell where the advertising reflections ended and reality began.

At least I had a free room. I was living for nothing in my mate Ken Fletcher's room in the Grand Hotel near the harbour on Kowloon Side. I had assumed my standard of living would fall once I reached the poor Far East, but instead it had jumped. Our hotel room had its own bath-room and lavatory inside, with maids to make our beds and Chinese boys to clean our shoes. The room didn't cost Ken anything either, because he was a good mate of the hotel owner's Chinese son, Victor Sun. They played tennis to-gether nearly every day.

I couldn't even tell the locals apart.

Shortly after our arrival in Hong Kong, Victor took us to the pictures to see a brand new James Bond spy film called *From Russia With Love*. He had to book the seats weeks before we arrived because the Chinese were so mad about James Bond: which I found strange. Why would the Chinese admire a British spy with a licence to kill any foreigner he wanted to?

The theatre was a fair way up Nathan Road in the Mong Kok area, so Victor drove us in the Sun family's large black American Chevrolet, and dropped us off while he went to find a park. The very fact that they owned a car showed the Sun family was rich. Hardly anyone, even the few British, owned cars in Hong Kong. It wasn't worth it because there was nowhere to drive. The whole Colony was less than twenty miles across and, of course, no one was allowed to drive through the Bamboo Curtain into Red China.

In Kowloon we were living on the Chinese mainland next door to 750 million Commos. No wonder my mother, Olive, wanted me to stay home, saying that, at 23, I was much too young to go overseas.

Being fresh out of White Australia, I saw Victor coming up Nathan Road several times before he finally arrived. But Victor didn't laugh at my natural mistake. He said he had the same problem himself when he first went to study engineering at Cornell University in America. "All of the Americans looked the same when I first arrived too," he said. He was right. I started to notice that the hordes of young American servicemen in Hong Kong all had crew-cut fairish hair, check bermuda shorts, small brown eyes, big watches, sunglasses, hairy legs, short sleeves, large cameras sticking out like a black paunch, a gold ring on one finger with a jewel in the middle.

My last interview for a job was with one of the bosses at the *South China Morning Post*, the English-language morning paper run by the British. I was desperate for work because, the way things were going, I'd be back home before Christmas. I couldn't just live in Ken's hotel room forever.

One of the good things about Hong Kong was that you could get shirts made to fit, something no one did in Australia. Plus they always sewed your initials discreetly onto the shirt pocket. For nothing. "HDL" my shirt said in black on the blue background as I examined myself in the Grand Hotel mirror. I had the initials sewn on the American way as the Chinese tailor, Harry, had suggested: using my middle initial "D" for Duncan, Olive's family name. It was moments like this when I wished I had a leather jacket, but I couldn't afford one yet. For some reason, the hotel mirror distorted my image so that I looked fat, whereas I was, in fact, too thin. Nothing seemed to work quite as well in Hong Kong as it did back home in Australia. But it was unfair to compare this poor Colony with Australia, which everyone knew had one of the two or three highest standards of living in the world.

I knew I was ready to roll when Fletch — lying back on his bed — said: "High Noon in Hong Kong," mimicking the local advertisement at the pictures for a brand of cigarettes: even though we didn't smoke. Ken was a snazzy dresser and was always at me to dress better. He bought his clothes in America when he was there with the Davis Cup team: classy lightweight dacron-and-cotton checked jackets in something called "Scotch pattern". You couldn't get them in Australia. But, even though he could afford it, Ken wouldn't buy a leather jacket because the smell reminded him of his schoolbag.

"Remember to lay it on thick," he said as I left the room, "but don't worry if you miss out. Something will bob up. I'll say three Hail Marys for you."

Above Carnarvon Road washing hung from bamboo clothes props sticking out from the sides of buildings, the only place the Chinese could dry their clothes since they didn't have backyards. Left into Nathan Road, past Chinese mothers in pyjama pants and tops with babies slung over their backs in hammocks. Around the world-famous Peninsula Hotel to the Star Ferry where huge jelly-bean-shaped double-decker green and white ferries connected the two halves of Hong Kong: Kowloon, where we lived among most of the shops and hotels, and the small Island to the south where most of the offices were.

There was no bridge: the only way across the clear green harbour was by boat.

When Hong Kong Island was founded as a British Colony in 1841 it was described by critics of the decision as "a barren rock". But the British man who claimed it, wrote in reply:

One day from this rock
a million lights shall glow;
And through this harbour 10,000 ships
Go marching to and fro.

4

I only knew this because, that morning, the *South China Morning Post* (which I had under my arm tucked inside my blue scrapbook) said so. It was a story announcing that, during 1964, for the first time more than 10,000 ships had visited Hong Kong harbour within one year. And there were certainly more than a million lights. I had thoroughly read the paper that morning because I knew newspaper people love to think everyone reads their paper front to back.

From the lower deck of the ferry the Island rose like the tip of a mountain out of the sea, smothered at sea level by skyscrapers. Residential towers scattered up the sides. Every now and then on the steep hillsides were shanty towns so big that you could see them from Kowloon. Made out of all sorts of rubbish ... tin, cardboard, plastic, canvas ... these crowded illegal towns survived with no running water or sewerage, home to refugees from Communism with nowhere else to go. Every year tens of thousands more Chinese fled to Hong Kong from Red China. It made me realise what a flat empty continent we inhabited in Australia. And how lucky we were to be so far away.

Outside the newspaper office on the footpath, several elderly Chinese women in conical hats tied under the chin sat on their haunches selling mostly Chinese-language papers. I marvelled that they could spend several hours in that position, when I couldn't sit like that for more than a few seconds.

Once inside, my arms involuntarily trembled at the elbows as I was ushered into a large teak-lined office with a ceiling fan where a tall, elderly Englishman stood at the deep window in sunshine so bright he was hard to see. With an upper-crust accent he greeted me without a handshake and called me "Lunn", which was off-putting. By his questions I could see he didn't really like Australians. I couldn't even get him to have a look at my three-inch thick scrapbook.

Every time I opened the scrapbook up at a story he moved quickly away from the desk and back to the safety of his window.

Then, suddenly, he said the paper had had a lot of trouble with Australian reporters. Not only did they break contracts and leave Hong Kong, but one Australian had recently bashed up the *Post's* sub-editors just because they said his story was no good. Worse still, when the executives tried to restrain him, an Australian sub-editor had shown no loyalty to the newspaper at all and had, instead, taken the Australian renegade's side.

His company now had adopted an iron-clad policy of employing no Australian journalists. "Under any circumstances."

I assured him that there were no fights in the sub-editor's room at the *Courier-Mail.*

He paced around in and out of the light of the window looking at me. Again he refused the offer of my scrapbook, even though I had it opened at my story on the failed world record table tennis attempt in Brisbane: "The half-way mark (ping) to the world record (pong) has been (ping) reached (pong)." It even had a photo of myself playing the man attempting the record.

The Englishman said he would like to give me a job because I seemed a reliable fellow, if I could just somehow disguise my identity from the Editor.

"I'll tell you what," he said at last. "Let's pretend you've never been in here today. You go away, grow a beard, and come back in a month and say that you're a South African, and we'll take you on."

The only chance left now was to try to find an Australian reporter called Steve Dunleavy. His name seemed to crop up whenever I mentioned newspapers in the Colony. Apparently this Dunleavy owned his own small paper, so Victor said he might need some help. But no one seemed to know where he lived. All they could tell me was: he can be found any time "after dark" having a drink somewhere in the strip of nightclubs along Nathan Road near the harbour. The trouble was that at night Nathan Road became the most crowded and, it was said, the most exciting street in the whole of the Orient.

Dunleavy had been a famous reporter in Sydney, where he always, but always, beat rival newspapers — and even sometimes the entire New South Wales Police Force — to front page stories. Or so I was told. If the police refused to make a statement, Dunleavy would get the story anyhow: because he knew how to talk police language, saying to witnesses "Good evening. I'm a Police ... (whisper) reporter". And, when this didn't work, Dunleavy would put on a hat and trench coat, walk over to the youngest policeman at the crime scene and, with the hat brim pulled right down at the front, say authoritatively: "Dunleavy, Paddington, Constable. What's going on here?"

As luck would have it, by the time I got back to the Grand from the *Post*, Fletch had somehow found out that Dunleavy had taken a job at the "Firecracker Bar": a popular nightclub which overflowed with people of many nationalities every night of the week in the basement of the massive black President Hotel just around the corner in Nathan Road. This seemed strange. The only function a reporter could possibly perform at a nightclub would be public relations.

Or else, maybe he wrote the advertisements?

It was near midnight. The nights were starting to cool off because it was now November. All I knew about Dunleavy was that everyone said: "You'll know him when you see him".

Hong Kong always contained thousands of sailors from the many warships that parked in the harbour, and tonight was no exception. As I approached the Firecracker, thinking about how I would start up a conversation with a stranger, half a dozen English and American sailors staggered around on the wide footpath outside. A British sailor dashed inside the Firecracker and returned wielding a gold chair upholstered with red velvet. He swung the chair wildly at his American opponents, but missed so often that finally he threw it: and missed again but broke the chair. An American picked up the gold remains only to catch his foot in the now mangled frame. Though hardly a blow had landed it was clearly a dangerous situation so, along with many Chinese, I watched from inside one of the numerous shop doorways nearby.

A low, distinctly Australian twang sliced through the Oriental night air:

"When do Laurel and Hardy arrive mate?"

The deep resonant voice came from an immaculately dressed man who sauntered out of the Firecracker Bar into the midst of the action. He was addressing the sailor who had his foot stuck in the chair. He held the jacket and waistcoat of his tailor-made dark blue suit back at the waist and I saw the initials "SD" embroidered on his shirt pocket.

So this was him.

He was handsome, though a bit of a Brylcreem Bodgie. In contrast to his expensive clothes, SD's dark hair was so long on top that it flopped a little at the front and curved up over his collar at the back. He looked about 26, three years older than me. His only imperfection was a slight kink in his hooter: and you didn't have to be a rocket scientist to work out how he must have got that kink.

Dunleavy's words stopped the men, who looked up under the flicking glow of a thousand red, green, and blue neon Chinese advertising signs at the Australian figure with his forefingers in the tiny pockets of his waistcoat — which he had now, for some inexplicable reason, done up: as if it was some sort of battle armour. There he was, bathed in a rainbow of Hong Kong's iridescent surreal lights: a lone dandy who dared insult six professional warriors beneath the drips of air conditioners which muffled the clack-clicking sound of Chinese women playing mah-jong.

"What did you say?" challenged a British sailor as all six advanced menacingly towards the confident intruder.

"I said," replied SD very slowly, "when do Laurel and Hardy arrive ... mate?"

Surprised by the exact repetition of the insult, the sailors stopped dead. "Well you're no help Aussie," said an English sailor, "why don't you stop making smart cracks and give us a hand." Dunleavy stepped recklessly into the centre of the melee, touching the right side of his nose with the outside edge of his right thumb, as champion boxers are wont to do, and helped a couple of the men — mostly much bulkier than himself — to their feet.

"Let's face it, none of you could fight your way out of a paper bag," SD said. "Now, matey, you Poms are going to have to pay for the broken chair, which belongs to the bar."

The drunk Americans staggered off while the British sailors pooled resources to pay up. Then Dunleavy disappeared inside, counting the money as he strolled back through the doorway under the pink neon "Firecracker Bar" sign.

Following him, I joined a couple of hundred people sitting in smoky semi-darkness around tables. A Filipino rock band on stage belted out the latest hits: led by a beautiful teenage guitar player with long black hair falling below her waist: almost reaching the bottom of her short, short white dress. All of these bars and nightclubs in Hong Kong had Filipino bands. But there were no strippers, because the British authorities who ruled Hong Kong wouldn't allow it.

For a while I listened to the music, wondering how to approach SD. A Beatles song took me home. I was a Beatles fan. Not only had I mimed their records in a black wig on stage at Milton Tennis Centre but, six months ago, I had seen them live at Brisbane's Festival Hall. The Beatles were the biggest thing in Australia that winter. It was impossible to get in unless you queued for days. But I was lucky. The manager of Festival Hall, Bert Potts, had nicknamed me "pink cheeks" because of what my mother, Olive, called my rosy cheeks.

"How would you like to see the Beatles, pink cheeks?" Mr Potts asked one night when I was covering the wrestling. He let me, and five of my friends, sit on a cramped ledge and watch the second concert for nix. When Paul sang "Hey Jude" the audience of mostly girls went berserk screaming. Every few seconds one would run at the stage pointing at him and calling his name and fainting in the arms of waiting police.

Then I spotted Dunleavy through the thick smoke. He was sitting at a table with several people, including the most alluring girl I had ever seen: a Chinese girl with an hourglass figure in a silver cheongsam which wrapped around her like a butterfly's chrysalis. Newspapers always gave the "vital statistics" in inches of any good-looking girl who appeared in the paper, and this one looked 36-24-36: which was considered ideal because the hip measurement equalled the bust.

It turned out that Dunleavy didn't write the advertisements for the Firecracker Bar. He was working as a casual throw-er-outer. The people at the bar said bouncer was a job which suited Dunleavy because he was a fantastic fistfighter. They said Dunleavy himself called fighting "going the knuckle".

Watching him move around the nightclub smiling, chatting, amusing, and touching people, I was reminded of my uncle, Cyril Duncan, who Olive said had defeated Aborigines in the ring. Like Uncle Cyril, Dunleavy stood with his weight on one side or the other, always slightly side-on, as if he was about to push a car up a hill. I noticed how the whole time he talked, Dunleavy's eyes never left the object of his attention. Whereas I often wondered what to do with my hands, and clung selfconsciously to drinks, Dunleavy's arms hung confidently beside a strong lean frame: secure in the knowledge that they could be up at the first waver of an eye.

He dressed like I wished I could. Shoulders filled the jacket to the extreme edges so that the suit dropped straight and uncrumpled. A red silk handkerchief, elongated slits on either side of the back of the jacket swinging cape-like. Plus a ring on a little finger. A ring was something we had been taught in Brisbane that only girls wore: except for the Phantom skull rings we sent away for as kids. Now, suddenly, even a ring without a skull looked he-manish.

When the band finally took a break, I walked over to introduce myself. Not that I wanted to, but if I was ever going to get a job overseas it had to be done.

"Er hello, Steve Dunleavy?" I said, noting that he had blue eyes like myself and a dimple in his chin: though his wasn't as pronounced as mine.

"Sorry to butt in on you like this. Look, you don't know me, I'm a friend of Kenny Fletcher the Australian Davis Cup tennis player. Anyway, I'm an Australian reporter, and so far I can't find a job in Hong Kong."

Dunleavy smiled: "I'm a bloody Australian myself, Hughie," and held out a more slender, harder hand than I was expecting. "You're not from Sydney are you."

How could he know?

"Great town Brisbane," he said with a radio announcer's voice. "A big country town growing up frontier-style. Lots of top journos come out of Brisbane to Sydney."

I told him of my four-year cadetship on the *Courier-Mail*, and the unfinished university degree after five years of study at night. I had come to the Orient to write some big stories.

"Getting university degrees in journalism, Hughie, is like getting a university degree in driving racing cars. Some can — some can't. And most of those who can won't take the necessary risks to win," Dunleavy said, eyeing me like a boxer.

I explained that I had a large, blue, linen hardcover scrapbook which contained all my 268 published newspaper stories: even the sports results I had typed out. On the first page was my only by-lined feature (on night sport in Brisbane): plus, the latest entry, my recent eight-story coverage of the Toowoomba Carnival of Flowers. "Ah yes, that wonderful weekend when all the sweethearts and sweet peas, and the guys and the gerberas, gather in Toowoomba: Gateway to the West," he said, and laughed. He even talked like he was writing stories.

I hadn't brought the scrapbook along, because it was too heavy. But I could be back with it in less than ten minutes.

"Journalism isn't about scrapbooks, Hughie," Dunleavy said, now looking a bit irritable. "Scrapbooks are out of date by the time the story's been pasted inside. Scrapbooks are for librarians. As a reporter you're only as good as your next story — not your last."

He generously invited me over to his table.

"Not another bloody Aussie journo," said a blond bloke with a long thin scar down his left cheek. "The Colony is crawling with them these days." His name was John Ball, an Australian journalist himself. According to journalists back home, the only way for an Australian to make a name as a reporter was to work overseas. Since most went to Fleet Street in London, I was surprised to find so many Australian reporters here in Hong Kong.

"So how do you like it?" John Ball asked.

Far more exciting than Brisbane, but I hadn't realised that Hong Kong was actually on the Red China mainland. Using the knowledge gained from four years in the army cadet band at school, I said: "The Red Chinese would only have to march straight in to Hong Kong. Nothing could stop them."

"That's true, Hughie," said Steve. "They say here that one phone call from Chairman Mao would be enough to see the white flag go up."

"That's why Americans get paid danger money here," said John Ball matter-of-factly.

"But it can't be too bad, can it, because Australians and British don't get any extra," said Dunleavy laughing.

They said I could drive out and see the 17-mile border fence between Hong Kong and Red China, about half an hour from the Firecracker Bar.

"I wouldn't mind going in there for a look," I said, trying to impress. "It sounds like a good story."

"Forget it, mate," said Dunleavy. "Australia doesn't recognise Red China exists. We recognise a large island off the coast of China, Formosa, as the real China now that the Communists rule the mainland."

"It's like recognising Tasmania instead of Australia," said John Ball.

When I told them I had just been knocked back at the *South China Morning Post*, Steve said I was lucky. "That's not a newspaper," he said. "It doesn't reflect what is happening in this great city. The *Post's* only good for cricket scores and what's happening to Princesses 'back home' in jolly old England. Out here we've got the Americans bombing North Vietnam; the Indonesians going ape in Malaysia; the Red Chinese testing nuclear bombs and threatening the United States and mumbling about the British even being here — and over at the *Post* all they can think about is how the Chelsea bloody Flower Show will go off next year."

Steve's own paper was called *American Tourist*. He said shops wanted to reach the American tourists, so he was filling a niche in the market. He wrote it, laid it out, and organised the printing all by himself. Steve knew photos too because, he said, his father was a press photographer in Sydney. If he needed any help on the paper, he called on his old mate here, John Ball. "But I think I can do something for you, Hughie," he said, winking generously with his right eye. "Leave it with me, and drop in again in a fortnight. But please, please, don't bring your bloody scrapbook." And he leapt up to do a circuit of the Firecracker, striding out as if trying to use every muscle in his body.

As I emerged back onto Nathan Road I felt euphoric for the first time since coming to Hong Kong.

Nathan Road was once known as "Nathan's Folly" because it was thought to be far too wide for the tiny Colony. But, now that millions had fled the 1949 Communist takeover of China 15 years ago, Nathan Road was just wide enough for the traffic in a city bursting with refugees and tourists. There were more shops in this one long, wide straight flat road than in the whole of Brisbane put together. There were more jewellery shops in Hong Kong than there were streets in Brisbane. And every jewellery shop, and every bank, had an Indian in a turban with a shotgun standing outside.

All the apartments had steel bars on the windows in various patterns, whereas back home we didn't even lock the back door when we went out. But according to Steve, the biggest danger of all — Red China — was not completely tucked safely away behind the Bamboo Curtain like I thought. The Communist Chinese, or Chicoms to those in the know, owned a skyscraper right smack bang in the centre of Hong Kong. It was their headquarters in the Western world.

This building resembled a fortress, and was said to be full of spies.

Not only was it guarded by thick stone walls and high steel gates, but also by two human-sized stone lions: perpetual sentinels to protect the Chicoms inside from the evil spirits that surrounded them outside in capitalist Hong Kong.

2 The Yellow Reds

Fletch always said his ambition was to become "a rich eccentric". Now I could see where he got the idea: living in international hotels during five world tennis tours since he was eighteen.

We ate like kings in the Grand restaurant from a six-page menu whenever we liked. Fletch just scribbled "K. Fletcher" on the bottom of the bill. While the hotel did our washing overnight, we went out to nightclubs with Victor — to the Bayside or the Latin Quarter — where Filipino groups belted out *I Left My Heart in San Francisco* over and over again for the elderly American tourists who, apart from the Chinese, dominated Kowloon. We got so sick of that song that we sang it as badly as we could in our dark corner: "... *high on a hill it calls to me ... and those little cable cars ... climb halfway to the stars ... above the blue and windy sea ... when I come home to you, San Francisco ...*"

Thus I rarely surfaced before noon — by then Fletch had already left to practise with Victor, or to coach. When he suggested I get up earlier, I used my father Fred's excuse: "I'm not sleeping, I'm just resting my bones." Fletch was always on at me to get up and write home to Mum and Dad, but so far there was nothing much to tell them.

What Ken didn't understand, was that I wasn't sleeping: I was thinking.

If I couldn't get a job, maybe I could survive by writing feature stories and selling them back home. No one in Australia knew what Hong Kong was really like. It wasn't at all British. It was Chinese: except for the numerous cricket clubs. Local products did bear a Union Jack with a tag

15

saying "Empire made," but only because Hong Kong goods had a world-wide reputation for shoddy workmanship. The streets swarmed like a school playground at little lunch, and the Chinese walked so slowly that you had to keep walking around them. Men sucked air in noisily through their noses, then wound up more air in their lungs, and spat big gollies loudly onto the road. This noise was heard so often that Australian reporters called it "the Hong Kong national anthem". Above the streets, workmen put up new 30-storey skyscrapers by climbing around bamboo scaffolding that was tied only with vine.

If you multiplied all the skyscrapers in Sydney by five thousand, then you would get some idea of what a tiny part of Hong Kong looked like. Brisbane was so small that you had to pay a penny to go up in the lift to the top of the City Hall tower to look down on the city.

Chinese girls often came to mind as I rested. They were exotic for an Australian. No gloves, stockings, or hats: just shimmering cheongsams, like Suzie Wong in the film. Cheongsams were a uniform for the girls in Hong Kong, except that they came in a range of satin-sheen rich colours, particularly pale blue, and invariably they had an intricate small pattern, like gold dragons, sewn over the material. These knee-length sleeveless silk frocks were so tight around the ribs that, while they emphasised the bust, the girls could only walk with the help of a split up both sides. The length of the split changed with the fashion, instead of the length of the frock.

On weekends, while not resting my bones, I watched the cricket on the picturesque Kowloon Cricket Club oval through a chain-wire fence from the footpath. Most cricket grounds back in Brisbane were covered in charcoal filling and didn't even have a dressing shed, but here there was a two-storey white stucco colonial clubhouse overlooking the entire soft green field.

It made me want to join the club, but it cost several hundred dollars: plus large annual fees.

16

Despite that, one afternoon I walked into the clubhouse off the street just for a look see. I found the dressing sheds underneath just as an assorted group of men were getting dressed after practice. The next thing I knew I was introduced to the captain. He was a tall Englishman with black hair and very sallow skin. He seemed more like an Indian.

"Well, Lunn, you're in luck," he said. "We're playing the Hong Kong Cricket Club Sunday and we could use an Australian, because we're facing a beastly drubbing."

Our club had two teams, the Saracens and the Crusaders, who were the firsts and the seconds. This mob were the Crusaders, the seconds. Which suited me, since I wasn't very good.

Sunday morning the KCC members and me caught the ferry across to the Island. The Hong Kong Cricket Club did not allow Chinese or other Asian members, though the club didn't object to them playing at their ground for other teams. This was an elite club run by British Colonialists since the previous century, whereas our club had lots of cricketers of all nationalities. Our best cricketer, for example, was an Indian, and our team's wicket-keeper, "K.K." Kwan, was famous. He was the brother of Nancy Kwan, the Chinese girl who played Suzie Wong in the film. Nancy got all the good looks, plus the figure, because K.K. had the crumpled look of a wicket-keeper even when he was dressed up to go out on the town.

The Hong Kong Cricket Club ground was immaculate. A small wooden, colonial grandstand on the northern side curved around next to the clubhouse, catching the sun in winter and avoiding it in summer. The field was right in the centre of the office area of Hong Kong and was said to be "the most expensive piece of sports field, dollar-per-square-foot, in the world: including New York".

Europeans slipped down to the club from work in nearby office buildings to sit in the grandstand and eat club sandwiches for lunch. But it was difficult to catch skied balls because of surrounding skyscrapers. On one side of the cricket ground was the City Hall, and on the opposite side a building towering above the ground at least 30 storeys high with a huge sign in English saying "HILTON", which meant it was a hotel. Across a narrow road on another side of the ground was a discernibly different building from all the rest in Hong Kong, a building a dozen storeys tall that looked like a stone citadel. Three heavy steel gates with Chinese writing on the top — one of them curving aggressively out towards the street like a pot belly — guarded a driveway. The building took up a whole block. With its tiny windows set deep in the stone, from the cricket field it looked like it wanted to be alone.

This was the Communist Chinese building in Hong Kong, their window on the Western world. Strategically overlooking the harbour and Western warships, it was called the Bank of China Building. The Hong Kong Cricket Club disliked their neighbours so much that they had a rule that if you could hit a six across Des Vouex Road and break one of the windows you would get twelve runs, plus free drinks for a year.

Fat chance.

Even though I had played cricket all my life, I had never hit a six. Most Australian cricketers boasted they had hit a six at some time in their lives: and could give date, place, and time. But every time I stood in the middle of a cricket pitch I could see there was no way I could hit the ball hard enough to clear the distant fence on the full.

As I fielded over near this Communist building, I wondered how Red China could afford a site opposite the most expensive sportsfield in the world. And why were they willing to let Great Britain keep this infinitesimal part of China on the basis of an ancient treaty that the Communists didn't accept: while allowing themselves to be the target for English imperialist cricket balls?

At least the balls were red.

Red was the best colour for the Chinese because they considered it lucky. However, red was especially revered by the Chinese Communists. Not only was it lucky, but it was also the colour of their doctrine. Red was so important to the Commos that, according to a local Chinese paper that day, China wanted to reverse their traffic lights so that green was for stop, and red was for go.

For the rest of the afternoon I couldn't concentrate on the cricket and let the Crusaders down by fielding badly. Shadowy black-haired figures moved back and forth behind the small deep-set windows high above. These were the Communists I had prayed as a Catholic to convert; and — as a 13-year-old Australian army cadet armed with a .303 rifle — trained to fight: once the Yellow Peril inevitably swept south. Yet here they were, watching me play cricket in the centre of the most Capitalist city in the world. Things outside Australia were much more complicated than I had expected.

When I got back to the hotel that evening I found out that the best way to be remembered was to turn a country into a Republic. I couldn't get into the hotel foyer. Every entrance to the Grand, except for a narrow path, was blocked by hundreds and hundreds of buckets of flowers. It turned out that our hosts, the Sun family, were direct descendants of Sun Yat-sen: a man revered by both Communist and Capitalist Chinese because he started China's first Republic. By overthrowing inherited royal rule in China, this Sun became known as "the father of the Chinese nation". Today was a Sun Yat-sen anniversary, and, by sending flowers, the Chinese in Hong Kong were paying their respects to the Suns.

"Victor is a big lardie-dah in this neck of the woods," Ken said. "His father's grandfather was Sun Yat-sen's older brother, and backed him financially. To the Chinese, Sun Yat-sen is a cross between Saint Peter and the Archangel Gabriel."

Yet, despite this, it was still too dangerous for Victor, whose Chinese name was Sun Bit-Shing, to go into Red

China to visit any of the many memorials there to his great-uncle.

Once a week, Victor's father invited us out to dinner with the family, each time to a different restaurant to check up on the opposition. Mr Sun taught me how to eat the Chinese way, insisting that you couldn't claim to be adept with chopsticks until you could pick a single toothpick out of a jar-full. Once I mastered this, I learned that the Chinese considered it impolite not to cover your mouth with the other hand while using a toothpick. Mr Sun also taught me the traditional custom of tapping the table with your finger-tips while someone poured Chinese tea into your cup. When you stopped tapping, the pourer knew to stop pouring.

The Suns loved to trick us, though they couldn't get me to eat any thousand-year-old eggs. The yolks were black, not yellow; and the white was a translucent green. They claimed these eggs were really "only a few months old".

A bald man, Mr Sun was much bigger than either Ken or me and he drank more tea than Olive, though he never used a cup. He carried a tall glass filled to over-flowing with boiling green tea as he worked in the hotel, holding the extreme top edge with the fingertips of his free hand.

One night after we'd finished eating, Mr Sun asked what we thought of the meal. When Ken and I both said it was delicious he asked what we thought we had eaten.

"Chicken?" I ventured.

"Something Chinese and horrific I bet!" Ken said, knowing the Suns better than I did.

It was a snake.

"You couldn't say a worse thing to us fair dinkum Australians," Ken said, poking out his tongue. "We were brought up spotting red-bellied blacks and death-adders down at Ekibin Creek. To us snakes mean two things: fangs and poison."

Mr Sun offered us a yellow-green drink in a tiny glass. With the family urging us on around the round table we sipped the queer tasting stuff.

Victor asked Ken if he liked it.

"Can I tell a lie?" Fletch said. "I don't like the way it's shaping up."

Ken was right.

It turned out it was snake bile, which Mr Sun said was good for male fertility. The Chinese paid big money for it: maybe that was one of the reasons Hong Kong was growing so fast. Mr Sun built the Grand as a seven-storey hotel, but within two years he had to add the 14-storey annex where Fletch and I were living. He said lots of six and seven storey buildings in Hong Kong had been knocked down in 1960 to be replaced by 15-storey buildings: only for these to be knocked down in 1964 to put up 30-storey skyscrapers.

The Grand was on a triangular site where several roads met, and Mr Sun said he got in a Chinese expert to tell the architect where the hotel entrance should face. No Chinese ever built a building, no matter how big, without such expert advice. Thus he loved it when I told him how Olive chose my father's "Lunns for Buns" cake shop in Annerley, Brisbane: "Fred," she said, "take the one with the worn step."

One of the reasons the family was so pleased to put us up was that Ken was a famous tennis player from the world champion tennis and sports nation: Australia. Every day he and Victor went off to practise at the South China Athletics Club, a club full of Chinese originally from Shanghai.

"It's like as if Australia was over-run by a revolution, and some of us escaped to New Zealand and all the Queenslanders joined the same tennis club," Ken explained.

While Victor and Fletch played tennis, I talked to Victor's brother, Peter Sun, in his hotel office behind reception. Peter was in charge because he had a degree in hotel management from America, which seemed a weird thing to study at university. Sometimes I wrote letters for him because, I was surprised to find, he thought I could do them better. Once I demanded new door-knobs from an American company for all the doors in the new 14-storey annex because the anodised plating had started to come off. I thought I should help out because Fred wrote a long letter from his cake shop:

"Dear Hughie," he started, in surprisingly good handwriting, "whilst it is very good of the Suns to let you stay at their hotel it is unfair on them for you to stay too long. Whatchamacallum helps those who help themselves."

Peter asked if I would write some advertisements for the hotel's new basement nightclub, *The Grotto*. Designed like the Phantom's cave, the walls and roof resembled giant boulders.

"What's in a Cave?" said the heading on my first advertisement. This was a reference to Shakespeare's "What's in a name?" but no one in Hong Kong seemed to get it.

The next week I changed it to: "Hong Kong has a Cave! Visit *The Grotto, the nightclub with a difference*. Drink and dance 2 p.m. to 2 a.m. Music by the Checkmates, Peter and his Trio, and star vocalist Sylvia." Peter added a drawing of a caveman with a club in his hand. The *South China Morning Post* wouldn't give me a job, but they were publishing the advertisements I wrote.

While we talked in his tiny crowded office, Peter explained things I didn't understand about Hong Kong.

The thing the Chinese revered most of all was, strangely enough, the dragon. So much so that the emperors were also seen as dragons. "Dragons are supernatural beings here," Peter said. "Fearsome in appearance, they are seen as great protectors."

This mystified me completely. I thought that these firebreathing small-winged monsters with long tails only existed in English fairy stories. But Peter said dragons were so important to the Chinese that workmen building a new road through Kowloon (which meant "nine dragons") had stopped work the previous week because they had hit rich red earth and thought they had cut the back of one of the nine dragons.

"They were too upset to continue."

The British seized Hong Kong with warships more than 100 years ago, during the reign of the last Queen of England, Victoria: which was why the harbour was called Victoria Harbour, and the peak on the Island, Victoria Peak. Under a lease agreement negotiated later, Hong Kong had to be given back to China on June 30, 1997.

"That is why Chinese call Hong Kong 'lent place'," Peter said. It made me wonder why people were building all these skyscrapers if they were one day going to get kicked out by the Reds. Still, it did seem a long way off.

The following weekend I prevailed upon Victor and Peter to take Ken and me for a drive to the Communist China border. We drove out through "the New Territories", Hong Kong's tiny version of the bush: a green barrier smaller than the city of Brisbane, between Kowloon and the frontier with China. It was mainly low-lying farms growing rice and vegetables for the city, with the occasional isolated high-rise resettlement village for refugees. The worst thing was the smell of shit everywhere. Fletch explained that, unlike Australian farmers, the Chinese didn't hestitate to use human excrement as fertiliser. No wonder that the milk bottles in Hong Kong contained a message in red on the glass: "Guaranteed TB free", which put me off drinking milk.

To get to the border we had to negotiate a curving road up the side of a peak covered in white cloud and, as I sat in the back of the Sun's black Chev and we ascended into the mist, childhood memories came flooding back.

During the annual army cadet camps at Greenbank near Brisbane from 1955 to 1958, Australian army officers warned us about the threat of the Yellow Peril and how we had to be ready. Then it had only been a couple of years since half a million Red Chinese soldiers in padded jackets surprised the world by invading Korea and pushing the United Nations forces — which included Australian Diggers and the might of the United States of America — back hundreds of miles in no time at all. After that, people in

Australia talked about "Red Aggression". This undeclared war between the Communist world and the West became a suspicious stand-off known around the world as "the Cold War".

"You'll be fighting for this land you're standing on," one army officer shouted at us on a parade ground in the Greenbank bush as he drilled us in the use of our .303 rifles: how to keep them clean and shoot them straight. The Chinese, we were told, had their eyes on Australia because they had run out of space, and we had such a big land with so few people.

One army intelligence officer told us in a lecture in a tent that there were a hell of a lot of these Yellow Reds. In fact, there were so many Chinese Communists, he said, that if they marched past twenty-five abreast "you would never, ever, see the end of the line, no matter how long you waited". This was because they would take so long to pass, and were multiplying so quickly, that the column would go on forever.

I was a bit confused by this because my classmate Jim Egoroff, who I sat next to at school, was born in China, and was a Russian: yet he was in the army cadets with us — in the Mortar Platoon firing bombs at sheets of corrugated iron representing a Communist camp.

Victor parked on a hillside and we looked down into Mainland China. All we could see were more green hills without trees and rice fields, with the only visible building one house in the middle of a paddy. I expected to see concrete bunkers and artillery pieces and telescopes and tanks and thousands of British troops in trenches, .303s at the ready. But there wasn't even a river. Coming from a country that didn't have any national borders, it seemed strange to have a mere fence separating the world's two warring ideologies. A small shack nearby held just two Hong Kong Chinese policemen, immaculately dressed in khaki shorts with black revolver holsters. They weren't going to stop 750 million Reds.

In fact, this little fence didn't even stop unarmed individual Chinese from entering Hong Kong.

Every year thousands of private enterprise Reds got around this border by floating into Hong Kong from Communist China on rubber car tubes, or rafts made from ping pong balls, or swimming through the night despite the sharks. Or by cutting through the fence. If these refugees got into Hong Kong proper they were allowed to stay, but if they were caught in the border area they were returned to China because the British were trying to keep in good with the Reds.

This border fence had only one purpose — to stop Chinese escaping to Hong Kong.

You'd have to be crazy to want to go the other way.

3 Dunleavy's Going Rate

In the fortnight since my last visit to the Firecracker Bar I had heard a lot about Steve Dunleavy. He wasn't only famous in Hong Kong, but also in Sydney. An Australian sports writer, who interviewed Ken, said Sydney was "too small a town for Dunleavy".

"Dunleavy always travelled on high octane. He partied and consumed all night and worked all day as if he could still remember the Irish potato famine. It was always a source of wonder to Sydney editors that Dunleavy could invariably get an interview with someone — even when they had refused all requests for other interviews. Plus, of course, the family photo album."

Apparently Steve was just as good a reporter on the phone as he was in person.

"They used to say 'put Dunleavy on a phone and he'll bring you back anyone in the world, dead or alive'," the sports writer told me, not altogether admiringly. "Dunleavy interpreted the legal phrase 'in the public interest' very widely saying, 'I reckon it's in the public interest if the public are interested'."

This bloke didn't seem to like Steve very much, so I thought he was probably jealous.

I knew I was.

He said Steve was such a desperado for a scoop that in Sydney he wasn't above flattening the tyres of opposition reporters, or putting the only public phone in the suburb out of commission: after he had phoned through his story.

I could never stop another reporter getting a story, but I wouldn't help an opponent either.

"Would you believe that Dunleavy once slashed the tyres of his own father's car to get a beat on a big breaking story?"

It just couldn't be true. I didn't believe it. No one would do that to their own father.

"Well, Dunleavy did say later that he hadn't known that his father was driving that particular newspaper vehicle that day," the sports reporter said, grudgingly. "But still, he did it alright."

When I returned to the Firecracker Bar to see Steve I brought Fletch along. I wanted to see these two famous Australians meet. We found Steve at the bar with a group of Yanks who were talking about the reaction time of racing drivers. As we waited to one side in the semi-darkness, so as not to interrupt, the tallest American, who was standing up, waved his glass of bourbon around as he explained to his fellow-countrymen sitting on bar stools how modern car brakes were much more effective than people realised.

"Most of the distance travelled before stopping is taken up by the reaction time of the driver," he said.

Apparently losing his grip, the American dropped his glass. We all looked down to see it smash on the floor. But it didn't. While everyone else still sat with arms folded, Steve had plucked the glass out of the air and in one motion put it back on the bar. Without spilling a drop.

"You ruined my show, Aussie," the American said. "I was trying to illustrate that human reaction times are too slow to do that. How you did it sure beats the hell out of me. If you ever want a job as a racing driver, just let me know."

Steve saw us and hurried over through the smoke, his confident arms kicking back the flaps of his brand new pin-striped tailor-made suit coat. There was nothing about Steve Dunleavy that said "employee".

He seemed very, very pleased to meet Ken.

"Fletch," he said. "Fletch, Fletch, mate. I know: the tennis rebel. Good to meet you. I've seen you play at White City. Like your Dacron American jacket. Very cool."

Steve wanted to know why Ken had chosen to live in Hong Kong, when it wasn't exactly known for champion tennis players? Ken said it was an exciting town.

Dunleavy was curious. It was as if he were interviewing Ken.

"What's so exciting?" he asked.

"Well, my first night here — in 1963 — I got hit over the head with a full bottle of beer by a bar girl," Fletch said.

"Not bad excitement," said Steve.

"When she hit me I hardly felt a thing, just the glass showering down on me," Ken continued. "It was a large brown bottle of San Miguel and there was blood on my neck. I picked her up and shoved her along the bar knocking all the glasses off just like in an American western." An English barrister with Ken had stood up in the centre of the nightclub and said "everyone please remain calm".

"He thought we were in bloody parliament or something. Bodyguards came from everywhere and I had to fight our way out."

Dunleavy was sympathetic.

"Australians will always fight to defend their honour," he said gravely, tugging his shirt sleeves to keep the shape of his suitcoat just right: as if talking about fisticuffs might ruin its trim. "Fighting is an Australian tradition. It's a really beautiful thing, if it is done right, and for the right motives."

Being a top reporter, Steve wanted to know why Ken had fallen out with Australian tennis officialdom, and Fletch explained that he was banned from Davis Cup team selection because he broke an embargo on overseas travel to accept an all-expenses paid invitation to play in the Caribbean: "The LTAA wanted me to apologise, but I wouldn't. Australia is a free country."

"You're what I call a good story, Fletch," Steve said. "A walking front page picture-story. None of this tennis robot stuff, like Laver and the rest of them."

The good news was that Steve had lined me up a job. An Australian journalist mate of his, Graham Jenkins, needed a reporter.

"Never heard of him," I said, as the Filipino band struck up *I Left My Heart in San Francisco*.

"No, but he's heard you're in town," Steve said. "He wants some good Aussie journos around, because he's going to start a proper newspaper and knock off the other garbage."

Steve drew closer and put his arm across my back, as if protecting me: "I've told him you're the hottest piece of reporting property to come out of Brisbane since Hughie Dash in the '30s, so I don't want you to let me down."

"But Steve, you can't say that. You haven't seen my scrapbook," I said.

"Forget the scrapbook, Hughie. You'll like Graham, and he'll like you. That's what matters. You're both Aussie journos so there's Cultural Compatibility with some capital Cs. Just remember the two most important words in Australian journalism: 'get there'." I'd never heard this theory before, and I was about to ask what it meant when Steve said: "Get there. You know, always beat the other mug," and he winked warmly and smiled his rugged, winning smile.

Graham Jenkins, Steve told us, made his money with a magazine called *Young Hong Kong*, which printed every story twice: once in English, and once in Chinese. It was in English from the front cover to the middle, and in Chinese from the back cover to the middle: because the Chinese read from right to left. "Graham could see that a million young Chinese in Hong Kong were desperate to improve their English. So this way they could actually enjoy doing it."

The magazine was a huge success, so Graham had decided to start an English-language newspaper aimed at the Chinese.

"The Chinese know they're not going to learn English reading Chinese-language papers. And they can't read the bloody *Post* because it is full of cricket and rugby scores and bridge parties," said Steve. "So he's planning a thin, bright tabloid in English using only very simple words and short sentences with lots of pictures. It won't have many pages, so he can sell at one-third the price. Within a month I predict he'll out-sell the other English papers combined."

Just then a group of American servicemen, who had finished singing *I Left My Heart in San Francisco*, called out something strange:

"Say Steve. What's the Going Rate tonight?"

"The Going Rate tonight, gentlemen is," Steve said, and then hesitated momentarily as if doing sums in his head while he brushed his long hair back with the heels of both strong hands … "is two Irishmen, four Scotsmen and five Englishmen."

This amused the group of Americans vastly. Steve explained to us that, whenever he was having trouble with visiting servicemen, he always explained what he called his "Going Rate": how many men from various countries an Australian like himself was worth in a fight. So tonight he was as good as any two Irishmen, any four Scotsmen, or any five Englishmen. And he obviously wasn't expecting anyone to challenge it.

"Say, Dunleavy," called another American in the group, "you didn't say what's the Going Rate for us Americans?"

"Oh Yanks," said Steve. "Yanks? I didn't say, because … the Going Rate is always the same for you. You Americans can write your own ticket."

And everyone, including Steve, laughed.

I was amazed he could get away with it, but it seemed no one was game enough to take him up on it. I was also glad that he was an Australian. Ken liked him too. "That Steve Dunleavy," Fletch said as we walked home up Nathan Road, "he's got all the props."

Next week I met Graham Jenkins. Being an Australian, he was much less formal than the man at the *Post*, and much younger. He said to call him Graham, and sat comfortably on the corner of his desk. He didn't want to see my thick scrapbook either: even though I had once again lugged it on the ferry and right across town to his office.

Graham said he was going to call his paper *The Star*, and he wanted me on the reporting staff. The problem was, it wasn't starting up until at least May 1965, six months away.

"Steve tells me you're good, very good," Graham said. "So I've lined up a job for you in the meantime on some magazines run by an old Pommie mate of mine, Max Schofield. But, remember, *you're mine.*"

Graham packed me off to *Far East Trade Press*, Alexandra House, 113 Des Voeux Road, on the Island — a massive triangular building covering a whole block just behind the new luxury Mandarin Hotel which looked north to Kowloon. This company published two magazines aimed at builders and engineers: a monthly *Hong Kong & Far East Builder*, "the oldest trade journal in the Far East", and a quarterly, *The Far East Engineer*, "the only trade journal devoted to the profession in the Orient".

Max Schofield was a short, ruddy-faced man with thinning crew-cut grey hair. He had an impressive moustache like that of the captain of a Spanish galleon, and a loud voice to match. Though he wasn't anywhere near as formal as most Englishmen in the Colony, he still insisted on calling me "Lunn".

"Now Lunn," he said, "Jenkins tells me you're a cracker writer from Australia, one of the best, which is just what we need here. We're re-styling and re-naming our two magazines, and we are making them both monthly. Plus we're about to start a third magazine. We've got plenty of sub-editors, but no specialist writers. So welcome aboard."

Without even opening my scrapbook, which I had discreetly placed on the blotter on his desk, he gave me a job at $HK2,000 a month as an assistant editor, payable in advance. We shook hands, and he handed over the cheque. I said I was surprised it had all happened so quickly. That he hadn't shown me a copy of one of the magazines, or even looked in the scrapbook to see my work.

Trade magazines weren't the sort of journalism I had been trained for.

Mr Schofield laughed uproariously at this, so that the opaque glass around his office shook. He would probably have laughed even more if he knew I wasn't a cracker writer. "No, Lunn. I don't advertise for staff. I head-hunt the people I want. I knew all about you before you even arrived, and you were what I was looking for. It's called having a nose for staff," and he touched his reddish nose and laughed.

I couldn't help liking him. He wasn't at all like an old British Colonial businessman. He said the re-styled monthly magazines would be called *Far East Architect and Builder*, and *Far East Engineering and Equipment News*. The first would be posted out monthly to 5,000 architects and builders throughout southeast Asia; and the second would be posted off to 5,000 engineers.

Mr Schofield said this was called "controlled circulation to qualified readers".

"So no one actually buys the magazines?" I asked.

"The magazines, Lunn, are posted out to the people who *want* them. As we say in our brochures, 'we don't scatter: we distribute'. This appeals to our advertisers because they thus know exactly who the magazine is reaching."

"But Mr Schofield," I said, "if they don't buy the magazine how do you know they read it?"

Mr Schofield leaned across his wide desk and wiped the bottom of his Spanish moustache with the thumb and forefinger of his right hand:

"I know you top writers want all the details. That's good, Lunn. So here is how it works: instead of selling to any old individual who happens to wander in to the paper-shop off the street and sees, say, the *Far East Engineering and Equipment News* on the shelf and it takes his fancy — for whatever reason — the magazines go straight to the readers the advertisers want to reach. That's why these magazines have been successful since 1935, long before you were born my boy. Be reassured: no one can knock back something for nothing once they've got it in their hands. Besides, many professional men write in complaining that they don't get one."

Some *Far East Trade Press* customers were, he said, more than happy to pay for these magazines, which they had to do if they didn't live in the controlled circulation area of Malaysia, Singapore, Thailand, Vietnam, Japan, the Philippines, Borneo and Hong Kong.

"We've got readers — engineers, builders and architects — back in your country in Australia, and in New Zealand, who pay in advance to make sure they get a copy," Mr Schofield said proudly. "But only, of course, on condition that I enclose a copy of *Playboy Magazine*," and again he threw his head back and laughed until his moustache quivered like a mouse's whiskers.

Ever too vigilant Australian and New Zealand Customs officers, Mr Schofield explained, could always pick out a mailed copy of the latest edition of *Playboy* from the United States, no matter what envelope it was in, because each month they established exactly how much the latest edition of the girlie magazine weighed.

"But they can't hope to pick it up when *Playboy* is enclosed with one of our magazines in an envelope marked *Far East Trade Press*," he said.

I liked him even more after that. A real cheeky old rascal. Mr Schofield himself added the *Playboy* to the Australia-bound envelopes each month, after sending out a boy to get the latest edition.

"We are disseminators of information," he said. "So we try in our own way to stop the censorship of information, which holds all mankind back."

Having explained how the company worked, Mr Schofield took me past some Chinese secretaries into a large rectangular room with windows at one end. Three men sat at similiar-sized desks, two facing the front away from the windows and one side on. This was the entire editorial staff. One was an English science graduate, Ken Archer, who was my age and had the same name as a famous Test opening batsman from Brisbane. There was a slightly older, married Englishman, Arthur Barnett, who was editor of the architecture magazine. And up the front, of all people, John Ball, the fair-headed, Australian journalist with the thin scar on his cheek I had met with Steve Dunleavy.

There was a spare desk at the back against the window where I would sit, starting Monday.

As I left, Mr Schofield's secretary handed over a letter of appointment. We worked six days a week, including four hours on Saturday, and the only holidays were two weeks a year "in Hong Kong". So there was no going home. The letter said I would be required to write articles for both journals "which are being re-styled".

However, I was surprised to see a paragraph at the bottom: "Early in 1965 you will work in close association with Dr Arnold Hsieh. You will show him how to do sub-editing, make up, layout, and other aspects of publishing of which he will not have an intimate knowledge for our new *Far East Medical Journal*." This, I presumed, would be mailed out to 5,000 unsuspecting doctors in the Orient. I was only 23 and had no idea how to publish a magazine. But I resolved to say nothing.

On the way back to the Grand I met up with a young Englishman, David Bonavia, who had advertised in the *Post* for a flatmate. David was just out of university, had a short cow's lick haircut, and was wondering what to do with himself. He spoke and wrote Chinese perfectly after studying the language for years.

Over lunch he taught me to count to ten in Chinese "yut, ye, sam, say, mmm ..." and showed me what he called "the logic" of Chinese writing. Writing "man" was just like drawing a stick human figure with two legs; big was the symbol for man with a broad stroke across the middle of the upper half; and sky had another stroke across the top. A river was three parallel squiggly lines "as a child might draw a stream", David said. I recognised the symbol for "big" because it was on just about every neon light in the colony. The Chinese were obviously impressed with anything big.

David Bonavia was in Hong Kong to learn more about the Chinese and China than he could at university. However, he wanted to live on the Island, while I wanted to live in Kowloon. So David wrote a note in Chinese which he said to show a taxi driver if I ever needed to find him.

That morning a room had been advertised for rent in a flat in Chungking Mansions, a very wide skyscraper on Nathan Road just next to the Bayside Nightclub and around the corner from the Grand. I could see immediately why the owners had found it necessary to call the building a mansion. The concrete exterior was filthy, and the interior was totally run-down. The building had so many entrances and lifts and twists and turns that it was hard to find a way around the hundreds and hundreds of flats and guest house apartments sub-let and sub-sub-let inside. But the rent was only one hundred Hong Kong dollars a week for a room right in the centre of Kowloon.

There were various lift-wells, so I had to search for the right one in alley-ways that smelt of human sweat and curry. The ninth floor brought a surprise when a Filipino man opened the door: I could tell because of the moustache and the classy way he dressed in a fine white cotton shirt, black trousers, gold jewellery and shining black pointed leather shoes. His name was Roxas, and he was a trumpeter in a band playing the big hotel nightclubs in Hong Kong.

Roxas said he was making plenty of dough, but the rent — even in this dump — was so high it was killing him. So he and his wife had decided to rent out their second bedroom to cut costs a bit.

I told him I had been a trumpeter in the school army cadet band and he showed me his instrument, which gleamed like Chinese gold.

"It's worth $20,000, so don't drop it," he said as he handed it over. It seemed far too fine and precious to reside in Chungking Mansions.

Roxas showed me the room. It had an old wardrobe and a large made-up double bed beneath a steel-framed window with no awning. The green wall below the window was stained by stormwater all the way to the floor and the paint had come off. There was no other furniture, but I didn't need anything else.

The trumpeter's wife was an Australian — a tall, slender dark-haired woman with skin that was as pale as his was dark. Over a cup of tea she said she had met Roxas while working as a model in the Orient. Now they were saving to get a nest-egg together. There would be no meals or laundry included with the room, but I could use the kitchen if they were out. I paid five weeks rent in advance, but she got my name wrong and wrote the receipt out to "Mr Hugh Lynn" before attaching a green fifteen cent Hong Kong duty stamp which had an English crown incongruously sitting on top of some Chinese writing

Back at the Grand, Ken was pleased I had finally landed a job and had managed to get a room just one minute away from him. He'd always known I'd get a job soon enough.

I carried my port and portable typewriter around to Chungking Mansions, to a room which seemed a long way from home. Funnily enough, as I lay on the double bed, I didn't feel at all homesick. I was exhilarated. I could now do anything I wanted, without listening to anyone. I could bring girls home, I could buy a radiogram or a tape-recorder, I could learn Chinese or French without doing exams, I could stay out or come home whenever I liked. I could work hard and become an expert at editing magazines. I could leave the light on all night if I wanted.

It was a wonderful feeling and I almost floated off the bed. For the first time completely free; living with people who didn't even know my correct name. No big brother Jack to worry if I was doing the right thing at work. No young sisters saying prayers that I would find a girlfriend, as they had been doing (at Olive's instruction) for the last couple of years before I left Brisbane. No parish priest wanting to hear my Confession. No three-hour university night lectures. No assignments. No exams.

And heaps of room in my first-ever double bed.

After a couple of hours I realised I had to work out what I really wanted to do with all this freedom. The first thing was to post my skyblue scrapbook home. Jack was wrong in urging me to take it with me: no one overseas wanted to see a journalist's scrapbook.

Then, if I was going to get a girlfriend, I needed to buy some contraceptives: something I had never done before. The one thing I knew about life was that, whatever bad cards I had been dealt, at least I wasn't a girl. I could never have faced being a girl and getting pregnant and having a baby.

With some trepidation I entered a busy Nathan Road chemist shop. As I found my way through the floor-to-ceiling shelves loaded with Western medicines, make-up, and hair oil, I realised the day I had feared for the last five years had finally arrived. Under my Catholic religion, using contraceptives was an out and out Mortal sin. Worse, merely to buy contraceptives and carry them around with the *hope* of using them was in itself a Mortal sin. The Church had commanded that we avoid, not just sin, but "occasions of sin". Chemist shops, I guessed, were — like bad company — occasions of sin.

Even *planning* to buy contraceptives meant that impure thoughts had not just flitted uncontrollably through my mind, but had been "harboured". So a pre-meditated intention of sinning had been committed.

Thus, without doing anything at all — except moving in and out, in and out, of these tight aisles — I was already sinning. Probably over and over again. There would be no extenuating circumstances: I couldn't plead a momentary failure of will when confronted with the irresistable body of a maiden: not if I was mischievously carrying the fit instrument of ill with me.

No. Buying contraceptives fitted perfectly the Church's definition of the classic Mortal sin: "planning to knowingly and willingly consent to something which you believe to be a Mortal sin". It might even negate the holy sacrament of Confession completely: because, for Confession to work, you had to promise, and believe, that you would not commit that same sin again.

Ever.

Which was worse? Hell for eternity under the Devil and his angels, or to get a girl pregnant and marry her forever with no hope of divorce. Or worse still, to turn her overnight into a disgraced unmarried mother. There was no hiding it. Every time a girl married in Australia everyone marked their calendars to see if a baby arrived — as it often did — "three months premature".

No wonder my palms were sweating. But I was still determined to get some contraceptives, despite the words of Bishop Fulton Sheen which kept echoing inside my head: "You can't call it Birth Control because there's no birth, and there's no control."

The only positive was that nobody knew me. I was concentrating hard, because I was looking for something I had never seen in the packet. I knew they were called "French Letters", though I had no idea why. I had seen them blown up like white balloons at university parties and imagined they worked something like the device Uncle Les wore if he cut a finger on his scythe — a leather sleeve that fitted over the bandaged finger and was then tied off around the wrist.

Hong Kong chemist shops were nothing like those in Australia, where the windows were full of giant clear glass bottles each containing coloured liquids, and where the smell itself was healthy. Here you could hardly see into the shop for opaque jars in all colours and small white cardboard boxes and there was no distinctive antiseptic smell. The chemist weighed items using a long black ebony stick with string, hooks, and little bell-shaped weights. He then toted up the bill on a wooden abacus quicker than any cash register.

I could just see the chemist at the end of an aisle, a young Indian bloke about my age. Had this been Australia he would have been wearing a white coat, but not in Hong Kong. Indians always wore dark clothing. With his dark blue long-sleeved silk shirt, oiled back black hair, and pointed black shoes he looked like a man of the world. Hadn't I seen lots of Indian men walking around Hong Kong holding hands? That was something you never saw in Australia.

He was momentarily alone. Though he didn't know me from a bar of soap, my pink cheeks still blushed as I stopped him setting out a display of Tiger Balm jars.

"French Letters?" he said, confused.

I looked around to see if anyone else had come in.

"Contraceptives," I whispered in a confidential tone, the back of my left hand cupped around the edge of my mouth.

He nodded, went away, and returned with a packet of large black tablets.

"No. No," I said, "not tablets. I want something for the boy to put on."

"Ah," the chemist said, black eyes lighting up with recognition. He returned with a jar of clear ointment, holding it up and saying "for the boy, for the boy".

Here I was, in the middle of the decadent Orient, throwing religion and conscience out the window trying to buy contraceptives, and all this Indian chemist could sell me was some medicine.

I decided to try somewhere else: there was plenty of time because I hadn't yet met any girls.

Later that evening, as Ken and I left the Bayside after celebrating, a beautiful Chinese girl caught up with us from behind and started talking. I thought she was lost. But she wanted to know where we were from. She was unusual in that she wore black trousers and a white knitted top instead of a cheongsam. She was a happy girl with bright eyes and bounced along as she walked, talking to us, looking in shop windows, and asking questions. Though her English was difficult to understand, when she talked it sounded like singing.

She was about our age, and Ken smiled and laughed as she asked how long we'd been in Hong Kong. She'd never heard of Brisbane, but was interested when I said Ken was a famous tennis player. To my surprise she walked with us all the way back to the Grand Hotel, and even followed us inside the bright spacious foyer. She took my arm and touched my cheeks with both hands and laughed, saying something in Chinese. Here I'd spent five years since school trying to find a girlfriend in Australia, and within a month of hitting Hong Kong a beautiful girl follows me home.

I knew already I was a bit of a hit with Chinese girls. I found out at a Dim Sum restaurant which overflowed with probably a thousand Chinese eating at once. Scores of teenage girls walked around the room with small, round bamboo baskets of hot food piled high on trays slung around their necks: each screaming out above the din the Chinese name of the dish they were carrying. If you heard a dish you wanted, you waved to the waitress and she dropped a basket on your table as she passed. It was very, very fast and efficient and, at the end of the meal, you were charged according to the numbers of empty bamboo baskets on your table.

But when I arrived, the waitresses stopped walking around yelling out and instead all gathered around looking at me: smiling, whispering, and giggling with their hands over their mouths. I had no idea what was happening, but Victor explained they were delighted with my pink cheeks, which to the Chinese were a certain sign of a brave, handsome, faithful man.

Back in Australia when I was sun-baking at Surfers Paradise a girl I was keen on said in disgust: "you are turning puce!" But here in Hong Kong my pink skin was in. Victor said you could always pick the hero in a Chinese Opera because he was made up with lots of rouge. It was a Chinese tradition dating back thousands of years.

I couldn't help saying that it seemed a bit silly to always have a hero with pink cheeks.

"No," said Victor, "it's the same as American westerns. The good guy always wears a white hat, and the bad guy a black hat. The hero rides a white or palomino horse and wears one gun, and the bad man rides a dark horse and wears two guns."

He had me there.

So history was working for me with the local girls. This pretty girl was so besotted that she followed us to the hotel lift and, instead of saying goodbye, took us each by the arm and pushed the lift button using the point of her pink umbrella.

"Now, Hughie," Ken said gravely, "you know that she's a prostitute, don't you. She's nice but, quite pretty really."

I was so surprised that I couldn't think of anything to say.

The lift arrived, and Fletch turned to me, laughed, and said: "Dear Mum and Dad ..."

4   Orphaned at Christmas

A few weeks after I started work on the trade journals, Mr Schofield poked his ruddy nose and Spanish whiskers around the corner of our office, yelled out "Lunn" and disappeared. I wondered what I had done wrong.

I had never worked so hard in my life. I was writing a feature for the engineering journal about a new machine that could continuously weld a pipeline out of flat steel over any length. Plus I was trying to track down before Christmas the designer of Hong Kong's traffic pagodas. These stood in the middle of the forty-four busiest intersections like large versions of Brisbane's helmet-sized "dumb coppers", forcing cars to go around them.

At peak hours Chinese police in their khaki shorts and shirts stood high, cool and dry inside the white pagodas directing traffic. The Professor of Architecture at Hong Kong University, Professor W.G. Gregory, had praised the pagodas in a speech reported in the *Post*:

"Contrast our concrete jungle with these point duty policemen's shelters which have style, character, and a taste of the traditional. Whoever it was who designed the pagodas deserves a gold medal."

I liked them myself. They were exactly what we needed in Brisbane, where the only thing that protected traffic policemen was some fancy footwork and a white pith helmet. The pagodas looked nice too, like small white Chinese lighthouses in the middle of intersections. Tourists from around the world were always photographing them: either with police or themselves inside.

I was hoping Mr Schofield might know who designed them and deserved a gold medal. But he wasn't interested.

"Stick to buildings, Lunn," he said. "We write about buildings, big buildings, not traffic stands. The bigger the building the more the architects like it. What about that Fu Centre which at 34 storeys will be the Colony's tallest. Get on to that right away."

Mr Schofield also told me to get a business card but I was dubious of the value of these small white rectangles of cardboard showing your name, workplace, and telephone number.

"You might not need them in Australia, Lunn, but in the Far East a gentleman always carries a calling card — just as he always wears a jacket after eight," Mr Schofield said. "Every businessman in the Orient has one. Anyway, I hear you need one more than most." At this he threw his head back and laughed so much I was looking at the roof of his mouth and all his fillings.

He had obviously heard I hadn't been able to line up any interviews with Hong Kong Colonial Office officials.

"It's not like working for a newspaper where everyone jumps to attention when you ring," I said. "They just don't care about journalists from trade magazines."

"It's your name, Lunn," Mr Schofield said. "On the phone 'Hugh Lunn' sounds like 'Hoo Lan'. They think you're Chinese. You couldn't get a much more Chinese name than 'Hoo Lan'. Don't tell them your name my boy, just say you're an Australian reporter and watch them jump to."

I told him my sister-in-law's name back in Brisbane was Lyn Lunn.

When he had recovered sufficiently, and had wiped his eyes with the large white handkerchief he kept nearby at all times, Mr Schofield sent me off to see our printer, a Chinese businessman in Ship Street. The boss said to make sure I got a card with English on one side and Chinese on the other. I already knew that was how it was done in Hong

Kong, because Fletch had a card saying on one side: "GRAND HOTEL, Ken Fletcher, Public Relations", and on the other side was a lot of vertical Chinese writing including "big big", the only symbol I recognised.

I couldn't find the printer in Ship Street. Finally, in desperation I took a chance and stepped through a man-sized hole that had been smashed in a brick wall. I couldn't see a thing in the total blackness. There were obviously no windows. It was so stuffy I could hardly breathe, and I tripped over what felt like loose bricks on the concrete floor. As my eyes slowly adjusted from the bright light outside I could see some faint lights further in. Two reading lamps reflected off black steel linotype machines where two Chinese printers sat setting type in English, without having a clue what the words meant. It seemed to be the basement of a partly demolished, deserted building. These printers seemed to be living like rats. Back home politicians talked about "the sweat shops of Asia": now I realised it was true.

Paul, the businessman who occasionally dropped into the office to collect layouts and copy, was still dressed in his dark suit, white shirt and tie, despite the breezeless conditions. He took me into his tiny office around a broken-walled corner and I wrote my name out carefully under his only light, a reading lamp, while he wrote the Chinese translation for the back.

As he drew the symbols, Paul smiled, holding his slender right thumb up at my face saying "Dai yut", which I now knew meant "number one". It was the best thing you could say about something or someone in Hong Kong.

"Your name 'Lunn' translates as 'Dragon'," Paul said. "Dragon is best possible name. And 'Hugh' translates as 'pillar'. So you are 'Dragon on Pillar'. Dai Yut. And this is Year of Dragon: very, very good for you."

He gave a long, slow, serious bow of his head, the light from his glasses reflecting once they reached below his desk lamp.

I was very pleased to have such a good name to go with my formidable pink cheeks. In fact, I felt a surge of pride.

This piece of good fortune was confirmed when Paul gave the details for my card to one of the printers who held it up under his lamp. The printer turned and nodded saying: "Ho, Ho." Which meant "very good".

At least being a Dragon was better than being a Devil, like all the other Westerners in Hong Kong, including Max Schofield. Our Chinese secretaries said the locals referred to Westerners as "gweilo": "foreign devils". They tried to convince me it had become a favourable term in recent years, but I doubted that. I thought the Chinese in Hong Kong were not happy about living in a British Colony. Like Aborigines in Australia, they never got to vote. Even after more than 120 years of Colonial rule, Hong Kong was still run by a Legislative Council appointed by a Governor, who was himself appointed by the Queen of England. There were no political parties, and the police force was run by the British: all white policemen had the minimum rank of Inspector. It must have been strange to be Chinese and have an English Queen.

Most were happy living under this arrangement, so long as they didn't have to live under Communism. The thing that pleased them was that, like Australians, they had passports with the word "British" on the front — "British Hong Kong" — because it meant that, when Hong Kong was handed back in 1997, they would be allowed to go and live in Britain if they wanted: "Britain would never hand us back to the Communists".

Most hoped that, instead of having to go and live in the cold and wet of England, Britain would negotiate a settlement with Red China to allow Hong Kong to exist as a separate country. "China needs Hong Kong as a window on the world," the Chinese were always saying. Though, except for the formidable Bank of China Building, I couldn't see any evidence of such a need.

It took me a while, in between researching tall buildings, to track down the designer of the forty-four traffic pagodas. He wasn't even an architect.

Arthur May was surprised when I turned up a few days before Christmas at his sixth-floor Island apartment on a weekend (because this wasn't an approved story I decided to work on it in my own time). He was a former English Colonial public servant who drew up the pagoda design in 1952 while working as an electrical inspector for the Hong Kong Public Works Department. Luckily for me, he had decided to stay in the Colony after retirement.

"There are not many people who know I designed it," he said as he stood in the doorway, then the full impact of a Professor of Architecture saying he deserved a gold medal for his design which had become a "world landmark" hit him. He sat down on a sofa as his proud wife rushed over and held both his hands at once.

"I always had ambitions as an architect," Mr May said wistfully. "When they asked the public service to come up with design ideas I thought an Oriental touch was a necessity — thus the pagoda-type roof."

He said he gave the pagoda a base two foot six off the ground, so that the traffic policemen would be visible to all motorists, and used six ordinary waterpipes sloped outwards to hold up a roof six foot seven in diameter, to give the policeman inside plenty of protection from the elements. The curved panels between the horns of the roof carried the rain water down the waterpipes: "thus preventing the policeman from being hidden by a wall of water during a tropical storm".

The roof was insulated and had a flashing red light on top; there was a fan under the floor blowing air up the policeman's shorts; and a bulb hidden in the sloping ceiling illuminated the policeman.

It was the only thing Mr May had ever designed, so I began the story: *"Not many men have made a world hit with their sole piece of architecture. Even less have received no acclaim for their accomplishment."*

"Lunn!" boomed Max Schofield's voice half an hour after I handed the story in on Christmas Eve. This time he came to see me and, in front of the other three, waved my story about saying: "Where's the story on the Fu Centre?"

I was still working on it.

"You didn't do what I said. I told you we weren't into the traffic direction business. This isn't the Police Gazette."

The other three looked determinedly down at their work, and I blushed red. I thought it was the best story I had even written.

Mr Schofield wasn't finished with me yet: "However, I admit, Lunn, that I had often wondered where all those pagodas came from myself, and you writers do have your way with words. Nice to see, too, that the lad stayed on instead of running off home. It's more of a human-interest story really, a story on a human scale. A bit of a *Playboy* interview. Seeing as we are making a fresh start under a new masthead let's start a human-interest column, cleanskin, right-hand page: 'About People, By Hugh Lunn'."

Getting my own column was the most unexpected Christmas present I had ever had. But, otherwise, Christmas in Hong Kong was disappointing: no Santas, no pine trees, no Holly. Because Hong Kong was a British Colony I expected Christmas to be celebrated like we did at home. Olive always cooked a few chooks with lots of roast potatoes for Christmas dinner, and Fred baked and then iced a giant cake which he carried dramatically into the breakfast room on the fingertips of his right hand yelling out proudly "yahoo". Then, in his white apron, Fred would sharpen his long knife on a round piece of steel held out in front of his stomach, and carve up the chooks.

I had sent plenty of Christmas presents home: a carved camphor chest for Olive, a modern "neck watch" for Sheryl, a toy dog called Sniffy for Jack's son Stephen, and, for Fred, one of those new Japanese watches they hadn't yet seen in Australia: a Seiko with not only the time, but the day and the date as well.

"Dear Herb," I wrote in the watch case, "Merry Christmas. Seiko claims this was designed by an architect. Every time you look at the time you can think of me. Don't worry."

I added "don't worry" because, ever since I'd left home in October, I had received nothing but worry letters from Olive. Especially since I mentioned that I wouldn't mind going into Red China for a look. Olive needn't have worried because, when I dropped in to the Bank of China Building one day — between the two stone lions guarding the front — I didn't even get past the woman in the foyer. She looked at my passport and said I couldn't go into China because I was from a "renegade country".

"You must understand, you Australians are all poisonous weeds," she explained with a smile, as if passing a compliment.

Olive was worried that Red China now had the atomic bomb. Gay told me to stay away from Singapore because people had been killed in race riots. Jack said things looked bad in Vietnam following a coup, and the bombing of the northern Communists by the Americans. Then, to cap off 1964, just before Christmas Australian and British troops went into battle against the Indonesians who, under Communist influence from Russia, had landed troops in Malaya.

Mum seemed to have the idea that the whole Far East was blowing up, whereas all these events were hundreds of miles away and Hong Kong was a carefree city. She said the Australian government was so worried it had re-introduced compulsory National Service.

The funny thing was that, while they were all worrying about me, I was worried about Fred. He kept having to stop cooking because of nose bleeds, and he wouldn't go to the doctor, saying: "Those fellas always find something wrong with you." I had seen Fred have one of these nose bleeds just before I left. It forced him to sit down in his apron on the flour bags — white flour in his black hair — outside the kitchen. I'd never seen him like this before. Then, when he felt a bit better, he made a plug of grease-proof paper and stuck it up his nose so he could get back to making the pies.

Christmas morning, Ken came around to Chungking Mansions with a gift that had arrived at Grand Hotel reception wrapped in green and red Christmas paper. He had a big smile on his dial because he had saved the present up for the actual day.

Inside was a book called *Poetical Works of Lawson* with a notation from Olive saying: "Dear Hugh, you might like to travel a part of the Hinterland with Lawson."

Mum loved Australian bush poetry and she told me to read the chorus of the first poem in the book:

Oh, he rides hard to race the pain
  Who rides from love, who rides from home;
But he rides slowly home again,
  Whose heart has learnt to love and roam.

It looked like she was still on about me wanting to go into Red China.

Ken had arranged something special for Christmas Day, but I wasn't looking forward to it. On his two previous trips to Hong Kong, he had taken three Chinese orphans out for the day from Saint Paul's Jesuit Orphanage, Causeway Bay. Because it was Christmas he had arranged to do so again, and he wanted me to go with him.

Ken was quite religious compared with me. He knew, for example, that the Church did not list sex as the worst sin: "The two worst sins are Calumny and Detraction, because they are sins against Charity." He was always asking questions about religion, like what would happen on the "Last Day" when everyone rose up and we were re-united with our earthly bodies.

"Which body do you get back well?" Ken always wanted to know: "your 18-year-old body or your 88-year-old body."

A former altar boy, Ken could somehow remember exactly the lines we had learned at school about what Christ would say on the Last Day, and would sometimes recite these with great dramatic effect: "And Jesus will say to the good 'Come Ye blessed into my Kingdom'. But to the evil he will say: 'Depart from me Ye cursed into the everlasting fires of Hell that were prepared for you, the Devil, and his angels'."

Even Fletch's jokes usually had a religious background. Like the one about the Catholic who died and went to Hell where the Devil said he had to choose one of three rooms in which to spend eternity.

"The Devil opens the first door," Fletch would say, already bursting with laughter at his own joke, "and thousands of people are standing on their heads on red hot coals begging for a drink. 'No thanks, not that one,' says the Catholic. Behind the second door everyone is standing on their heads on sharp spikes cutting into their bleeding scalps. 'No thanks, not that one either,' says the Catholic. The Devil opens the third, and last, door and everyone is standing up to their waists in shit, but they are sipping on nice cups of Bushells tea from the finest bone china. 'Well this isn't too bad, considering,' he says, and takes up his position sipping tea and smiling at those around him. Then suddenly one of the Devil's leading angels bursts in wielding a long whip and shouts: 'OK. On your heads fellas, tea break's over'."

Thus Ken tried hard to be good. He was always talking about looking after those less well off than himself, particularly kids.

"It's not a question of being lumbered with them but," he said. "They really look forward to it. Hughie it's Christmas, and life has gone off the boil as far as they are concerned. If it wasn't for the Church they'd have nowhere to live."

I didn't like the idea because, when I was a boy, Fred and Olive had the same bright idea. We took two boys from Nudgee Orphanage out with us six Lunns for a Sunday drive when Fred took a rare day off from his cake shop. They wore a khaki uniform, and they got in the road of our family outing. But Fletch argued that we should be trying to do God's work on earth. I put all this down to Ken being an only child. With an older brother and two younger sisters, I never felt lonely. But I knew Ken did. He had a little piggy doll he used to sleep with at Annerley as a little boy, and one night in the Bayside nightclub he told me: "That little pig. I can still see the look on him: a sort of nice smile."

In his first year of school at the Convent, Ken used to be so scared of the nuns with their crucifixes tucked like daggers into the front of their black belts, that he ran away from school every day for the first year, and his parents had to keep taking him back. His mother, Ethel, said that every morning at about eleven she would see a little blonde head bobbing past the kitchen window, and she knew Ken had shot through yet again. But he was tough. Even though he got a belting from his father, he would still run away again the next day.

Ken said we could be like Guardian Angels to these orphans, and he was still able to recite the prayer we learnt at the Convent:

Oh Angel of God, my Guardian dear;
To whom God's love commits me here.
Ever this day be at my side
To light and guard, to rule and guide
  Amen

Next thing I knew, early Christmas Day, on my one extra day off, I was on the Star Ferry heading for Hong Kong Island, as if I was going to work. I dressed in my grey Beatle suit because it was a cold, windy, winter's day, and Ken wore the heavy brown suede jacket he'd bought in Spain.

The ferries were a bit like a Brisbane tram, with narrow slat seats to cool the body and a timber floor: except for the "Beware of Pickpockets" and "do not spit" signs in both English and Chinese, and the huge coils of thick rope we had to step over. But, like the trams, the driver sat up the front in a special steel cage by himself and they could be driven from both ends. Also, like the trams, you didn't need

51

a timetable because another ferry was always on the way. At the pier, Europeans in long white uniforms stood in the green alleyways that funnelled people in. They counted everyone by looking at each face while pressing a small silver counter in their hand. They must have got to know every face in Hong Kong.

The ferry cost hardly anything, but down the bottom deck was half-price. All the Europeans and well-dressed Chinese went on the upper deck, and Chinese Coolies sailed on the bottom. I preferred the bottom: it was closer to the water and every day as I went to work I was the only European surrounded by the poorest of the world's poor. But with the sea spray in my face, heading for an island of skyscrapers, I felt like a King for ten minutes every day.

Ken had a habit of often bringing religion up at the oddest times and, instead of enjoying our Christmas ferry ride, he suddenly expressed surprise that we didn't hear anything about Jesus between when he was the child in the Temple "until he is wandering around the place doing miracles".

"I wonder where he got to?"

At the orphanage it was strange to see a Chinese dressed in the uniform of a Catholic nun. Ken had dealt with this nun previously, and she brought out the three Chinese orphan girls Fletch had taken out the previous year, and they rushed forward to greet him while giggling so much that I could see one girl had no top teeth. The orphans spoke only Chinese, so we had no idea what they were saying. He said the one that wasn't saying anything was deaf and dumb: "She's the happiest of the lot of them but."

The nun then announced that one of the girls had that morning stolen a pencil, so would not be allowed to go. The little girl started screaming. Ken pleaded with the nun to let her come, saying that after all it was Christmas, and forgiveness was a sacrament of the Church. But, being a nun, she wouldn't change her mind.

There were lots more orphans milling around. I didn't like the place because Fred had told me a hundred times how terrible it was when he was brought up in an orphanage in Western Australia. He said the people in charge ate most of the food.

"I've got Hughie to help me, Sister," Ken said, "so give us a few more well."

We ended up with five Chinese kids, three boys and two girls. I couldn't tell if they were six-years-old, or eight, or four, and I couldn't ask them: since they couldn't speak English.

Because Ken said they had to wear hand-me-downs I was surprised how well dressed they all were. They had neat haircuts and didn't look at all hungry.

Unlike Brisbane on Christmas Day, all the shops were open, and we stopped to buy the orphans Christmas presents. Ken bought each boy a toy helicopter, and each girl a toy red telephone. The helicopters gave Ken a good idea: to take them out to the aerodrome to see the jetliners taking off and landing. By the time we got there the kids were carrying plastic bags full of presents, and I soon ran out of coins because all five wanted to look through a coin-operated telescope on the Observation Deck at Kai Tak Airport.

The Suns put on a special Christmas lunch for the orphans in the Grand Hotel dining room at their family table. I invited along the young English editor from work, Ken Archer, who had only recently arrived in Hong Kong.

Arch soon had all five orphans climbing all over him. The two girls never stopped laughing all day, but the boys seemed to get bored after lunch when they finally stopped playing with their helicopters, and Arch stopped taking pictures with his brand new Japanese Minolta camera.

So Ken let them play with his electric train set. Since I'd moved out of the hotel room, Ken had bought a train set. You couldn't walk in without tripping over train lines, signals, tunnels, sleepers, goods yards, and shunting engines. The trains ran all around the room and under both the beds. Ken's father was a Queensland Railways train driver and Ken wanted to be one too because his father used to take him on trips in the engine and let him blow the steam whistle. Toy trains were too expensive back home, and were only wind-up anyway. But in Hong Kong electric train sets were very cheap, so Ken had indulged his childhood fantasy.

Soon the orphans and Arch were operating the points to divert trains on shortcuts, or into one of the four stations. Fletch kept an eye on the transformer because he said if too much electricity got through the trains would "go into orbit".

While the others drove trains, I put some twelve-inch long-playing microgroove unbreakable records on what Ken called his "James Bond record player" — because it looked like an ordinary port until you opened it up and found a small radiogram inside.

In particular, I played *When Irish Eyes are Smiling*, by Bing Crosby, which I had given Ken for Christmas. I picked this record out at Moutries because Ken had sung it on our way up to Hong Kong in the near-empty Qantas jetliner, urged on by the stewards.

But the number we liked best that Christmas of 1964 was towards the end of the record: *The Isle of Innisfree*. As that song played, for the first time I wished I was back in Brisbane. Ken, banished from Australian tennis and so conscious of his Irish heritage that he often said "the whole world should be Irish", sang along to words that seemed written for us:

"And when the moonlight peeps across the rooftops of this great city, wond'rous though it be … Precious things are dreams unto an exile, they take him o'er the land across the sea … But sure a body's bound to be a dreamer, when all the things he loves are far away …"

5   Of all the Gin Joints …

My Russian classmate from schooldays, Jim Egoroff, arrived in Hong Kong just after Christmas wearing thongs, shorts and a shirt. Normally Jim dressed very formally in suit and tie, but not when on holidays. The heels of his thongs were already worn paper-thin, Jim being so big and so active that he was the only person I knew who could wear out a pair of rubber thongs. He reckoned thongs only lasted him a fortnight.

"I'm glad to see you didn't over-dress to travel overseas, Jim," I said as we shook hands, because on a jetliner you were supposed to wear a suit.

"Don't worry mate," Jim said, "it's just my Australian heritage."

Having crushed my hand inside his mighty brown paw to teach me a lesson, he added: "In any case Lunn, you dog, you forget that I have of been here before in 1950 when we escaped from China. Anyway, all jokes aside, how have you been going these couple of last days."

Jim had come up to stay for a few days of the Australian holidays, partly because I'd promised to line him up with a few girls. Which wasn't going to be easy. But Fletch said he knew a couple of good lookers who worked as ground hostesses at the airport. I also wanted to introduce Jim to Steve Dunleavy if I could.

It was great to have Jim in Hong Kong because he would make sure we ate well, he'd tell some of his funny stories, and let me know how the Lunns were getting on back home. I already knew he had manufactured some special shampoo for my blonde sister Gay. Jim said he had tiled our kitchen floor for Mum, and had promised to line our unlined bathroom walls for her with a new product, pink and white Tilux. He was always doing things for Olive, ever since he fixed her washing machine when he was twelve years old.

Jim was doing well in Brisbane, building cold rooms and twenty-foot long shop refrigerators. "Refrigeration has at last come to Brisbane mate," he said. "Every Tom, Dick, Harry, or his dog wants to get refrigerated. That's why I decided to have a holiday, because this year I have of built up quite a large egg-nest."

He now even had employees. It was hard to imagine: one of us hiring and firing people. Controlling the lives of others. Jim even had his own private secretary, no less, but said she slowed everything down because she kept having trouble with her boyfriend.

"Apparently this boyfriend's eyes were rolling around at women and other loose things. So she complained to me about him having goo-goo eyes," Jim said. "But it had nothing to do with me, and her hard ravings were boring me to tears on a daily basis. So during the pre-Christmas rush I said: 'We're a bit busy today. Why don't you take the rest of the day off?' "

I asked Jim if he had sacked his secretary, and got one of his ambivalent answers.

"Whatever," he said.

Like me, Jim marvelled at the myriad buildings, people, and shops as we headed for the labyrinthine ways of Chungking Mansions and up to my room, where Roxas had kindly provided a sleeping bag for Jim. Once unpacked, Jim looked hard at me through his black eyebrows, as he always did when he was going to make a serious announcement. Hong Kong, he said, had really gone ahead since he had been here as a nine-year-old boy fourteen years before when his family fled the Reds for Australia. Nodding his head up and down gravely, Jim said: "Lord and behold, I told you before Lunn, Brisbane is only a fish-and-chip shop, but you couldn't believe me. Instead of going ahead, the place has gone back to the dogs."

Jim was still inventing things, even though no one had ever taken up his award-winning schoolboy design of refrigerator doors that opened when you said "open" and shut when you said "shut". He had recently made something that just might put Brisbane on the map.

"In any case between you and me confidentially," Jim said quietly, "I really, really honestly believe this will be a beauty. Everything is push-button these couple of last days, except taps. So I have of made a push-button tap!"

Without thinking, I inquired if it worked.

"You are a low-down dirty dog, Lunn. You wouldn't know your fist from your fingernails. Of course it works. Like a real little beauty, using only mains pressure."

Jim just happened to have a tap with him and, before I could stop him, he was in the kitchen ripping off Roxas' cold water sink tap with the monkey grips he always carried in his hard black briefcase. Ever the complete businessman, Jim not only carried papers in his briefcase, but also spanners, screwdrivers, and packets of photographs.

It was terrible to watch the old pipes of Chungking Mansions bending beneath Jim's indelible force, as he took no notice of my cries to stop. Rusty water oozed out the side like ointment from beneath a bandage. Then, suddenly, the old Chinese tap was in Jim's claw. Out of the briefcase he pulled something strange. I couldn't work out what it was until my mind re-adjusted. It was half a tap: a spout, with the turning attachment on the top missing.

Jim screwed this doover to the pipe, turned the water back on, pressed the top, and, after a half second delay, out came the water as from a tap. He pushed the top again and, after another slight delay, the water stopped.

"Did you ever had, Lunn?" Jim said, laughing proudly at his brilliant invention.

He cleaned up the mess, and threw the push-button tap back in his briefcase where it disappeared among all the tools.

It was only since I'd come to Hong Kong that I'd realised how difficult it must have been for Jim when he arrived in Australia from China as a New Australian called Dimitri Egoroff. He not only had to get a new first name — an Australian one — but to learn English. Not just well enough to count to ten or order a drink, but to understand Shakespeare, Milton, and Bryon well enough to get into university. In China his parents had lived in an all-Russian town called Harbin, so Jim only spoke what he himself called "the basics of the basic" English when he arrived aged nine.

I had tried to learn some Chinese but had picked up just a few words. "Wei" was the same as "hello", so from the first day in the office I said "Wei" whenever I answered the telephone. There was "dorche" for thanks, which was important for being polite. Every time someone in the office, even the Englishmen, helped me, I said: "dorche" just for the practice.

"Ay yah!" I recognised because, whenever something unexpected happened in a film, the whole theatre — they were always full — would yell out "ay yah!" It was what you said if something went wrong. "Ay yah!" was a sort of exaggerated version of "good grief!"

Although I could count to ten, and knew the word for dollar was "mun", in three months I hadn't learned enough to speak sentences. But still, Jim, being an engineer, was impressed to hear I was writing for an engineering journal.

"I'm glad you're not loafing, Lunn. I don't want to insult you, but you might learn something useful."

Jim knew I was never any good at Physics or Chemistry at school because we were partners in science experiments. So I was happy to admit that writing about architecture and engineering worried me. Jim wasn't often sympathetic but, whenever he could see a need, he always came up with some sound advice:

"People always get into trouble whenever they try to be too smart, Lunn. Just make sure you stick to the flat and narrow."

The next evening I took Jim to a Russian restaurant near the Grand where Ken and I often went for crabs claws. Even though Jim had never been to Russia, I thought it might make him feel more at home.

It was a bad choice. Two men in white suits sitting behind Jim had a long, earnest conversation in a foreign language. After we had eaten, Jim swung around and spoke to them in Russian. The one facing me went red, and the other spoke Russian — like loud whispering — vehemently at Jim. The pair picked up their small-brimmed felt hats and left.

Jim said there was no problem: "I heard them speaking Russian and, just for fun, I said: '*I am an Australian Russian spy. So you had of better keep quiet. I only have limited time, I'm being watched*'. And, lord and behold, they abused me. So I told them not to mix up their intentions with their capabilities."

As we ate, Jim revealed he was doing just about as well as me in the girlfriend stakes. When I left Brisbane three months before he had a striking looking girlfriend, a beauty queen no less. I remembered he took her to a film about Russia and afterwards he said: "We were sitting there having tender moments when she held me so tight that I thought she must of have been scared."

She had since given him the flick.

"Cutting a long story short, I had of given her a gift of ten driving lessons for her birthday, and went off to Sydney for work. When I came back, Lord and behold, she had of become engaged to the driving instructor."

Jim said it showed how women always thought ahead: "There has got to be a reason behind a woman's brain. In any case I suppose she wanted to make sure her kids learnt to drive properly."

I felt Jim was more upset at this rejection than he was saying. I knew how I would feel. Olive always said it was best to "talk things out", so, as sympathetically as I could, I said that I supposed Jim was pretty angry with her for taking advantage of his famous generosity.

"She made me feel very little, but if you are a wolf you have to lead a wolf's life. If she was being shot, I'd save her," he replied gallantly.

Even though we had sat next to each other at school for nine years, we had never shared a room. Even in the army cadets we never shared a tent because I was in the Band and Jim was in Intelligence, and then Mortars. So I was surprised when, before we went to sleep, Jim said he wanted to take maximum advantage of his three-day holiday: "So please make an effort to get up and wash yourself."

Getting up early was alright for Jim: he claimed he only needed three hours sleep a night. But all of us Lunns needed at least nine hours to feel human.

I kept some soya milk and corn flakes in the kitchen for breakfast, but to my surprise Jim wouldn't eat any.

"That's chickenfeed Lunn. Why don't you eat a proper meal of steak for breakfast? What I am trying to tell you is this: no wonder you're so thin and weak." So we decided to have breakfast at the President hotel across the road. As Jim showered, I noticed he shampooed his whole body, and then, to my surprise, he put some sweet smelling perfume under his arms.

"It's underarm lotion Lunn," he said.

That was a new one to me.

When I asked why he shampooed the hair on his chest, Jim replied: "When you wash a dog you don't just wash its head."

I dressed in my blue suit for work and Jim put on one of his classy white suits with a black shirt and, after our Presidential breakfast, we walked to the ferry, slipping around the hundreds of slow Chinese like we were in a speeded up film. I saw by the Star Ferry clock tower that we were running early, which I hated. So we diverted to the lush foyer of the Peninsula Hotel which was one of the most expensive in the world.

"There's still plenty of time to run late," I said.

"You Bastard Boy, Lunn. How many times must I tell you to buy a watch. I know you don't want fidgety cogs and wheels to control your life, but you should of have known the time."

On the ferry ride, as Jim admired the view across the harbour I told him of the terrible experience when I wandered into the foyer of the Mandarin Hotel on my first day at work, and suddenly realised I was surrounded by a hundred Japs. My pulse raced, my face flushed, I wanted to run out: as if I was in great danger. The only explanation I could offer was that these were the first Japanese I had seen since World War II when the ultra-evil crooks in the *Batman* serials at the flicks were always Japanese, who said things like: "Ve must turn zee Batman into zee Zombie and get zee atomic raygun at all ze cost."

Somehow I just knew Jim wouldn't be able to walk past the scores of rickshaws which were always parked outside the Star Ferry on the Island side. Rickshaws were man-powered vehicles for short pleasant journeys in central Hong Kong. They had one wide passenger seat between two wheels, a fold-up semi-circular top to protect the passenger from sun and rain, and each was powered in and out of the traffic by an old Chinese man in shorts, loose shirt and sandals. It was like a small sulky pulled by a human being instead of a horse. The rickshaws were made of wood and painted mostly red, with large black bicycle wheels.

"Come on Lunn," said Jim, giving the owner a bundle of ten dollar notes, "get in."

I tried to talk him out of it, but he said: "Are you an idiot or what? Get in before I get annoyed again with you. Are you a fair-weather friend?"

So I did as I was told.

For the benefit of the toothless Chinese driver, Jim pointed to the corner and back. Then he squeezed his huge muscular frame in between the two wooden handles protruding some distance at the front. I could tell by his stance, one leg back and one forward, that he just had to show the Chinese how fast these unusual machines could go. Jim wasn't the type to train by lifting weights in a gymnasium. His method was to push his car around the block every morning.

"The only trouble, Lunn, is that these couple of last mornings people are being too nice. They have of been stopping to help me."

Jim was three times the size of the average Chinese rickshaw puller and was used to pushing a giant American Plymouth Belvedere around the block at Kangaroo Point in Brisbane. So the red rickshaw must have felt like a toy as he took off on the circular road that led into Hong Kong's business district, with me hanging onto the seat. So fast did Jim take off that the pram-like quarter-circle canvas lid collapsed backwards so that I was suddenly riding a careering topless rickshaw. Every time Jim hit the slightest bump the sprung rickshaw bounced in the air. Once I came down on one of the red timber mudguards as we raced along the road past hundreds of slow-moving Chinese in the morning peak hour. By the time Jim turned back at Connaught Road everyone was watching, so I pretended I was whipping him along and, working in unison, we gathered tremendous speed like we had when we won the inter-school three-legged race a decade before.

As we swung around the circular drive I saw Max Schofield's unmistakeable Spanish moustache coming towards us in the crowd. He gave a little wave as we careered past and called out "Good show, Lunn".

The rickshaw driver was relieved to get his machine back in one piece, and Jim was elated by the laughing Chinese faces that surrounded us outside the Star Ferry terminal.

"Did you see them, Lunn," he said, "they were rolling themselves."

The driver became anxious again when Jim pulled some tools out of his briefcase and started work on one of the wheels. "Tell him it has of pulled to one side, Lunn," Jim said, putting his left arm tenderly on the driver's shoulder and calling him "mate".

Since the driver spoke no English, and I could not speak Chinese, I didn't know what to say.

"Wei, dorche, ay yah!" (Hello, thanks, good grief!) I said, which seemed to make both Jim and the rickshaw driver happy.

The rickshaw ride was such a success that I thought I might give it a go myself. "You get in this time Jim," I said as he finished fixing the wheel.

Jim picked up his briefcase and headed for the centre of town saying: "I wouldn't mind not seeing that, Lunn."

We arranged to meet Ken for a Dim Sum lunch, and for once I was able to impress Jim, signalling the girls who walked around calling out the names of my favourite Cantonese savoury snacks, which by now I recognised. Because of my pink cheeks, I always got served immediately.

"Har Gau" was the best: four delicious white steamed shrimp dumplings. "Cha Siu Bau" landed us two white steamed barbequed pork buns, and "Shiu Mai" got us steamed minced pork.

Jim for once was satisfied. This was real food.

"We would of have had made our fortune if we sold this tucker in Australia instead of pies and sausage rolls," he said.

We finished off with three hot custard tarts: one each, and wiped our faces with the inevitable boiling hot face cloths provided in all Hong Kong restaurants after meals.

Over several hot bowls of Chinese tea, Ken told us he had taken our Chinese friend Billy Lee Long — a fourth-generation Queenslander from Cairns — to this very restaurant the previous year, and Billy, who spoke no Chinese, was asking all the time: "What's going on Fletch? What are these sheilas yelling out for?"

And Jim told Ken of the rickshaw ride: "You should of have seen us Ken, whooosh. No one could believe it."

"You're lucky you both didn't end up a couple of cot cases," said Fletch.

That afternoon Jim rang me at work.

"It's Jim out here Lunn," he said. "I'll meet you after work at the Peak tram."

We used to catch the tram together after school in Brisbane, but this was no ordinary tram. It travelled almost vertically to the top of Victoria Peak on Hong Kong Island, the slope pushing us heavily back into our seats and making my palms sweat. Each of the stations told how far we had to fall back down. The first was Kennedy Road station: 184 feet. It was said that once upon a time no Chinese were allowed to live above this level. But that was no great loss to the Chinese because, although the views were fantastic, the peak spent most of the summer shrouded in mist, which made mould grow on shoes and clothes in the cupboards.

Bell Road: 314 feet. After this it got so steep that everything else in Hong Kong looked straight, but we felt crooked.

May Road: 590 feet. By now we were almost tipping over backwards. What a contrast with the Salisbury-Clayfield tram. This tram seemed to be suffering in a bid to make progress. The skyscrapers now looked as if they were leaning over.

Barkers Road: 1,190 feet. Jim still watched impassively out the window as Hong Kong began to glitter below in the dusk, like fireworks at the Ekka.

The Peak: a lookout at 1,300-feet where we looked down on the roofs of all the skyscrapers and the hundreds of ships in the harbour. Jim pointed out all the American and British warships — and an Australian — each with a string of lights strung from the front up over the central structure to the back.

"If the Commos want to win World War III they just have to bomb Hong Kong at Christmas time," I said. It seemed to me we were not very well prepared for war after what

64

happened at Pearl Harbour the year we were both born, and in the Gulf of Tonkin a few months ago when the North Vietnamese launched a sneak attack on an American warship patrolling off their coast.

"Forget it, Lunn," said Jim, "a few boats won't make any difference with the weapons now being invented every day."

True to his word, Ken lined us up with a double blind date and booked us a table at a posh restaurant on the Island at the Mandarin Hotel. I thought it would be too expensive, but Jim, as we got ready in my room, said it was important, now that we were in the international community, to show we were prosperous and successful. He insisted we wear suits, and both put on his underarm lotion.

"It gives you intelligence status, Lunn."

The airport ground hostesses looked knockouts in their tight cheongsams and Jim was the perfect gentleman, helping them both on and off the ferry. I never knew until that night that Hong Kong harbour could get so rough.

On arrival at the Island, bamboo poles were used by the Chinese ferrymen to catch the three-inch thick ferry ropes to tie them to the piers, because they were too heavy to throw more than a few yards. The ferry was pitching up and down, so the shore man only got hold of the one rope, which he quickly wrapped around a foot-thick steel post to pull the ferry closer and get some more ropes attached. As the boat pitched down and backwards the three-inch thick rope tugged and then snapped, and the whole ferryload yelled out in unison "ay yah!" like a chorus. The water churned as the underwater propellors spun furiously to try to give the driver some control.

Jim rushed forward, saying "give me that dirty great rope" and lifted up a ten-yard section and hurled it through the air so that the rope easily reached the men on the pier. The girls — and all the other Chinese on the ferry — were impressed. But Jim ruined all his good work at dinner. Chatting up girls had never been one of our strong suits, probably because we had been educated at a boys-only college. Our teachers, the Christian Brothers, knew nothing of girls, and so they taught us what to say and do at dinner parties from a book called "Christian Politeness and Counsel for Youth". There was only one piece of advice on what to talk about at dinner with girls: "It is OK to talk about the flower arrangements, but never the food."

Luckily, one of the girls was a Catholic. So instead of talking about the food, Jim showed his knowledge of our religion: "Brother Campbell told us that if the Pope says Grip-U trousers are the best, then he is not being infallible." Jim felt it was best to be honest with them: "Cutting a long story short, we are slightly dubious characters. But I have to tell you: everything bad I have of contracted, I have of contracted from Hugh."

After a while he had the girls rolling themselves.

He told them about the Australian recipe for an omelette: "First, borrow some eggs," and explained the difference between Eno's and Epsoms Salts: "Eno's is what you have in Heaven; and Epsons is what you have in Hell."

They were both laughing at everything he said.

I could see he was white-anting me with both girls at once, so I advised them not to take too much notice. "Jim often carries on like this. He can't help himself. It's his Russian background."

"I don't want to insult you Lunn, you gutter snipe," Jim replied, reaching out to grab me by the front of the shirt, "even though you are a worthless wretch, I'd be very nice to me if I was you. Otherwise I will tell these pretty little girls some stories about you, that you are not a very savoury character ..." and he opened his dark eyes wide, raised his dark eyebrows at them, and then narrowed his eyes and looked at me as if holding back something very, very sinister.

Both girls looked at me as if I must have committed some horrible crime. Jim relented at the last minute and laughed, saying: "I was only having a swing on him." But he said he wanted them both to know that I knew absolutely nothing about women: "And even when he knows something about them, he won't tell me."

Inevitably, Jim fished around and around until he finally put his foot in it. One of the girls wasn't hungry and, as always, Jim had ordered enough food for four Jims: and 10 normal eaters. So the feast was going to waste.

"Do you want something else before you starve to death?" Jim asked one of them politely.

"You're a big girl … I mean, you are not a young woman … do you want a glass of water?"

"Leave her alone," the other girl said. "You Russians are always picking on people."

"So young and so untender," said Jim, quoting Shakespeare's King Lear, as he was wont to do. "I am sorry girls, my English has gone down the dumps lately."

Never one to leave well enough alone, Jim told them his apocryphal story — though he seemed to believe it — about compulsory chest X-rays in Australia. No one in Hong Kong had heard of such a thing and, though the programme was aimed at wiping out TB, even the Chinese thought it was an authoritarian step to take.

"This is honestly, honestly true," Jim began, which immediately made me suspicious.

"Because of huge queues for these X-rays in those last days, you always left your shirt on for X-rays to save the nurses time. Cutting a long story short, I had of bought one of those new modern shirts with a vertical metal thread in the material, and I forgot I had it on. The nurses were pretty little girls and took my X-ray and, by the time I got home, there was an ambulance waiting to take me to hospital. I tried to get out of it, but they said I must be put away in quarantine: they had never seen lungs so diseased with TB. They wanted to know if I felt alright and wondered how I could still walk. 'Walk mate?' I said. 'I can run out of sight'. They were amazed.

"When I got to the hospital, doctors looked at my chest X-ray in the light, trying to work out how I was still alive.

Being an engineer, I soon worked out that the many tiny holes that showed up in my lungs on the X-ray was where the metal threads on the back and front of my shirt crossed over each other."

Soon after this we headed for the Firecracker, alone.

Jim said of the two girls, misquoting Tennyson: "God in his mercy lend them grace, at least they had a lovely face".

I was hoping to introduce Jim to Steve.

Steve might be pretty tough, but Jim cracked Queensland nuts between his teeth — which always made me wince — and walnuts in the palm of his hand. He had a simple way of looking at his enormous strength. He said human muscles were like timber, and there were three types of timber where he came from: "hardwood; hard hardwood; and hard, hard hardwood".

Jim, always the facer card in any pack, added a new dimension to our group and, because he and Victor Sun were both engineers, they had a lot to talk about. Fletch explained to Jim that, unlike Brisbane, there were no topless acts because the British Colonial Government wouldn't allow them. But there was a dance hall up Nathan Road where you could pay girls for a dance.

"It's no Cloudland but."

Jim then told us he had once met a beautiful girl in Brisbane: "One thing got to another and, I couldn't believe it, she said: 'Do you want to watch me get undressed at eight o'clock tonight?' I was really, really honestly surprised. Then I have of found out she was a stripper at a nightclub. I went to see her. She had of had beautiful breasts, both of them."

Victor was interested to hear that Jim owned a Plymouth Belvedere back home, since Victor drove an American Chev. But Jim said the Plymouth "got broken" in a car accident just after Christmas. It was in for panel-beating and that was one of the reasons he had gone on holidays.

"I had of been rear-ended by this pretty little girl from Switzerland," he said. "It was a real scene. My clothes were torn and we were stuck together for some time. But I pulled out, and she backed out."

I couldn't stop myself from laughing.

"I know you are a little bit of a pervert, Lunn, with your lewd thoughts," Jim said, feigning anger and holding out his hand like a steel claw, "but this is honestly, honestly true. She had of just bought a Hi Fi unit, a stereo one, and — because her car was broken — I drove her home to her place and plugged it all in for her."

Victor looked inscrutable.

"Is this story second hand?" he asked Jim.

"Second hand?" said Jim. "Second hand mate? I got it from the horse's mouth."

A voice boomed out from some British servicemen at the next table in the cramped nightclub.

It sounded like "bullshit".

Sensing trouble, I told Jim to ignore them.

"They don't call me 'bastard features' for nothing, Lunn," Jim said. "I too have whiskers."

Whenever Jim was really angry, he didn't go red or become animated like other people. He got a very melancholy look on his olive face, as if he were genuinely sad for the people who had upset him: and I think he was. Also, he moved more slowly instead of faster.

Jim sauntered glumly around the adjoining table, deliberately leant one large arm on the table with his thick fingers spread so the servicemen could see that each finger was the size of a Cavendish banana. The candle lit up the wide scar down the length of Jim's nose.

"Have you of been upset about something? Or are you speaking from experience? Is there something you would have liked to stand up and discuss?"

"Forget it chum," said the biggest of the Brits.

"I'll make sure you forget it," said Jim, reaching for him. "You have of taken the bait by the hand."

"We haven't done anything, we're just talking among ourselves," said the one who yelled out. "What's the trouble?"

"You tell me, then I'll tell you, then we'll both know," said Jim quietly.

Ken urged Jim on from our table: "It's 'High Noon in Hong Kong'."

"As I was saying before that rude interruption," Jim said, "I have decided to dig my heels in the sand. Do you think I shouldn't of."

A young Englishman with a strange accent tried to speak: "But, but …"

"But me no buts," said Jim.

"Give over stranger, give over. We ne'r meant nought," said the Englishman.

At which Jim, used to Australian English, turned and looked around the nightclub, which had gone totally quiet, and said: "I must find out who perverted the Queen's English."

Our table, and the ones nearby, burst into laughter: and Jim's mood turned.

"You have of missed the giggles," he told the sailors seriously. "Never miss the giggles."

At which moment, Steve Dunleavy appeared out of the smoke in an off-white suit like Humphrey Bogart in *Casablanca*, except he wasn't smoking.

Steve pushed his hair back between his fingers with both hands as he arrived, unbuttoned his coat and pulled the sides back, and with his left hand took Jim by the arm just above the elbow and turned him around.

They were standing in one another's space.

"I liked that, pal," Steve said coldly. "Very good. Very good. But stopping fights is my job."

I leapt up and introduced them, explaining that, although Jim was Russian, he was in fact Australian, and Steve was a friend of ours.

Steve stepped slowly back and shook hands with Jim, who wasn't sure which way to react to this confident, handsome stranger who had laid hand on him while he was in fighting mode.

"A Russian, huh," said Steve. "A Russian. Well, Hughie, tell him we don't have a Going Rate for Russkys, yet."

And Steve disappeared back into the smoky mist.

Jim asked who he was.

I explained that Steve was a top journalist by day, and a freelance nightclub throw-er-outer by night.

"When you meet him again, Lunn," Jim said gravely, "don't put a step out of place."

This sounded like a strange thing to say about a nice bloke like Steve. So I asked Jim not to be so coy, and for once to say what he meant.

"Bugger-me-dead Lunn, as I always say: don't ask for trouble unless you need it."

6 Tea for Three

When Fletch found out that Jim and I had failed to win on with the two hostesses he was very disappointed.

"You're proving hard to place, Hughie," he said.

Ken wanted me to get a girlfriend because he had found one: a beautiful Burmese girl called Pamela d'Castro who looked like a China Doll. Now that they were an item, Ken kept leaning across asking her to put her small nose into the space between his left eyeball and the bridge of his nose.

When she did this he would turn and say to me: "Perfection son, perfection."

But I didn't want to know.

Ken always reckoned there were two lucky girls in Hong Kong "walking around with no idea that us two big Lardie-dahs are about to arrive on their doorstep. We can't miss out with our reputation for putting one over." But I said I'd believe that when Queensland won the Sheffield Shield.

All I could hope was that my girl was still walking around the Colony somewhere.

After six weeks in Chungking Mansions, I moved out into a two bedroom flat with my English workmate Ken Archer. The flat was way up the end of Nathan Road on the top floor of a four-storey building at 48 Ho Man Tin Street, so Fletch reckoned we'd moved to "the end of civilisation". But this wasn't a problem, because Arch had just bought a white MGA sports car, and things had turned around on the girlfriend front.

One day, early in the New Year, I got talking to a Chinese girl in a jewellery shop near the Grand and asked if she was on the phone. She was a good sort, her jet black hair emphasised by the white plastic hair band that held it in place. She wore black spectacles that pointed out and upwards at the sides, and spoke English like a native. Her name was Emily, and, when she said she was really a singer but couldn't get a job because of all the Filipinos, I said she could sing for me if she liked. I'd be very happy to listen.

She shut the shop and, as clearly as a magpie, sang Western hit songs like *It's Almost Tomorrow* and *Hey Jude*. She moved so quickly I was starting to believe those stories that Chinese girls in Hong Kong were after a Western husband to take them away from the dreadful poverty of the East, so that they could send money back from a rich, prosperous country like Australia.

Emily liked to kiss, but always did it with a lolly in her mouth. I didn't mind, because it doubled the taste sensation. She seemed to be able to kiss without breathing, but I had to stop to blow my nose, which she thought was very funny.

Ken wasn't impressed.

"She's not my cup of tea," he said, "a bit of a pushy bird really. Just because you find a girl very disturbing doesn't mean she is the one you should do a line for. We all get carried away sometimes, but in the end it's the personality you have to live with."

I had also become friendly with Babette Wolfe, a 19-year-old half-English and half-German girl. I got off to a bad start with her at the Kowloon Cricket Club when we met: "English and German: now there's an unlikely combination so soon after World War II," I said. She wouldn't speak to me after that. But when she did, Babette told me it was a difficult way to be brought into the world. She didn't know if she was German, or English. She didn't feel she belonged to either side. Then she cried. Even though I was still in my cricket clothes I put my arm around her and walked her home.

Babette's English father, an officer in the British Forces defending Hong Kong, sat in a single lounge chair in the tenth floor apartment looking out over the harbour while listening to a tape recorder. He was a British army language expert who spoke Chinese, German, Russian, and was learning French by listening to tape-recorded lessons. It was easy, he said, and would only take him three weeks of concentrated effort.

Babette clearly wasn't impressed. But I was. I had always wanted to learn French, but boys in the C class at school were not considered smart enough to learn such an exotic language — unlike the As and the Bs. The Cs had to do Latin.

I resolved straight away to learn French from tapes, just like him.

The day Arch and I moved into our flat, I dropped into an architect's office looking for a story. I was greeted by a receptionist with kissable lips, tanned brown skin and black hair cut straight across at shoulder level, with a fringe to the eyebrows. Ken said you knew a girl was the one if you felt like kissing her.

This girl looked for all the world like Elizabeth Taylor in *Cleopatra*. I hung around after the interview and chatted. She seemed to laugh happily at just about everything I said. I liked her voice, which was delicately clear and quiet, like a series of little church bells rung by an Altar Boy at Mass. This girl was very confident, and didn't seem to mind wasting time in the office when she should be working.

"No. I run things in the office. You can stay," she said and laughed.

Every now and then she had to answer the phone, "Wei", but each time I waited around until she had finished. It wasn't rude, because, since she was talking Chinese, I had no idea what the conversation was about.

"You seem to have a lot of time on your hands," she said.

"I have today," I replied.

Her name was Jeanette Joyce Jones, which seemed a strange name for a local Hong Kong girl.

She was 21, two years younger than me, and I just knew she would have a boyfriend. But the way she moved her long brown fingers as she talked into the phone — illustrating each point even though the caller could not see her — mesmerised me. Her hands made everyone else's seem like hunks of meat. She made me think of what Ken always said: "You have to get a girlfriend who puts a spring in your step."

I asked Jeanette what she did in her spare time.

"Tell fortunes, read cards, have fun."

"All you Chinese seem to be in the fortune-telling business," I said, congratulating myself on the quick quip.

"I'm not Chinese," she said.

What a blunder. She had black hair and brown skin, but no wonder she looked like Elizabeth Taylor, and not Nancy Kwan. I thought she would be very annoyed, but she was not fazed one bit by my stupid error.

"Have you just arrived? How does an Australian man find life in mysterious Hong Kong?" she asked.

I told her that I kept getting mixed up in the northern hemisphere and kept thinking east was west, and west was east. "It's because all the maps have Hong Kong Island on top of the mainland; whereas the Island, being south of the mainland, should be on the bottom," I said.

"No. You're right. It should be on the bottom, but it isn't," she explained.

Plus I kept running across words I didn't know. Not just Chinese words but words like "godown" instead of warehouse. It made writing articles hard work.

She asked if she could have a look at my left hand. She held it so softly I could hardly feel her.

As she took the hand she started to laugh. "Yes, you have never done any hard work in your life."

I had, often.

She said hands never lied.

"Your life is all here. These hands are so soft and unspoiled, like a baby's. No marks, no scars, no callusses, no thickening."

She touched the finger next to my little finger. This would tell if I was artistic. I wasn't.

She passed me her left hand, and the end of the same finger seemed to bulge imperceptibly each side at the top next to her fingernail. Which showed she was artistic.

"I like to draw," she said, flicking her hair back very seriously. "Now you can give me my hand back."

I hadn't realised, but I was still holding on to her artistic finger: the one with the tiny bulges I had to imagine to see.

Jeanette examined the palm of my left hand. As she twisted the hand around under the desk lamp to see the creases more clearly, she really did look like Elizabeth Taylor. Then she bent towards the hand. All I could see now was her gleaming black hair absorbing, then reflecting, the lamplight, but I could feel her tautness across the desk.

I hoped her boss wouldn't come out.

A change in her voice brought me back. It had grown strangely deep.

"I am looking at your lifeline," she said. "No. It shows you will be in great danger. You must be very careful, or you will not live long."

She looked at me with pity in her face.

It enabled me to look deep into her eyes, hoping for the faintest smile, or a hint of revenge for my gauche remark about Chinese.

But nothing. Her dark eyes easily overpowered mine with their intensity. To break the spell, as she held my hand tightly between hers as one would a relative in shock, I said I didn't believe all that Oriental clap-trap.

"You can't tell the future from lines on the hand," I scoffed. "No one knows the future."

She didn't let go.

"No. You can," she said softly, her slender right forefinger running slowly down the lifeline. It would have tickled in a different setting.

Jeanette pointed to the wide crease running in a curve from between thumb and forefinger to the wrist. "This is the lifeline. Its length foretells life. Some are short, most run to near the palm. But look at yours: there is a big island in the middle which you must get around, or else you just don't continue."

She was right. There *was* a fat little island, but I pointed out that the line continued around both sides, and joined up again to run down to near the wrist. She pointed to the thumb side of the island, to where a spur ran off: and stopped dead. We looked at each other across the desk: me and this foreign girl I had just met who knew my future.

"I suppose a girl as beautiful as you are has got a boy-friend?" I said.

"No, you are right," she replied, "I have been out with a doctor recently."

"That's good to know," I said, as casually as I could, "because I can perform a few operations myself."

She laughed, stood up, picked up her handbag and said: "Well come on. Let's go then." I was amazed by my power, until I saw two hours had passed and it was already five o'clock. Everyone was leaving and shutting up.

I took Jeanette for a cup of tea at the Peninsula, and then went shopping for kitchen utensils and bed linen for the new flat. Since Arch had found the flat and a servant, this mundane job fell to me.

Not only did the Chicoms have a bank in Hong Kong, it turned out they also had a huge store in the middle of Nathan Road. Jeanette said to go there because their goods were very cheap, and you could buy everything from a fork to an antique jade statue. So the store was a sort of Communist Woolworths.

The Red Chinese, despite their anti-Capitalist philoso-phy, had covered the outside of their store with more advertisements and red signs than you ever saw on a store in the West. The shop covered three floors: each half a football field in size. It was cash-and-carry serve-yourself so I set about getting four of everything, except for the potato peeler, a tea-pot and a kettle.

There were hundreds of statues, thousands of pieces of jewellery, and square yards of figurines from Mainland China — all to sell to Hong Kong Chinese and decadent Westerners.

But not to Americans. American tourists to Hong Kong were forbidden to return to the United States with goods which were made in Red China. They could only buy ivory chess sets, or jade jewellery, or Chinese chests, or carpets, or paintings, or antiques if the item was accompanied by a duly signed authorised Certificate of Origin stating that the item was manufactured in Hong Kong, Formosa, or elsewhere in southeast Asia.

Of course, these Certificates of Origin could be purchased on every corner in the Colony, and were advertised on every shop: except the Communist Chinese Store. But, even so, this Communist supermarket was the one shop in Hong Kong where there were no Americans. In fact, I was the only European. Which was a bit of a problem, because I couldn't find a kettle anywhere.

After searching the entire top floor, elbowing my way through crowds of Chinese workers out doing their night shopping, I asked a shop assistant for help. But I had no idea what the Chinese word for kettle was. The Commo shop assistant ended up walking around the kitchen section holding up items which he thought I might want. When I indicated, by miming, that what I wanted could hurt my hand by being so hot, he held up a toaster, then a hotplate, then an egg-beater. Finally, when he had moved some distance away, he held up an aluminium kettle from behind a counter.

At least I knew the word for "yes" in Cantonese, and so called out: "Hi", "Hi", which meant "Yes", "Yes".

His reaction was unexpected. The shop assistant started waving the kettle and his other hand above his head and shouting out in Chinese.

"Hi," I yelled louder, thinking he didn't understand my Cantonese.

I wasn't going to miss out on what looked like the last kettle in the store.

"Hi."

Another male shop assistant ran across in front of me and waved his hands, palm outwards, backwards and forwards in front of my face as if begging me to stop. Faced with this frantic activity, other shoppers moved away and then turned to watch, as if admiring a painting.

When I went to speak again, the man with the kettle ran over and held out his left hand, pulled the top of the index finger backwards with the middle finger of the same hand, and pushed his right hand index finger in and out between the two.

I wished I could leave immediately, but bought the kettle without saying another word.

By the time I got home, very late, Arch was dying for a cup of tea on our balcony.

There was a large bedroom at the front of our flat with its own small patio looking across the railway line to the playing fields of a Catholic college, a rail line which once ran from Hong Kong to Paris: before the Chicoms took over. The door from our steep irregular stairwell opened into the large lounge. Behind that was a tiny bathroom, and then an even tinier stifling bedroom with just enough room for a single bed. The one little window in this second bedroom opened only into an interior air well so you looked out to a view of other flat windows. Beyond that was the kitchen, and then the usual Hong Kong monastic servant quarters out the back on the small roof, where our servant, "Ah Ping", had already moved in.

These servants were known in Hong Kong as "Amahs". They were elderly Chinese women in black pants and white tunics who worked as servants in all Western homes in Hong Kong. Everyone had an Amah, even if they didn't need one, because they cost practically nothing and all home units for whites had a tiny room and toilet out the back for the Amah.

These old Chinese women did all the shopping, cleaning, washing, and cooking so that Westerners could enjoy being in charge. They were said to be infamous for always making a little extra on top of the shopping bill, which they salted away. Thus, many were quite well off in Chinese terms. But they bought food so cheaply at the markets — since they were expert bargain-hunters — that it was said to still be much cheaper to let them do the shopping.

Amahs had become a tradition in the Colony because there were large numbers of Chinese women who had never married, or were widowed and childless. There didn't seem to be a widow's or aged pension in the Colony of Hong Kong. So it was considered to be practically a public service to employ one.

Ah Ping spoke English better than Chinese businessmen and immediately took over our household. She was broad in the hips and very narrow at the shoulders, which gave her an earthy solid look. But this was softened by the thick grey hair pinned up behind her neck. She had gold in her large yellowing teeth which protruded slightly and gleamed whenever she gave her big laugh at whatever I said: her leathery face well creased with happy laugh lines.

I expected these servants to be unhappy with their lot in life, yet Ah Ping and her Amah friends were always laughing. Ah Ping seemed to like us a lot, but, being an Australian, I found it difficult having a servant and could not get used to her calling me "Master".

However she insisted.

"You Master," she said every time I tried to stop her, and she laughed with her eyelids pulled tightly together to let me know she thought she was putting one over.

The flat was furnished with cheap, timber 1950s furniture and Arch and I tossed for the right to take the best bedroom first — then month about. I won. For the first time in three months I was living in more than one room. And with a large balcony with a view. But I felt a little guilty because at work Ken Archer was the boss and yet here he was installed in the tiny, airless second bedroom.

But Arch, who was the same age as me, always played things very fair. He was a hockey player and, to my surprise, he said Australia had a great hockey team. I didn't even know we played men's hockey or had a team, but he said we had beaten England seven-nil at the 1964 Olympics which, in hockey terms, was a real thrashing. So he was impressed by Australians and willing to give them best.

Even though he was one of my bosses, I liked Arch because he had given me the confidence to experiment with my writing on the trade magazines. I wrote a story for him about one of Hong Kong's biggest builders, Paul Y Tso, a 61-year-old lawyer who graduated in Shanghai in 1930, built the Merdeka bridge in Singapore, and wanted to build a tunnel under Hong Kong harbour for cars to drive across from Kowloon and back. Most people didn't believe it could be done: but Arch went for it in his magazine.

I described Mr Tso's neat office and the way he was dressed — "dark suit, dark tie, black horn-rimmed glasses" — and Arch said straight out how much he enjoyed the story.

"You write like Ian Fleming in the James Bond books," he said.

No one had ever praised my writing before, and I kept repeating that phrase over and over again in my mind. After that I felt able to describe people and places my own way, and to put myself in stories to make them more interesting: instead of writing lifeless reports like they taught us to do back on newspapers in Australia.

Someone else who had a lot of confidence in herself was the beautiful Jeanette. The week after we met — because I hated buying clothes — she took me to a Chinese tailor and ordered a brown three-piece silky suit with a charcoal fleck and leather buttons, giving extensive instructions to the tailor in Cantonese while he was measuring me up.

Every now and then she covered her face with her very long fingers because she was laughing so much at whatever it was she was saying about how my suit should be shaped. I wanted one cut in the Steve Dunleavy style, but Jeanette said broad shoulders and big flaps wouldn't suit me.

She had a slightly strange way of putting things. When I asked anxiously "Why not?" she answered "Why Yes?": which left me confused, and without a reply. Then she laughed at the brilliance of her own reply.

That night, with me in my new brown suit, we went over to the Island for our first proper date, and I invited Fletch and Pamela along to celebrate. On the ferry I told them all the story of the kettle, and the strange reaction of the Commos. Jeanette said that Chinese, unlike English, was a tonal language. Thus, exactly the same sound said in a different tone had an entirely different meaning. So it was difficult for a born and bred foreigner to speak any of the Chinese dialects with any great degree of certainty.

She said I was saying "Hi", the correct word for yes, but with the wrong tone.

When we were alone up the front of the ferry, I asked what I had been yelling out in front of perhaps a hundred Chinese. Jeanette placed her elegant left hand just below her belly — palm down, fingers close together — and whispered demurely from under her black fringe:

"You were saying … a woman down here."

Jeanette promised to teach me some more Cantonese.

"What's the Cantonese for 'beautiful'?" I asked.

"Ho Lang," she said.

"Well you are Ho Lang," I said.

But I had the pronunciation wrong again.

I had inadvertently called Jeanette "a good dragon". Which would have been a much bigger mistake back in Australia.

Everything went very well until we were on the way back on one of the last ferries. Suddenly, I was aware that Ken was pulling awkward faces: his eyes darting swiftly from side-to-side, his chin tucked into his neck, his mouth pulled down at the sides. We had known each other since before memories had started, so I knew immediately that he wanted my eyes to follow his to disaster. I looked across the narrow aisle to see, sitting just across from the four of us, and carrying a pink umbrella — of all the ferries to walk on to, in all the harbours, in all the world, on tonight of all nights — the prostitute who had followed us home to the Grand three months before.

What if she saw us and said hello? What would Jeanette think?

Then Ken said aloud, without looking at me: "Dear Mum and Dad ..." and we both burst out laughing.

Jeanette and Pamela wanted to know what was going on and our laughter attracted the attention of the girl. She looked straight at me. Then she looked away. She had forgotten us.

The next Friday night Jeanette was coming to see our flat for the first time. I took an unofficial day off work to get a haircut — even though Indonesia, supported by Red China, had withdrawn from the United Nations. That was the good thing about working for trade magazines: no story was big enough to stop you getting a haircut.

Unlike in Australia, the barbers in Hong Kong were women and, after cutting my hair, mine massaged my head, neck and shoulders.

Then the other Australian in the office, John Ball, took me for a steam bath, which he said was the only way to feel really refreshed in tropical Hong Kong. John was an expert on how to stay cool in Hong Kong. He always wore a silk cravat instead of a tie, because he said it kept the neck cool.

At the steam bath, we were the only white people. They moved us from one small swimming pool of hot water to the next, each time into much hotter water. The last pool was almost boiling. After an hour, two small, muscular Chinese men escorted us behind curtains. We lay face down on two long narrow tables and each got a massage. Then they both climbed up on the tables and walked up the middle of our backs. My back cracked a few times, but it never hurt a bit. As we left, I had never felt so light in my life. I didn't know if it was because of the steam bath, or the prospect of Jeanette's visit.

There was a television in the lounge room of our flat, but there was never anything interesting on Hong Kong's Rediffusion TV, unless you wanted to see John Wayne talking Cantonese. So Jeanette and I chatted while looking out over the rail line which ran all the way to Peking, Moscow and Paris.

Ah Ping was dancing around the flat because one of us had finally brought home a girlfriend. My younger sisters prayed that I would one day get a girlfriend, at Olive's request, but now Ah Ping was taking what should have been Mum's share of the joy.

"Good Master bring girl," she kept saying, as if it had something to do with her.

Ignoring Ah Ping, who clearly liked Jeanette immediately, I told Jeanette I found it annoying that I couldn't catch the train through Red China to Paris like people used to before the Communists took control. It would be a cheap way to get to Europe, and a great story. Then I could go to 85 Fleet Street, London, and get a job with Reuter.

To my surprise, Jeanette said: "No. No, I think you will do it."

I wasn't sure if this was a prophecy, or not. Before I could ask, she moved inside and spoke to Ah Ping in Cantonese and sat down at the round pine table Arch had bought and placed as a dinner table at one end of the lounge room.

I was just about to ask her, when there was a knock on the door. I was annoyed at the interruption on this night of all nights.

Arch was supposed to be deliberately staying out.

As Ah Ping opened the heavy wooden door, Jeanette and I heard her say: "Hugh Lunn not here. Master he go away. Not here. Go away, far."

What was Ah Ping on about? It seemed she really had taken over our lives.

But she was too late.

Striding through the doorway with an unhappy look on her face, and wearing a plunging white blouse, was Babette — with Ah Ping angrily shepherding her backwards.

I only just resisted the temptation to say "What are you doing here?"

She'd come to see my new flat.

Not knowing what else to do, I invited Babette to come in, introduced the two girls to each other, and we all sat down at the round pine table.

"Babette's father is learning French," I said, to try to start the ball rolling.

But Jeanette said nothing. I thought about breaking the silence, but couldn't think of anything to say. I was going to ask Jeanette to tell Babette's fortune. But it didn't really seem a good idea.

There was another knock on the door. This time I was really looking forward to Arch's return. He would be perfect. He would even up the numbers.

This time Ah Ping said: "You want Master? You want Hugh Lunn, Master? Please to come."

Standing in the lounge with a smile on her full lips — and, of course, sucking a lolly — was Emily, the singer, wearing her pointed black glasses, white head band, and a very tight cheongsam.

Ah Ping padded down the hall to her quarters, deliberately giggling loudly enough for all to hear.

I'd gone for five years in Australia hoping to win on to a girl and get one into a flat of my own, and now, here in Hong Kong, it had finally happened: except that there were three exotic girls representing five nationalities in my flat all at once.

I introduced Emily to the other girls, who said little. This time I had a good idea: with Ah Ping hiding in her quarters I went off to the kitchen to use the Communist kettle and whistle for the first time, and made a pot of tea for the three of them. I took as long as I could, but they were all still there when I returned with the Communist tea pot and cups on a tray. I tried talking about subjects that would interest all three: like the upcoming Chinese New Year, and the snap of cold, wet weather. But we drank our tea in silence.

My guests made excuses and left in reverse order, until there was just Jeanette and me. I noticed that she had made no attempt to leave, and I was glad she wanted to out-wait the others.

Later that night I took Jeanette home in a taxi. She lived with her parents in a flat near the top of a 14-storey building with views over the harbour. Her mother had come to Hong Kong from the Portuguese Colony of Macau, which had existed on the coast of China not far from Hong Kong for 400 years. The mother was also very beautiful and elegant, but shorter with even blacker hair. Even up this high, the unit had bars on the windows and Jeanette's mother said that the Japanese occupation during World War II was the only time Hong Kong hadn't needed bars.

"The Japanese strung thieves up by the thumbs in the city square," she said, "so we never had to lock our doors."

Her father said he lost all his money when the Labour Party nationalised the transport industry in England and so he left the country. He was a big fan of English comic actor Norman Wisdom and kept re-telling scenes from his movie *Trouble In Store*. And I had to laugh. But I didn't mind at all, even though I didn't like Norman Wisdom.

I danced out past the scores of large locked steel letter-boxes in the building entrance, and happily up the street to find Nathan Road several blocks away. I had to step around, or over, Chinese refugees from Red China sleeping on the wide cement footpath all the way.

Now I knew what Ken meant by saying I would be doing Catherine wheels when I met the right girl.

Halfway up, two little boys stopped me.

"You want young girl, Mister? Beautiful young girl, twenty dollars."

I laughed out loud, and kept walking.

They had no idea what I was chuckling about. In Nathan Road I jumped in a taxi and said: "Sei sup baht ho, Ho Man Tin Gai," and he drove me straight home.

7 Dog Teeth Hills

Dressed in her white jacket, Ah Ping reminded me of Fred in his apron and, for the first time, I could see why Dad had always called his apron his "badge of servitude". Every day Ah Ping took her white jacket off to go shopping, as if symbolising her escape.

She alone decided what we would have for dinner, and Ah Ping was such a good cook that we were pleased to leave it all up to her. I was glad now that we had her. From the day she arrived we always ate dinner at home.

One night Ah Ping brought home a two-foot long fish which she bought for the equivalent of two shillings at the market, and Arch, Arthur Barnett and me — with Ah Ping eating the boiled fish's head out the back — had a feast.

The next night I was in bed coughing and coughing and couldn't stop, as had happened once a year since I was a child. Ah Ping came to look after me in the middle of the night, just like Olive when I was a boy. Instead of arriving with aspirin, Vicks, and Kays Compound Essence like Olive, Ah Ping brought phenacetin, Tiger Balm ointment to rub on my chest, nostrils and temples, and a glass of warm water. I objected to the warm water because I was hot and wanted to cool down. But Ah Ping said: "Master drink water cold then Master must cough. Water not cold, no cough." And she picked up the glass and tipped it down my throat just like Olive did when I wouldn't take my medicine.

The warm water trick was one Mum didn't know, but this home remedy really worked.

Ah Ping seemed obsessed with how much money she thought I had. She seemed to think, like most of the Chinese in Hong Kong, that all Australians were millionaires.

"You Australie man. Plenty money. Lot money," she would say. And when I said I didn't have much money at all, she laughed so much that I could see her tonsils.

I said I had only just enough to fly home if needs be.

"Big money you Master," Ah Ping would reply, holding her ageing sides with the insides of the palms of both hands as she laughed.

"Big money Australie Master."

There was no way to convince Ah Ping that I was practically broke. I pointed out that perhaps she hadn't noticed but I didn't own a car; didn't even have a record player; didn't own any furniture; didn't even have a wireless to listen to. And she was the one with real gold fillings in her teeth.

"I sold my sports car in Australia to get here and now I don't even own a cricket bat Ah Ping," I told her sternly one morning, "so I have to borrow one at the Kowloon Cricket Club when I play today. Which the other players don't like. Touching a man's cricket bat is very much like touching him."

But still she wouldn't believe me.

"Dragon Master rich. In Club. Big nine-dragon cricket Club," she said.

Now she was calling me a Dragon too.

"No. Ah Ping," I said. "Master not join Club. Money fee too high. Club too much money for this Master. Club *think* Master Club member, but Master no."

As we had a cup of her strong green China tea, I explained how difficult this made my weekends because I couldn't sign chits for a drink or a sandwich at the bar, like all the other cricketers did. Ah Ping wouldn't know, but you couldn't use cash at these Colonial clubs. Members signed for everything. It was as if having to handle cash was beneath them. Instead they got a monthly bill: considered much classier than paying cash to Chinese waiters and then having to wait for the change.

I told Ah Ping how Master had to go without at the cricket club, pretending he wasn't thirsty or hungry all day no matter how hot Master got. Three times Master had let "KK" Kwan sign for a drink and club sandwich for him, without Master ever being able to pay him back.

Ah Ping was unimpressed.

"Master Dragon big Club," she said, and for days afterwards, every time she looked at me, Ah Ping said "Club," like a silly little sister teasing.

One good thing about being in — well almost being in — the Kowloon Cricket Club was that my cricket captain knew Hong Kong's Director of Civil Aviation, an Englishman in a white spotted blue bow-tie, a Mr Muspratt-Williams. He turned out to be very helpful, once he knew I was a member.

Mr Schofield wanted a cover story on Hong Kong aerodrome for the first edition of the newly named *Far East Engineering and Equipment News* monthly.

"Aerodromes are always big news, Lunn. Always have been since the War. And Kai Tak airport is one of the talking points of the East," he said. "It sticks out a mile-and-a-half into the sea, yet there is no alternative strip for cross-wind conditions. Plus there are city buildings at one end of the runway and water at the other. Ken Archer wants a story that will make engineers throughout the Far East sit up and take notice."

When I asked Mr Muspratt-Williams about Hong Kong's aerodrome he walked over and shut the door, as if he had been waiting for just such a person to appear in his office. He was a good-looking man with a grey moustache. His baldness, rather than subtracting, added to his handsomeness. It was like a statement that it didn't matter that he had lost his hair. He seemed to immediately trust me with all of the aeronautical knowledge available to the British Colony administration.

After a few minutes of niceties, he leaned gravely across his giant desk: "How do you stop a jet airliner loaded with hundreds of people when its brakes fail?"

I shook my head.

"With reverse thrust," he said, "that is, by reversing the engines. But what happens if both the brakes and the reverse thrust fail at once?"

"The jetliner overshoots the runway," I said.

"Overshoots the runway?" he said. "Overshoots the runway? You're a cricketer. You know how hard it is to stop a well-struck ball. Do you know how far an unobstructed, fully-laden, modern jetliner landing at 130 miles per hour would travel with no brakes or reverse thrust?"

No. I wasn't exactly sure.

"For six?" I opined.

"That's not as silly as you might think. The airliner would end up, so to speak, out of the ground. It is estimated that such an aircraft would, if unobstructed, continue for seven miles. Yet the distance between the end of our runway and the highly congested area of Kowloon City is just over three hundred yards. Loss of life would be catastrophic."

At this, Mr Muspratt-Williams stood up and walked around his desk and stared down.

"And that's where you are damn important. We have to know how to stop a modern jetliner in three hundred yards. It is basically an engineering problem. You have thousands of engineer readers. We need advice, guidance, or appropriate data to come up with the solution."

I didn't know what to say. I thought of suggesting Jim Egoroff. Then, even though I had never studied engineering, a Jim-like solution came to me.

"What about a twenty-foot thick brick wall at the end of the runway?"

Returning to the other side of his desk, as if he wanted to get away, Mr Muspratt-Williams said: "Build a brick wall to kill all the tourists. This place lives and breathes tourists.

Can you imagine what effect a twenty-foot thick brick wall at the end of the airstrip would have on tourism?

"What would the travel writers call it? 'The wall of death'?"

No, he said, what he had in mind was three hundred yards of soft ground — quicksand, or earth, or gravel — perhaps sloping upwards to make the airliner dig in and gradually slow, and then stop. But not sloping up too quickly, or the jet might be lifted back into the air to crash on Kowloon City like a bomb. Studies had shown the height of the ramp would have to be limited to twenty-four feet so as not to interfere with normal take-offs and landings.

Nets stretched across runways had been used to stop military aircraft, but giant jetliners would need strengthened wings not to be ripped apart when hitting the nets. And strengthened wings would increase aircraft weights, thus cutting into passenger numbers. Countries with isolated spacious airports, like Australia, would not want that. And what if the nets were accidentally activated when a plane was just taking off?

"The real answer is, of course, arrestor hooks because they work so well stopping planes landing on aircraft carriers. But these could not be added to existing passenger planes or they would rip out the sides. New planes would have to be designed for the stresses, and built with these in mind."

What a story.

As I caught a cab back to our flat late that afternoon because our office had already closed, I wished I was working for a newspaper again. I could see the posters in my mind: " HK PLANE CRASH RIDDLE", "DEATH FROM PLANE HORROR?", or, better still, "SHOCK AIRPORT CRASH PROBE".

Arch was thrilled when I told him of the story over one of Ah Ping's delicious dinners.

"Well done, Hugh. This is what we need for our new magazine," he said. "Every engineer in the Far East will want to have a say on this, and I know you will write it so well."

I was glad now I was working for his magazine. Arch was always so positive and encouraging about everything in his life. As Ah Ping served mango dessert, Arch said my story was worth at least four full pages as the main story of the month.

It seemed strange having a servant in such surroundings, I thought, as Ah Ping shuffled around the table muttering to herself about her Masters. Although Arch was talking about my wonderful story, I kept hearing Ah Ping instead: "Very sad two Masters, no wife. Two rich masters. Eat alone. Dragon Master plenty plenty girl, no wife ..."

Arch stopped eating and said he had thought of the heading: "The Problems of Stopping a Runaway Jet" — with a play on the airport word "runway".

It was hard to concentrate on writing the story in our office because all the Chinese girls at *Far East Trade Press* were so excited by the up-coming four-day public holiday for Chinese New Year and the 10 days of celebration. Normally the Chinese worked quietly away, but the closer February 2 approached, the more frenetic the office became. Each day the Chinese girls returned from lunch with new outfits and loaded down with food, decorations, flowers, firecrackers, fruit, plants, dwarf trees, presents, and red envelopes.

I had never heard of Chinese New Year in Australia, but it was as if Christmas, Guy Fawkes Night, the summer holidays, and Easter were all arriving at once. One of the days was so big it was called "Yan Yat" — "Everybody's Birthday".

Amid all this activity I finally finished, at great expense to the management, three thousand words on THE PROBLEMS OF STOPPING A RUNAWAY JET and, below Arch's heading, I wrote a series of sub-headings: "Arrestor hooks? Arrestor nets? Quicksand pit? Water?"

Just for a joke, I added: "Brick Wall?".

Late that afternoon the word "Lunn" again reverberated through the 'door from Max Schofield's office, and I hurried in to see what was wrong. Mr Schofield was in a bad mood, but not with me. An accountant in London headquarters had complained that our office had been extravagantly fitted out with teak.

"They don't know anything about the Far East back home my boy," he lamented. "Teak is like gold there, but it's the cheapest material you can get out here in the Orient.

"Lunn," he added unexpectedly, wiping the bottom of his moustache, "good show. How did you get him to say all that?"

Not knowing what to say, I diverted the conversation to how hard it had been to concentrate on writing the story with Chinese New Year starting.

"It's a tradition, Lunn, that the Chinese put over on us British a long time ago," Mr Schofield said gravely.

"You see, Lunn, we English have twelve months in our calendar, and, like we do with you, we pay everyone their wages once a month. The Chinese adopted the Western calendar years ago; they used to have thirteen months because there are thirteen new moons every year. We didn't mind them having thirteen months and being ruled by the moon, so long as they turned up at work on time on the right day.

"But then one day it turned into a jolly bad show. They said: 'We have thirteen months in our calendar, but you only pay us twelve times a year. We have to be paid thirteen times a year'. They were such good workers that they had the Dragon by its tail so-to-speak. So now, every Chinese New Year, the Chinese all get two months pay for one month."

I was shocked.

The nearest thing we had to that in Australia was every Christmas all workers got a small "Christmas Bonus" in that week's pay packet, but only if the company had done well. A holiday loading of 100 per cent! No wonder the Chinese were getting ready to go crazy.

That night Ah Ping, never being one to miss out on money, also claimed double wages.

"But you just started last month Ah Ping," I said. "You can't get double wages after a few weeks."

"Chinese New Year mean two wages, Dragon Master," she said. "You plenty money. In Club."

So we paid up, putting the second month's wage in a red envelope, as I had seen the Chinese do with all money gifts at New Year. This was said to make it "lucky money". And, in keeping with tradition, I made sure — despite the long queues — that all of Ah Ping's money was in new notes and new coins from the Hong Kong and Shanghai Bank.

"Kung Hei Fat Choy, Ah Ping," we said, handing her the red envelope: the Cantonese version of wishing someone "Happy New Year".

This meant something like "May your wealth increase" which, in Ah Ping's case, I knew would certainly happen.

Ah Ping held up the red envelope and danced around the room like a young girl, shouting: "Ah Ping in Club," and laughed as she paddled and swayed in her wooden sandals back out to the kitchen.

Within minutes Ah Ping was back carrying the tiny battered old cardboard port she had arrived with. Since this port held all her possessions, it looked like she was now walking out on us.

"Where are you going Ah Ping. We just paid you big money," I said.

"Ah Ping go Chinese New Year holiday," she said. "Spend big money."

I said honestly that I didn't think servants got holidays. At least not after three weeks at work.

"Kung Hei Fat Choy," she said, and clattered down the stairs like a seven-year-old.

Jeanette explained that Ah Ping would visit all the graves of her ancestors to make offerings of peach blossoms, and to clean their graves.

"No. You were right to let her go. This is an unbreakable tradition," she said.

The next day, February 2, was the first day of the second new Moon after the winter solstice which, Mr Schofield said, was why the dates for Chinese New Year changed every year.

But it always worked out at either late January or early February.

All Hong Kong was awoken by firecrackers. The Chinese bungers made twice the bang that the biggest made on Guy Fawkes Night in Australia and soon Nathan Road was inch-deep in crimson wrappers. The bungers kept exploding non-stop for two days. There were no sky-rockets or colourful firecrackers like at home, just big bangs to scare away the evil spirits. It emphasised, if it was needed, that Hong Kong was still a totally Chinese city, with an almost unnoticeable British presence. It made me wonder why the Chinese kept the British here, when they could so easily kick them out.

Mr Schofield organised a New Year hiking holiday for the whole office on an almost uninhabited island just off the coast of China to the west of Hong Kong: Lantau Island.

"We're better off out of Hong Kong over Chinese New Year," he told me. "Bring your walking shoes, a jumper, and be prepared to travel through time back a few centuries. Writers like yourself should see these things."

No one was game to knock the boss back, so everyone in the office — secretaries, journalists, advertising sales people, tea girls, cleaners — all anxiously lined up at the ferry pier waiting for Mr Schofield at seven a.m. on the third morning of the Chinese New Year.

We didn't recognise him when he arrived: trousers tucked into his socks, long walking stick, and a strange checked cap like Sherlock Holmes. Diagonally across his shoulder was a leather strap attached to a brown bag Robin Hood-style.

"Well my merry men, and ladies," he said. "Time to go a-hunting."

The only way to this isolated island was on a ferry headed for the outer islands, so our large group made its way on wooden walkways which rose and fell with the tide to the ferry . It wasn't an auspicious day to be heading out to sea to Silvermine Bay on Lantau Island, which was twice the size of Hong Kong Island and an unheard of part of Colonial Britain.

As we rounded Hong Kong Island the ferry rocked violently. There was a rainy mist, and dozens of boats were sounding fog-horns and bells. The backs of the ferry seat benches were designed to move back and forth so passengers could always face the way they were going. Now, because there were so few passengers, the backs swung violently back and forth. The diesel smell from the engine below the middle of the boat made me feel ill, so I moved up the front where the crew had lowered green canvas blinds to stop the ocean spray. There I saw Mr Schofield standing on the front riding the waves and smelling the breeze with obvious deep breaths.

It took an hour to reach Silvermine Bay.

Once on land, Mr Schofield took us into a small cafe in the tiny fishing village. The cafe had a dirt floor and a couple of brass spittoons. I thought they were for decoration, until I saw them used, often. After that I didn't eat anything, though Mr Schofield had a big feed.

"You'd better have something, young man," he said, tucking in to black-and-green thousand-year-old eggs incongruously with a knife and fork. "We've a long, invigorating walk ahead."

We set out in a long thin line on a narrow track around the side of a steep grassy hill with Max Schofield at the front, followed by the three Chinese office secretaries and the others, then Arch and me at the back. I could see that, for all his enthusiasm, Mr Schofield walked like a man who sat at a desk all day: slightly bent forward from the hips like he was still at his desk, falling a bit forward with each step rather than striding out like Arch the hockey player did.

It was such a beautiful walk along a track worn into the hillside. We looked out over the ocean all the way and I felt euphoric, and part of a team. How wonderful that I could see such things. Had anyone else from Australia ever been to this remote almost unpopulated island, I wondered? Certainly there were no signs of civilisation, and no other people. Hour after hour, with Mr Schofield leaning into the breeze out front, we wound our way up and down and around on the well-trodden path. But we never saw anyone else.

We were to spend the night at a Buddhist nuns monastery. After several hours of walking we started up a hillside, and by late afternoon reached a temple with a gold pagoda roof. At last, other human beings. Shaven-haired Chinese women in orange robes: the Buddhist nuns. These were nothing like Catholic nuns. They seemed far gentler.

Outside the temple I could see other women taking hand-sized hunks of something off a clothes line.

"That's your dinner Lunn," said Mr Schofield. "Dried mushrooms. Buddhists never eat meat."

"Then how do they survive?" I asked.

"It's an interesting thing about humans, Lunn m'boy. Nearly all of us kill and eat other animals, but the Buddhists have shown that man can survive without killing to eat. They make us look like damn barbarians."

Mr Schofield seemed to like people who wouldn't accept the normal rules. On the long walk across Lantau he told me the reason he was willing to put the *Playboys* in the envelopes was because he didn't think other people should decide what a man could read.

"Where does it stop?" he said. "First *Playboy*, next Chaucer, then Shakespeare."

After the six-hour walk I had never been so hungry in my life: and I was going to have to survive on mushrooms for two days. The nuns showed us where we would sleep, and to my surprise it was inside a temple where there were already nuns burning incense, and praying and hitting small gongs. My bed was a raised wooden platform with a four-poster net right around, and no mattress. So I was going to be sleeping on wood.

Mr Schofield was unimpressed with my complaint: "This is where they sleep, Lunn," he said. "They've given you one of their best beds. Mark my word, you'll feel chipper in the morning."

Dinner was the best meal I'd had since leaving home. I swore I was eating a large steak and not soya bean curd and mushroom. And, even more surprising, although nuns were praying and gonging next to my bed from dawn, I'd never slept so soundly except under anaesthetic.

This monastery was said to be halfway up the highest peak on the island, a mountain twice as high as Hong Kong Peak, more than three thousand feet above sea level. After a vegetable breakfast we headed for the monks monastery near the top, with Max Schofield pointing to a peak high above, which had one of those down-to-earth descriptive names Chinese give places: "Rotten Head Peak".

He also said to beware of large snakes. "This is where the Chinese chefs come to get their snakes," he said. "Some Chinese call it 'snake island' — so watch out they don't eat you." And he roared with laughter at the frightened expressions on our faces.

This was a much steeper journey, and again we didn't see anyone else. When we got to the monks monastery I was disappointed to see the mountain peak still high above.

It was early afternoon and, while the rest were too tired, Arch and myself set off up a long grass slope with no track to see how close we could get to the top. Several times I thought we were almost there, but always when we reached the top of the rise there was yet another peak ahead.

I was reminded of Pope's line: "hills mount on hills, and alps on alps arise."

Finally, we just had to be near the top. It was like we were above the world and there was so little land left that no more alps were possible. By now the slope had no grass and was almost straight up, so Arch edged to the right around the peak, slowly getting higher.

Just as he said he was almost there I came to a halt on a ledge no wider than four inches and, as I looked down, I realised in horror that I was standing on the edge of a three thousand foot drop. Even though we were well inland I could see the sea crashing on the rocks far below. I thought to turn back, but the ledge was too narrow to risk a return and there was nothing to hold on to.

Fixed like a fly on a wall. My wet palms couldn't find any rocks ahead to cling to. I looked down again, and this time my feet curled under at the sight, like two hands about to pick something up.

"I'm on top," Arch called from above. "It's incredible. I'm on top of the whole of southeast Asia. It's so beautiful."

"I'm stuck Arch," I said, trying not to show how scared I really was.

"Just keep edging around. It's only a few more paces," he said, leaning over from just above: though I couldn't risk looking up to see him.

My feet wouldn't move.

Had I done all those exams, fought all those State School Kids, written all those stories, and been born to Fred and Olive only to disappear off the side of a mountain on an unknown island in the middle of the Orient?

I reached up and grabbed the dirt of the side of the mountain and clawed and pulled, as Arch reached down and grabbed my stick from above, and saved me once again from myself. On New Year's Eve I had got drunk and Arch not only stopped me from drinking a bottle of gin straight, but cleaned up the mess I made on Roxas's floor.

In half a second I was up there with him looking down on the mountaintops below, looking across fifteen miles of ocean to Hong Kong in the east; looking at the hydrofoil in the distance heading for the Portuguese Colony of Macau away to the west on China's Pearl River; looking out to the thin line of blue hills to the north that was Red China. And now able to see and understand exactly why the Chinese had long-since called the jagged row of mountains on central Lantau: "Dog Teeth Hills".

Arch took a photo of me leaning on my trusty stick in my fire engine red cardigan with the mountains of Lantau Island way below. If I could get up here, I could get anywhere in the world. I felt I had already come a giddy long way from home.

8   Ken Lands on Zero

Mr Schofield had been calling me "Hugh" since our hike across Lantau Island. Now suddenly he was back to "Lunn".

"Sit down, Lunn, we have a problem here," he said, and, as I reached under the chair to pull it closer, I could feel my palms starting to sweat again.

"Wonderful story in this month's publication on the aerodrome," he said. "But Colonial Administration is a bit miffed. They don't like our idea of a brick wall at the end of the runway. Don't like it at all. They especially don't like us disseminating such an idea all over the Orient."

Now I was sweating all over.

"What I cannot understand," he said, "is how this 'brick wall' got in. There's no reference in your article to building a brick wall to stop errant aeroplanes: a wall which would, of course, merely end all tourist traffic to the Colony for evermore. Yet there it is in the headline."

He threw a copy of the opened engineering journal across the desk and I didn't have to look very hard to see in 24 point Tempo Bold lower case:"Arrestor Hooks. Arrestor nets. Quicksand Pit. Water. Brick Wall" next to an inch-high question mark.

"The Colonial Civil Aviation Office says no such suggestion has ever even been contemplated, let alone made. Now, Lunn, where did that 'Brick Wall' spring up from my boy?"

I thought about lying, but no doubt Mr Schofield had already checked the original story, which was always kept in case of errors.

"Well, Mr Schofield, you're not going to believe this."

"I fear that I am, my boy."

The brick wall had been purely my own idea. I had added it as a bit of a joke, expecting it to be cut out during sub-editing.

"Well I suppose it's a blessing in disguise, Hugh," said Mr Schofield, bursting unexpectedly into a smile as wide as his moustache.

"Your Brick Wall has got everyone in the Colonial Office talking about our magazine. Engineers from Cambodia and Thailand and Kuala Lumpur have written in to offer alternatives. They all say 'try anything, but WHATEVER YOU DO, don't build a brick wall'. People just love it when they think you're going to make an error of judgment. You've got people talking about us, and in the publishing business if no one is talking about you then you're in trouble. That's why there is so much interest in *Playboy* in that country of yours — because your government keeps banning it. Hugh my lad, good show."

And he deliberately held the *Far East Engineering and Equipment News* open and out at arm's length as if my four-page article was a girlie centrefold.

Lost for words at this praise, all I could think of was Ken's favourite saying: "Always strike while the iron is hot".

Fletch wanted me to join him on a gambling trip to Macau, the tiny Portuguese-owned isthmus on the coast of China forty miles west of Hong Kong. There were regular ferries because Macau's casinos were very popular with the Hong Kong Chinese since casinos were banned in Hong Kong. Ken reckoned he had a few betting systems worked out: "Imagine if we won a million dollars — no, hang on, two million dollars, because then we'd have a million to waste."

In any event, he had no doubt we could win my airfare to Europe to see him win the French and Wimbledon titles. "If you don't come, it'll be your miss-out," Ken warned. "And if you do come I feel I can win Wimbledon. What I need is a friend to back me up. I'm 24 and this is my best chance. I've gone close to making the final before, but loneliness and despair are a brutal combination."

What better way to go to Macau and win my airfare to Europe than on an all-expenses-paid trip for *Far East Trade Press*?

"Er Max," I said carefully, calling him by his first name for the first time: which made him look up.

"I was thinking. One way of getting people talking about our *Far East Architect and Builder* would be to do a series of articles from an exotic location. Like Macau. Few people have been there, yet it is a part of Asia that has been ruled by a European power for more than 400 years. Everyone knows what sort of architecture has evolved from mixing the British and the Chinese for 100 years in Hong Kong. But what happens when you mix the Portuguese and the Chinese for sixteen generations?"

Max wiped his Spanish moustache with thumb and forefinger as he talked: "You didn't have any particular Macau buildings in mind, Lunn?"

I had underestimated him.

"You know," he said, "people only go to Macau for one thing: to lose their money."

"Well Max," I said, "naturally I want to have a look inside a casino because, like *Playboy* magazine, and most other interesting things, casinos are banned in Australia."

This did the trick. Max stood up and leant across his desk and shook hands.

"I like it, Hugh," he said. "A free trip to the casinos of Macau for you, in return for three articles on Macau architecture for me. How's that for putting the odds in my favour?"

When I told Ken, he didn't seem at all surprised: "It's all down to Tuesday well," was all he said.

Outside the ferry terminal just up the road from the Island side of the Star Ferry, two Chinese men sat on the footpath selling passports. Since Macau was an international destination, we had brought our passports along:

plus medical certificates to show our cholera, smallpox and typhoid vaccinations. Ken said Hollywood had made a film about a man stuck on the ferry between Macau and Hong Kong for years because he didn't have a passport. Obviously, the film had inspired this business: passports of all colours — German, British, United States, and even Australian — were laid out for sale on the footpath in front of the two peddlers.

There were two ferries to Macau: the slow, relaxing ship-sized steamer which took four hours — the way I wanted to go; and the quick new-fangled "hydrofoil" which aqua-planed on steel flaps fitted like wings underneath — the way Fletch wanted to go.

Ken said the hydrofoil would save a total of five-and-a-half hours, even if it was more expensive.

It was hard to argue, since we were loaded down with so much dough that the extra fare didn't seem to matter. Max had given me a bundle of dollars for expenses, plus we had practically emptied our savings accounts because Ken's system of gambling required "a large bank".

As we boarded the hydrofoil, Fletch passed across what looked like leaves of spinach: five hundred unfolded American dollars, saying: "Hughie, on no account give me this money while we are still on Macau. It's my expenses to play the Philippines Championship next week."

I folded it up and put it in my pocket — the way Ken said was the safest way to carry money.

The hydrofoil sped smoothly over the water as fast as a car but, inside the cabin, the stale air and smell of diesel made me ill. We went up on the small bridge. It was better, but still uncomfortable because of the wind, sun, and sea spray. We couldn't even talk for the roar of the engines.

Macau wasn't what I was expecting. It was a tiny hilly headland with low, crowded European buildings. Nothing like Hong Kong at all. It even had some large ancient trees. I was particularly interested to see it because of Jeanette's mother's connection.

The Macau peninsula — only two square miles — stuck out like a finger and thumb from Communist China pointing south. It was joined to China by a narrow strip of land in the middle of which was a huge stone arch containing what was called the *Barrier Gate*. Beyond this gate was rural land in China.

Though Macau was also a free port, unlike Hong Kong there was no aerodrome and no wide, deep harbour: just a narrow creek with concrete guard post bunkers on the Macau side. Near the ocean was a long promenade behind a stone wall which looked like it was there to keep the sea at bay. The cobbled streets had long non-Asiatic, non-British names: Rua Do Almirante Sergio and Avenida Do Dr Rodrigo Rodrigues. The centre of the island was like the Italian towns in war movies: double-storey adjoining stone and brick buildings and stone and cement streets. There were hardly any cars. People walked everywhere.

We booked into the Estoril Hotel, a nondescript small building, and within minutes I was in a casino for the first time. We didn't have to go far: the Estoril had its own casino downstairs. I knew what a casino would look like because Ken had often described them. But I was surprised by the size, the glistening chandeliers, and the hundreds of Chinese desperadoes crowded around the tables. Green was the predominant colour, probably because all of the gambling tables had dark green tops. They gave the place the feel of a Fortitude Valley snooker room. We were almost the only Europeans.

"It's about time you learned some of these games," Ken said as we walked in.

Fletch explained in detail how each of the several games was played, and the systems he had learned to employ during his five round-the-world tennis tours with the Australian tennis team. Some of the games were played with dice, others with cards. But they didn't have "unders and overs" like at Catholic school fetes.

One of the card games was similar to one we played as kids: Twenty-one. Ken said this was "Blackjack" and the way to win was to try to remember all the cards that had already been played so that you knew if there were a lot of picture cards left, or aces. Plus he had a number of other rules like: always double on eleven; never sit on sixteen; always split a pair of tens ...

But the game we were really looking for was a French game which was, of course, banned in Australia: roulette. There were four of these roulette tables all going at once and each surrounded by Chinese. In the middle of each elongated narrow table was a giant wheel like the chocolate wheel at Catholic fetes, except it was very fancy. Plus it was lying on its back and had only thirty-seven numbers: one to thirty-six, plus a nought, which they called zero.

Unlike a chocolate wheel, the numbers were jumbled and completely out of order. Half of the numbers were black, and the other half were red — Max Schofield reckoned that was why roulette was banned in Australia.

Zero was green.

Even without looking, Fletch could tell me the colour of any number on the wheel. He said you could back red, or black, at even money: with a fifty-fifty chance of success — except for the nought.

"If it lands on zero then all of the money on red and black goes to the bank." Zero was there so the casino could make money. But, if you wanted, you could back zero and be paid the same odds as for any other winning number: thirty-five-to-one.

"Let's sit here a while. You'll soon get the knack," Fletch said. "There's plenty of time because the casinos open 24 hours a day."

The numbers were laid out on identical green mats at both ends of the wheel so plenty of gamblers could get chips on. The numbers were in three long rows of twelve. You could back one row of twelve numbers at two-to-one. Or you could put your money halfway in between two numbers and get seventeen-to-one if one of the two came up.

It was a complicated game, so I could see why Fletch needed systems. You could bet that an even number would come up, or an odd number; or on a small number, or a big. One of Ken's favourite methods was to back a particular section of the wheel: especially if the wheel was slightly unbalanced and the ball kept landing in that area.

Even though the numbers were scattered willy-nilly around the wheel in no particular order, Ken knew by heart which numbers were next to which. With his incredible memory he could name the numbers in their scattered order right around the wheel, colours and all.

Ken liked to bet on 26 (black), zero, and 32 (red) on the same spin, because that way he was backing the bank's own number, plus the number on either side on the wheel: just in case the casino was cheating. I couldn't see how they could possibly cheat.

A man called a croupier spun the wheel anti-clockwise and sent the larger-than-marble-sized ivory ball whizzing clockwise inside a round curved varnished timber frame above the wheel. As the very light ball lost pace it slid down towards the deep numbered slots but, as often as not, it hit a silver stop and flew back up away from the wheel and down again. When it hit the slots, which were travelling in the opposite direction, the ball bounced around before finally settling in one slot for all to see.

I couldn't help wondering why this game was banned in Australia. Everyone at the casino seemed to be having a whale of a time, some actually screamed out if their number came up. And, as Ken said, the atmosphere was much classier than at the racetrack.

Fletch had not yet decided on the best system. So, after lunch, he cased the joint while I went looking for the three stories for Max. I wasn't confident, so I wanted to start straight away. I walked along on the perfectly flat cobbles past hundreds of grimy-walled double-storeyed adjoining homes with long pinkish wooden shutters on the windows, upstairs and down. These windows were almost as long as doors, and the shutters hadn't been painted in years. Was I relieved when I found two ideas straight away.

The first was obvious. In the middle of town above scores of steps on a staircase a cricket pitch wide, was a pre-Captain Cook stone Catholic church — St Paul's. There was some strange architectural feature I just couldn't work out. The church rose from the hillside in five distinct stages. Ten giant round stone columns on large pillars divided three doorways. These held up ten smaller columns above, divided by three windows with curved tops. The third level was particularly ornate, rising and falling on the edges and covered in stone carvings. Six smaller central pillars here held up another level. Above this, high above, was a triangular peak with what looked a giant bird flying outwards from the middle: probably the Holy Ghost.

Being on top of a hill, the church dwarfed the surrounding area. But still I couldn't make out what was different. There were no steeples, but that wasn't it. Then I realised that I was looking up through this Cathedral straight to the sky above, because there was no church behind this facade. It had been burnt down more than 100 years ago. Only the stone front had survived, with the open window holes at the top gaving the church a human appearance — as if it was watching me.

Plus, it turned out that the Portuguese government in Lisbon had just sent a team of five architects to the colony to ensure that future expansion was in keeping with Portuguese ways: the perfect story for our magazine.

"How's it going Fletch," I said back at the Estoril, "what have we been on?"

Ken was concentrating exclusively on 6 of the 37 roulette wheel numbers, putting a small amount on each.

This was his "Catholic" system.

"I've been on three, for the three divine persons of Our Lord; seven, for the seven dolors of Our Lady; ten, for the ten commandments; twelve, for Our Lord's apostles; fourteen, for the Stations of the Cross; and thirty-three, because it was the age at which Jesus died," he said. "Can you think of any others?"

Even so, God wasn't on his side.

"I'm not even holding my own," Ken said, mystified.

But at least he didn't blame God. As Ken stood up from the table and collected his chips he said loudly enough for everyone to hear: "Trust the bloody Frogs to invent a game that drives you mad."

At the nearby north coast the other casino, the Macau Palace, floated on the river fronting the border with Communist China. While we stood at the roulette tables we looked out of the window into this country Australians weren't welcome to visit. It was just 100 yards, or less, away. We could actually see the Communists walking around.

So here was another mystery: if the Red Chinese left Hong Kong alone as their window on the West, then why did they leave Macau too?

"Look at them," Ken said, "they thought they were going to take over the world, and all they got was their hopeless, colourless lives. Anyhow, it's time to hit the casino in the leg. Let's get some scores on the board."

Ken, all done up in his white sports coat, his fair hair brushed straight back, his gold watch gleaming, chose a seat at one end of a high curved table behind which a girl was dealing cards. Each time, Ken was the last player to receive a card. This, he said, was vital. Being in the end position, he knew what cards had gone before. This was even more important in Macau than in Europe or America: because Macau only used one pack of cards. Elsewhere, casinos used four to six decks shuffled together, and even then they didn't use all the cards. So elsewhere it was impossible to work out what cards were left.

Ken was carefully watching all the cards come out: "At least in Macau you know if all four aces are out, or if you have a good chance of getting a picture card. I feel you can win here," he said. And he did, five hundred dollars in no time at all.

110

"This all goes well for my career, Hughie. I'm really thinking of becoming a professional gambler, if I can't win Wimbledon. I'd have to live here but. I couldn't stand the ferry trip back and forth from Hong Kong every day."

Fletch passed me four hundred dollars of his profit, and started again with the one hundred. "If I can build it up to five hundred again well and good, if not — finished," he said. When he lost that small bank we returned to the Hotel Estoril as winners.

That night back in our room Ken got out the book his father had passed on, a book of sayings that had been in the Fletcher family for a long time: *The book of Proverbs and Epitaphs*. "There are so many good ones," Ken said. "Listen to this: 'A hypocrite never thoroughly repents,' so it is no use a hypocrite going to Confession well. 'A wooden leg is better than no leg,' well that's certainly true. Hey, I don't believe this one: 'Choose a wife rather by your ear than your eye'."

I asked Ken if it contained any Chinese proverbs, and it did.

" 'A man without a smile must not open a shop', well they're right, they are so right there," he said. "It is important to have a pleasant disposition when you are dealing with the public. But here is the best Chinese one: 'The gods cannot help a man who loses opportunities' — Hughie you have to take your opportunities. Here you have the opportunity to come to Paris and Wimbledon with me. If we play our cards right we are in with a chance. And if you come to Europe we have the opportunity of conquering the whole world.

"Here it is! Look at this! This is the best one," he said, holding up the open, battered, brown book above his head: "'Without going, you can get nowhere'."

I wasn't sure I understood what it meant.

Next morning the five Portuguese architects were busy working in a run-down old double-storey stone building. I was surprised their government didn't provide better offices.

One of them was a woman. I thought they might be reluctant to talk to a journalist, but — because I was writing for a professional magazine — they were excited by the idea. Luckily, they all spoke English.

The architects said it was important to understand Macau's history before designing any buildings because it was unique as the oldest European settlement in southeast Asia. "Every city develops its own architecture based on the people who founded it — their thinking and their background — so, unless you are a conqueror, you should enhance the city and not pull it down," said Jose Manieras, and the others nodded.

They said their job was to make sure Macau did not fall prey to modern building methods which ensured all buildings, and all cities, were starting to look alike.

"Go into any modern hotel in any world city and you will now see the same mirrors, the same tap fittings, the same plumbing. The way it's going you might as well stay at home," Mr Manieras said.

The Portuguese architects took me back many centuries to the Chinese Goddess A-Ma: the patron of fishermen and seafarers who was worshipped in a temple on the island. So Macau was called "A-Ma-Cao" — Port of A-Ma. In the sixteenth century the Portuguese wanted to get in contact with China to trade, but China, even then, was a very closed society. Because of cyclones, the Portuguese only came to China in winter, so each year they had to set up temporary trading posts. After 40 years of this they agreed to help the Chinese wipe out the pirates who controlled the area, in exchange for Macau. Then the Portuguese set out to convert the local Chinese to Catholicism.

All of the Macau architecture took into account the cyclones — no high towers, no church steeples, roofs double tiled.

The architects said the taking over of Hong Kong by the British several centuries later made Macau a backwater. But the rise to power of the Chinese Communists in 1949 meant

112

a mass of refugees to Macau and a consequent building boom, which could not continue without ruining the architecture of the tiny peninsula. So Portugal sent out these architects to draft a town plan.

To show what could be done, they designed four projects — a block of flats; a Catholic church; a tower block on reclaimed land; and "two-storey maisonnettes for a back lane".

I had a brilliant idea. Would the architects supply me with a plan and model of each project? I wrote out a dozen questions: "What is the aim?"; "What is the best feature and why?"; "When will it be finished?"; "How does it fit with the traditional architecure of Macau?"; "Does it suit the Orient?" They readily agreed to do the work for me.

Thus I had lined up — including the Cathedral story — five features for Max Schofield, not just three, in less than four hours. Pictures, plans and all.

That afternoon Ken and I walked all over Macau like a couple of tourists, taking pictures and talking in cafes. It wasn't difficult because Macau was only a mile or so across. We sat on a stone wall by the water, ate the local dish of pigeon, took photos of the Cathedral facade, and talked about his imminent departure for the world tennis circuit. While Ken was excited about the night of gambling which was about to begin, he was unhappy that he could not imagine what he would do for a crust when he finished playing tennis. The reaility was, he said, unless he won Wimbledon he would have to get a job. Yet he wasn't trained for anything other than tennis.

His pale blue eyes stared across the sea into the distance.

Winning Wimbledon wasn't beyond him. One year, because he came down with Urti, he lost to a finalist he had beaten in straight sets in the Australian title that same year. Another year he gave a point away when he was just one game from an easy straight sets victory which would have put him in the last four — where he would have been favourite to beat Martin Mulligan on grass and play his old Queensland nemesis Rod Laver in the final.

What went wrong after he gave that point away I didn't know, because Ken wouldn't talk about it. But I knew it made him feel like giving tennis up.

As we talked down by the edge of the South China Sea, near the Pearl River estuary, I said that Ken Fletcher giving away tennis would be a great waste of talent. Hadn't tennis writer Alf Chave written: "They say that opportunity knocks only once; in Ken Fletcher's case it has almost battered down the door." Wasn't it time to take the opportunity?

Ken looked at me and quoted a stanza of poetry I had once quoted to him:

> We look before and after
> And pine for what is not.
> And our sincerest laughter,
> With some pain is wrought.

Now that he had experienced life outside the strict Australian tennis regime, Fletch was sick of the game. Tennis had been his life, day-in day-out, since he won the Queensland Under 12 title. So he was on the lookout for a new career.

While I was at work in Hong Kong, Fletch had been all over the Colony pricing women's beaded jumpers. He had played tennis championships in several African countries and reckoned there was a huge market for cheap beaded women's jumpers and cardigans. Because of the extremely cheap Chinese labor in Hong Kong, it was possible to buy a woman's jumper or twin-set covered in coloured beads and baubles, sewn in a pattern on the front, for much less than the price of an ordinary jumper anywhere else in the world.

"I've bought a lot of samples and I'm taking them with me next month," Fletch revealed. "I've got all the colours — from mauve to apple green — and all the designs too. I sent a twin-set to Mum to test the market, and she loved it. I've got so many that my ports are overflowing with them

114

and I've got no room for my tennis clothes … I can't miss out, they are so cheap."

I hadn't known Fletch was an expert on the fashions of African women, so I asked how much money he would make. Typically, Ken looked up at the clouding sky saying: "Divide by nine … no it doesn't go … put down the nought and carry the one … seven dollars U.S. profit per beaded jumper!" he exclaimed enthusiastically. "It's money for old rope."

It wasn't what I wanted to hear. I wanted Ken to become the world's best tennis player, and here he was wanting to become a fashion merchant.

"You'd be better off sticking to tennis," I said, not wanting to go on about it.

"I can't see where it's leading but."

I reminded him that, if he could just win Wimbledon — or even the French — it would mean a lucrative career forevermore with endorsements for racquets, balls, shirts, shorts and shoes. "Even hair oil if you want."

"Just win Wimbledon!" he replied. "You make it sound like I only have to turn up. I've told you before that you're the world's greatest off-court tennis player."

Ken was always sensitive to the fact that I didn't know what he had to go through to win Wimbledon. Once, when watching Ken play in Hong Kong, I asked him why they bothered letting old Spenser play, since he was getting on a bit.

"He's a good player," Ken said.

"Even though I'm not a tennis player," I replied, "I reckon I would beat him: if I only had some tennis equipment."

Ken pulled down his shark skin tennis shorts in front of everyone. Then he tore off his Fred Perry tennis shirt so he was standing dressed only in his jock strap.

He handed over his Slazenger Challenge racket.

"Come on, well," he said, "we'll see."

When I went to the net, Spenser hit the ball over my head. When I stayed back, he dropped it short. On top of that, Ken's shorts were too big and kept slipping down, and I didn't win a point.

"I knew you had no hope," Ken said afterwards. "But you Lunns are always skiting. Spenser is an old Shanghai player from way back. He's played every day of his life and has a tennis brain. At five-love you were looking a bit sick, Hughie. You've learnt your lesson but. I shot my mouth off with Harry Hopman once at squash. Here I was one of the best tennis players in the world and him a bloody old bloke in his sixties, and I said I would smash him. He beat me 9-1, 9-1. So I learnt the hard way too."

Thus I decided to say no more about the jumpers.

"You're dead a long time," Ken said. "I just can't see myself standing on a back court coaching some hopeless bloody tennis player for the rest of my life. I'd rather live on my wits. I'd rather be a businessman, or a professional gambler. I might make more money than I would at tennis."

We wandered all over the Colony because Ken wanted to see the memorial to Victor's great uncle, Sun Yat-sen, who had once been a doctor in Macau. It was an ornate three-storey white Memorial Home with two semi-circular front verandahs with dozens of barley sugar white columns. We saw half a dozen Catholic churches and a similar number of Chinese temples — including one with a round, smooth stone table out the front where the United States and China had signed a friendship treaty in 1844. That stone table seemed so strange now, because the U.S. and China were mortal enemies.

We came across a monument to Portugal's greatest poet, Luis Camoes, who had lived in Macau from its foundation, and an explorer we had learned about at school in Australia: Vasco da Gama.

By that evening Ken's attitude to life had totally changed. I could feel his excitement as we hit the Estoril casino with all our money in tow.

Macau gambled in Hong Kong dollars and, together with Ken's $US500 for the Philippines tournament and my *Far*

East Trade Press expenses, I had money folded in every pocket. I suddenly felt life had reversed ten years to when when Ken and I, as thirteen-year-old kids, went off to the Brisbane Exhibition with two-bob bits secreted in every pocket to gamble for boxes of *Old Gold* chocolates with other open-mouthed clowns. Except then we used ping-pong balls instead of chips.

Fletch, like Minnesota Fats in *The Hustler*, had prepared for the evening's battle with a shower, talcum powder, a shave, Old Spice after-shave, and his charcoal-and-white sports jacket. He looked every inch an international gambler: his confident smile, his clothes barely touching his light athlete's body. He made sure I got dressed up too, saying: "Let's make them think a couple of James Bonds have hit the floor, a couple of class horses from Brisbane who are going to hit them in the leg for a fortune. And remember, if we lose, we *are* gentlemen."

I hadn't contemplated the thought of losing before. Fletch was always so confident we would win.

Ken took a seat at the end of a curved wooden Blackjack table — to get the last cards — and said a cheerio to the other five players and the two beautiful Chinese girl dealers. He liked playing Blackjack in Macau because they allowed you to double on nine, ten, or eleven — instead of just eleven. Plus — unlike other world casinos — if you got a rotten card, and the dealer had a good one, you could surrender and only lose half your bet.

Here you were also allowed to hold your cards, whereas elsewhere in the world you couldn't even touch them. And the cards were dealt face down, not face up for all to see. This meant Ken could enjoy that special moment of picking the cards up while very, very slowly looking under the edge to see what treasures awaited.

The first card was a picture card, which counted as a ten. He squeezed the second up off the table, barely peeking at the top edge saying: "I want a ten — ow! I've come unstuck!"

It was a five. Blackjack disaster.

"Stiff luck," said Ken.

The dealer dealt from the shoe, so she couldn't pull cards from the bottom of the pack. She dealt so quickly that the other girl was kept busy loading the next shoe. After a few hours, Fletch was two hundred dollars in front, and switched to roulette to try out the new system.

Since half the numbers were red and half black, and each colour was dotted randomly around the wheel, it was unlikely that there would be a run of too many reds, or too many blacks. So we would put a dollar on red and, if it didn't win, double it. If it lost again: double it to four. If black came up yet again, we'd put on eight dollars. Only if five blacks came up in a row would we lose the next bet of sixteen dollars, which wasn't much money anyway.

One of the rules of Ken's system was "never let a run beat you" — always let it ride. We had to stay on our bet no matter what, even if we were a few bob down.

I felt like when Ken first introduced me to throwing bottle-tops at the local girls at Annerley. Now, just a decade later, "Bottletop Lunn and Bottletop Fletcher", as we used to call ourselves then, were tossing Macau casino chips around willy-nilly instead.

Playing an even-money bet, and doubling when we lost, it took a long time to win or lose. But slowly, ever so slowly, we built up our winnings.

By four o'clock the next morning there were hardly any other gamblers around and Ken talked to the croupiers on a first-name basis. They seemed very amused by our system and the intense way we stuck to it, no matter what.

Occasionally Ken would try to deviate, but I wouldn't let him.

By sunrise we had won $1,600 — a month's wages for me, after tax.

Then Fletch worked out that if we had started with a base unit of ten dollars, instead of one, we would have stayed in the game and be $16,000 up! Easily enough for me to fly to

118

Wimbledon and the French. So we changed to a unit of $10 and, an hour later — after eight blacks in a row — we faced a last bet of $2,560 just to win our original ten dollars.

We had already spent $2,550 in doubling eight times, losing $1,280 on the previous spin. Were we going to stick to a system that meant we could blow a total of $5,110 trying to win ten dollars?

Ken said we had to put it on, even though it was risking all on one spin of the wheel.

"We can't let a run beat us. Look at it this way, Hughie. It's match point against you in the final set at Wimbledon. All you can do is go for your shot. If you miss, well it's game, set and match. But, if you hit a winner, the pressure is back on your opponent."

So we risked all.

The little ivory ball bounced around the spinning wheel, leapt in the air, and landed in eleven — black. The ninth black in a row.

Ken turned to me: "On your head, Hughie, tea break's over."

The croupiers laughed as if they knew we were doomed from the start, which Fletch didn't appreciate.

By now there were some early morning gamblers around the table. The wheel spun again, the ball slowly lost pace and began to descend. Ken nudged me to let me know he was going to teach these smart Macau croupiers an international lesson.

As the ball hit a silver barrier and dropped towards the slots, Ken leant across to the chief croupier and said: "I'll have ten thousand dollars on ... Zero."

Everyone — the gamblers, the croupiers, the on-lookers, stared in disbelief down at the wheel as it spun noiselessly around with the ivory ball sitting in ... Zero.

The croupiers started to panic. In most casinos, Ken knew, last minute bets were accepted from known gamblers who had not had time to turn cash into chips. Fletch could argue it was a real bet.

They would have to pay out $350,000.

Ken had distracted the attention of the tired croupiers and started his sentence just as the ivory ball was about to fall. With the quick eye of one of the best net volleyers in the world, he timed it perfectly so that his last word was uttered the moment the ball tipped over the edge of the Zero slot.

Ken burst into laughter.

"Only kidding, mate, only kidding," he said, and we walked away as the Chinese and American gamblers laughed at the stunt and applauded the ruse, and the croupiers all sat down to recover their composure.

"I just wanted to wipe the smart-alec smile off their bloody faces," Ken said.

Just then an American tennis fan recognised Ken and asked what he was doing in a casino and not having a bet: "We're here to say a novena for all the desperate gamblers," Ken said, and the American believed him.

Since we were leaving Macau in a few hours, and might never be back, Fletch suggested one last small bet. So we returned to a different roulette table, "for luck".

As we stood watching the mesmeric ivory ball flicking around, Ken suddenly turned and said: "I've got a feeling. Quick give me that $500 I gave you."

"No way Ken," I said. "You told me not to give it to you on any account."

"But that was *before* we'd lost all our money. I'm going to get it back in one hit. I'm going to surround thirty-two, my old bet. I don't know why I ever changed."

The ball started to wobble.

"If thirty-two comes up I'll never forgive you," said Ken.

So I whipped out the money and he just got the bet on.

"Eleven, black," said the croupier, reaching out with his stick to drag the money in.

"Temptation is an awful thing, Hughie," was all Ken said.

Heading home on the cheaper, slow old steamer, we found our way slowly downstairs to a bar in what looked like one of the old Brisbane theatres I used to tap-dance in, red velvet curtain and all. As Ken said, we looked like a couple of beaten favourites.

Suddenly the velvet pulled back and, to our surprise, six long-legged Australian girls hit the stage and danced and stripped for the whistling Asian audience.

We couldn't believe it.

It would never have been allowed in Australia or Hong Kong.

But, as Fletch said: "I guess anything goes when you're out to sea but."

"These are fun days son," he said, suddenly bouncing back to life: leaning backwards on his elbows on the bar as if he owned it.

"While everyone else back in Brisbane is sitting in an office filling in forms, here we are living on our wits like a couple of soldiers of fortune on the High Seas."

9 Great Dragon Master Lover

Although it was no longer the Year of the Dragon, Chinese New Year had brought an unexpected bonus. It was now the Year of the Snake and, for the first time in 12 years, my birth sign had come up under the Chinese Zodiac. This was very propitious.

Jeanette said the Chinese considered people born in the Year of the Snake to be very wise. By my birthdate, I was a profound thinker, quick-witted, intelligent. "Snake people are also considered very handsome," she said.

That was what I loved about the Chinese. Thousands of years of civilisation to work out real insights into people. But I doubted that Snake men were also stingy, irritable, and hated to fail. I was used to failure — having failed grade 10, grade 12, and both university subjects in my first year.

Because I was a Snake and had been to Lantau Island, one night we went to see the live fat snakes for sale at the open-air night street-market in Kowloon where thousands and thousands of locals pushed past each other between footpaths covered with things for sale, all lit by kerosene lamps. It was near Nathan Road. Traffic was blocked off especially, which would never happen in Australia.

Some stalls played old Beatles records over and over again. *I Wanna Hold Your Hand, Love, Love Me Do: you know I love you* ... yet the Chinese surely could not understand the words.

At the same time, up the Harbour end, a few hundred Chinese of all ages watched a Peking Opera performed on the back of a truck with canvas for curtains, and no painted

122

scenery at all. They didn't need scenery because the actors wore fancy hats, crowns, fake coloured beards, and full length patterned multi-coloured gowns. It looked like a combination of pantomine, mad-hatter parade, dance concert, and fancy dress ball. But to the Chinese, apparently, the colour of the shining robes told them who was who: yellow for Emperor; red robe for villain.

The actors exaggerated every movement, but now and then they stopped completely still for a moment: like in a photo. When on the move, they rolled their eyes within faces painted with intricate geometric designs in bright colours from violet to pale green, plastered on thicker than paint on a Queensland verandah.

Jeanette said every adjustment by these actors, even the tiniest movement, meant something: a certain minute tug of a red sleeve with thumb and forefinger and all of a sudden the character is in disguise. The painted faces, the colours, the designs, revealed their role. Gold for a God, green for a ghost.

At first I couldn't believe that one earth could produce two such diverse musical types: the simple strumming rock-and-roll beat of the Beatles coming over the Market's loud speakers, and the high-pitched Peking Opera voices. Like cats fighting in the back yard, the opera singers never seemed to vary much: all accompanied by a discordant cacophony of gongs, bells, cymbals and drums.

Two years before, in Brisbane, one of my uncles had walked out on my 21st birthday party because we were playing the Beatles. It wasn't just the rock-and-roll he objected to. It was the way the Beatles looked. They didn't look like him, or me, with our short-back-and-sides, wide suit lapels and cuffed trousers. Like actors in a Peking Opera, the cut of their Beatle suits, the length of their hair, foretold their character. And, to my uncle, they were trouble.

Now I understood why the Beatles were such a hit with us young people: their very look set them apart from the older generation. To me, the Beatles used Peking Opera techniques. When Chinese wanted to show an actor was important in an opera they gave him a very long black beard. The Beatles had given themselves very long black hair. When the Chinese wanted to show a characteristic of an actor they added, or subtracted, something special from a garment. The Beatles removed their lapels.

They were playing an ancient role.

I pushed my way through the crowds just to confirm that the opera hero did indeed have red cheeks.

By now I had lived in Hong Kong long enough to distinguish Eurasians from Chinese, and locals from visiting Asians: especially the obvious Koreans. Even, I thought, the stockier yabbering Cantonese from the less loud, less argumentative, taller northern Chinese.

Many of the gutter-side Cantonese peddlers in the market were offering green jade. Not the noble figurines of soldiers and workers that were for sale to non-Americans in the nearby Communist department store; or the green and white chess sets of the tourist stores; but small items of jewellery spread on plain white pieces of cloth on the footpath. I liked the look of these because green had always been my favourite colour. I had thrown a lot of gibbers in Australia, but I'd never felt a stone like jade before: so smooth, so heavy, so hard.

Some jade was white, some grey or blue, or a mixture of colours. In the way of the Chinese, each was given its own peasant-like descriptive name: grey-and-white mixed was called Mutton Fat Jade.

Jade looked solid and royal: it was so hard that it could never be scratched. Especially hardened tools had to be used to carve it from the few jade mines deep inside Red China. According to the Chinese, these seams of jade were created thousands of years before from tears shed by dragons. Thus jade was valued more than gold, and the Chinese believed it offered protection from evil spirits. Something like Catholic Holy Water, I guessed.

The peddlers displayed slender rings, bangles, brooches and ornaments, all in green, which was rare and thus much more expensive. This was where the shrewd locals shopped, so I knelt down to buy a ring of Imperial Jade (emerald green) to send home to Olive: the price twenty U.S. dollars. But Jeanette stopped me, saying that much of the jade sold at markets was fake. After picking out a ring, she argued vehemently in Cantonese and eventually beat the price down by half to ten dollars. But, even then, she wouldn't take it.

"But I want it," I said.

"Yes, you do," she said, and walked off up the street.

After twenty paces the peddler came running after us yelling "Gau Mun" — nine dollars. Jeanette said you were expected to bargain with Chinese, but not enough to make them "lose face". I had heard this phrase many times in Hong Kong, but could never really get what it meant.

"If you bargain too far, you lose because they lose face," she said. "So do not claim victory , especially if you win."

It was better to pay a little extra, than to make a Chinese lose face.

"But how do you know when he has lost face?"

"Yes, that's right. You don't know," said Jeanette. "They can't say they have lost face, and they can't get angry — because that way they lose more face. The best way to know is if they smile."

At last I understood. "Just like an Australian footballer," I said. "When an opponent really hurts him, he smiles back to let everyone watching know he didn't feel a thing."

"No?" said Jeanette. "What a strange game."

Not as strange, I assured her, as one of the Chinese fortune-telling operations in the market. At the dark end of the street, scores of fortune-tellers exhibited sticks, charts, cards, and even birds: cages with one small live finch in each — with a stack of tiny bits of folded paper protruding through the cage wire. Each of these pieces of paper foretold a different fortune and yours was selected by the bird: for a price. Mine said: "A woman with a mole on her upper lip will have no difficulty snaring a mate." Well, I already knew that.

Jeanette wanted me to get my palm read again, this time by a professional. But because of the "period of great danger" in my lifeline I knew what she was up to and tried to get out of it. Also, she had foretold with a pack of cards that I would get a letter about a dark-haired older man who was very ill. I didn't like that sort of prediction and had tipped the cards over in anger.

"No, you must do it," she said.

I didn't reveal — in case it somehow got back to Max Schofield — that, at home in Queensland, telling fortunes was, of course, illegal. Under Section 43 of our State Criminal Code fortune-telling came under "Witchery, sorcery, enchantment and conjuration" — all criminal offences. Police even raided tea houses in Fortitude Valley where women read tea leaves for the customers. Bewitchment was considered as bad as the heinous Queensland crime of "defaming Princes". This was just the sort of Australian censorship that Max Schofield would love to add to his long list.

An old woman, dressed in black and sitting on a white stool, studied my hand: rubbing her stubby brown fingers, with long fingernails curling over and in, across the palm. From wrinkled folds of skin, the barely visible blurred dark eyes of the bent-over fortune-teller looked up into mine and foretold. I never heard a Cantonese word I recognised, but the crowd clapped joyfully.

"She said," intoned Jeanette, laughing enough to have to cover her face with her long hands (fingers separated and up), "that you will one day become a Great Lover."

It was a couple of weeks later at dinner with Arch and his American girlfriend, that Jeanette confessed she had slipped the fortune-teller an extra dollar to say that. Even Ah Ping got the joke and clattered around throwing her arms in the air saying "Dragon Master Lover," "Great

Dragon Master Lover". Ah Ping, wearing the white jacket she donned every night, had been singing and chuckling to herself all evening as she cooked: probably because for the first time we each had a girlfriend to share dinner. Ah Ping was not the sort of servant who waited on you, but that night she went close. Especially after Jeanette told us that Amahs had been around for hundreds of years and stuck staunchly together — because some Chinese women got such a raw deal.

"If not drowned at birth they are married off at a young age. Once widowed or divorced they can only become servants. So they stick together: like a trade union."

Yet still, despite all this, Ah Ping seemed to enjoy herself immensely: giggling and laughing as she went off to the markets every day in her black jacket and with the thin black handles of a large silver-and-black plastic bag over her little forearm.

I saw a lot more of Hong Kong after I met Jeanette, who, in my own mind, I thought of as "JJJ": her initials. Instead of sitting in nightclubs, we went all over the Island: the Tiger Balm Gardens made up of grotesque painted statues like giant dogs bigger than elephants; a seven-storey white pagoda; a walk on the hilltop behind the Peak, a temple of one thousand gold Buddhas. In a laneway behind some shops were dozens of skeletal old Chinese men sitting on their haunches smoking opium with spoons, matches and silver pipes. They never even looked up.

I learnt to speak more Cantonese: to say the word "Mmmm" through my nose: "Mmmm Ho," no good; "Mmm Goi," please. And "Ngoc" up the back of the pallet for I: "Ngoc Oi Ne," was I love you. "Ho ho" very good; "Gate door chin?" How much money; and "Joy Geen" — goodbye. Plus one I was to use often in the heat of Hong Kong: "Mmm Goi Ne Chang Jup" — Please, can I have an orange juice.

We didn't lose touch completely with the West. JJJ and I went to see sixteen-year-old Jamaican pop singer Millie bop

127

around the stage singing *My Boy Lollipop* "you make my heart go giddiup" at the City Hall, where we also saw Paul Newman and Jackie Gleeson shoot pool against each other in *The Hustler*: a special showing of the film for Westerners and cinema lovers. It didn't play at the usual huge theatres like the James Bond films because there were no spies and no sword fights to attract the locals: just two men tensely squaring off around the green baize. To get into Chinese theatres, Newman and Gleeson would have had to fight each other with their billard cues or, better still, the odd and even balls. But the European audience — starved of such classics — gave the film a standing ovation. It was the only time I had seen an audience applaud at the end of a picture.

Whereas in American action pictures actors always crashed to their death from rooftops, Chinese films invariably contained sword fights with reversed bits where the actors leapt backwards up onto high, tiled pagoda roofs. The films were often about what the translators called in the English sub-titles "filial piety" — a child revenging the deaths of ancestors. Often this revenge was left to a daughter, which made the film more exciting because she would have to outwit stronger male opponents. This meant using unusually small weapons such as purple darts, tiny daggers, or magic potions.

One film was about a famous one-armed swordsman. Of course he was too great a warrior to have lost the arm in battle: it was chopped off when he turned his back on a jealous woman. Even so, he was still the most feared fighter in all China's Middle Kingdom. In fact, this ancient Chinese warrior was so quick on the draw that no one knew what type of sword he used. Those who saw his weapon never lived to describe it. In the final scene, the one-armed swordsman faces his arch enemy alone in the moonlight upon a tiny convex bamboo bridge.

The one-armed swordsman pulls out his weapon for all to see.

"Ay Yah!" yells the audience.

It is like a long meat-cleaver with a sharp arrow-like point protruding forward from the top.

The arch enemy is in big trouble.

But, suddenly, from under his long satin cloak, the arch enemy produces his weapon.

"Ay Yahhhh!!!"

His weapon is exactly the same as the one-armed swordsman's.

As we criss-crossed Hong Kong, JJJ pointed out the Chinese letter-writers who served illiterates, and the foot-high tiny red-and-gold temples at ground level that went almost unnoticed in busy Hong Kong streets. These small incense offerings were for the spirits of dead ancestors and various Gods. Some of the unhappy spirits were known as "Hungry Ghosts", a much more malevolent idea than the Catholic "Holy Ghost". Incense was burned at these altars for these unhappy spirits — a bit like Catholics saying prayers for the Holy Souls in Purgatory. Of course, Catholics could also get a soul out of Purgatory by making someone laugh.

Fletch often said "Purgatory must be nearly empty by now" after we had all laughed at one of his jokes. And sometimes when Ken suffered in the heat during a long tennis match he said under his breath: "I offer this up, Lord, to get some poor bloody bugger out of Purgatory."

Hong Kong was a constant reminder that there were many suffering spirits on earth as well as in the Heavens. On the Island, poor people slept in a street of gold shops. One of the first sights I saw in the Colony was an old lady like Ah Ping in black pyjamas carrying a heavy load of wood up a steep narrow street being beeped out of the road by a Rolls Royce. And you couldn't miss Jeanette's next door neighbours. They lived under a kitchen-table-sized piece of brown canvas attached to the side of the tall building and sloping out almost, but not quite, to the gutter. So when it rained the water wet the footpath floor of their home.

Five children were born and bred under that sheet of canvas. The mother and father sat on their haunches under their canvas sheet home while the children played in and around the gutter. They washed their plates in the gutter, folded up their cardboard beds in the morning, and ate by kerosene lamp at night. Untold thousands were living like that in Hong Kong: surviving by being tied to someone else's building.Yet no one objected to their presence, as they would have in Australia. In fact, everyone — including JJJ's family — spoke of them with pride. They knew this family had nowhere else to go. That Mum and Dad were doing the best they could, surrounded by poverty and riches not even imagined in Australia.

Hong Kong shop windows over-flowed with gold and pearls and diamonds and jade and emeralds and carved ivory. I had never seen ivory in Australia. But in Hong Kong there was so much of it that every tourist shop sold sets of mysterious ivory balls magically carved one inside the other: up to six balls moving independently inside each other and sitting on a bakelite stand.

I bought an ivory chess set, making sure it was genuine ivory by checking for the distinctive cross-lined pattern on the bottom of each piece. The King was in the costume of a Peking Opera General and carrying a spear with a flag. The Castles were elephants. Each pawn was a different Chinese peasant. One set of the ivory pieces was stained brown, with tea. It was a thing of beauty I had never expected to see, let alone own and it gave me great pleasure until I happened on something much more magical and exotic.

One night in the night market, for a few pounds Australian, I bought one hundred exquisitely painted paper cut-out faces from inside Red China, each one showing the face of a different famous character from Peking Opera — each as famous to them as Robin Hood or Ned Kelly to us. In each case, a very thin piece of paper about the size of a small envelope had been cut into a face, the many fine cuts giving it three-dimensions.

Each face was painted totally differently using a multitude of strong colours which emphasised the sharp and intricate, not abstract, nature of the faces. So sharp that I could see the cut of the cloth; the expression on the mouth; the anger in the eyes; the hairs in the beard; even deliberate, painted distortion. Number ninety-one was from the Opera "A Journey to the West" a face described as "money-shaped spots on a leopard face". Number thirty-one the hero from a play about a walled farm.

Each was numbered and folded inside a piece of tissue paper describing the character: "the paper-cuts of painted faces: traditional facial make-ups in classical Chinese operas." The packets said the make-up worn by Peking Opera stars was to enhance the artistic beauty of the operas.

I was pleased to read what it said about red cheeks: "A red face symbolizes loyalty and straight-forwardness; a white one craftiness; a variegated one, courage; a small one, wit ... when embellished with head-dresses, moustaches, and beards, they become still more attractive."

Hundreds of colours in different geometric combinations: the forehead, the head-dress, the hat, the beard, the swords, the decorations, the pom-poms, the tassles. Somehow, tiny nicks of the the razor blade created curly hair, or sunken cheeks, or old age, or madness, or glumness. Even the thickness of the beard. And all the while the colours and their pattern told the character, the position, and the role.

In some you could see the slyness, or the goodness, straight away. For others you had to be Chinese to know. Some were bulbous and dragon-like, others toadish or monkeyish, another like a pig. Yet all created with the slightest stroke of a razor removing, not adding, a weightless whiff of paper.

Later I got eight paper-cuts of Chinese Fairies — like Dragons, something I didn't know that the Chinese had.

They weren't like our Australian fairies at the bottom of an English garden. These cuts were all the one colour, cerise. The seven male fairies and one female were all like Gods riding forth on a horse, or a donkey, or a large bird. Compared with these weightless pieces of painted paper, the expensive faces of carved jade or ivory sold to tourists were emotionless, expressionless, and worthless.

It was as if these cut-out people were alive: life by a thousand cuts.

I studied these Peking paper faces on my desk at work, and realised I had to do something. I typed a letter to the External Affairs Department of the Soviet Union in Moscow requesting a visa to enter Russia from Red China.

I thought it might make it easier to get to Peking.

10   Mr Kiat and the Fiction Experts

On the way to the Hong Kong Cricket Club to meet Arch for lunch, I stopped on the footpath outside the Bank of China Building for a moment. Then, once again, I walked between the two stone lions protecting the Communists from bad spirits. Through the giant timber doors into the monastic foyer of the almost glass-less Communist building.

I had been past this building scores of times since my abortive visit months earlier, without being tempted to enter. But this time I had something extra in my left pocket: a surprise.

A letter from Moscow. The Russians hadn't sent me a visa, but they hadn't knocked me back either. In English, the typed letter said: "If you get in to China, go to our Embassy in Peking and ask them."

This letter confirmed everything I had heard about the Communists: it was typed on a very old, almost brown, sheet of paper through a worn-out ribbon and contained spelling mistakes. Where letters normally had "Dear Sir" there was nothing: in fact no reference to me at all, except on the envelope. And they forgot to sign it, or to even type a name at the bottom.

It wasn't much to go on. It didn't even promise me a definite visa. But the letter did have a very official-looking red Soviet stamp — what the Chinese called a "chop" — and I knew from work just how much the Chinese respected documents, any document, with a chop.

Especially a red chop.

What better way to get some articles published in Australian newspapers than to travel through forbidden China.

Then I would only have to skip across Russia on the train to the centre of Paris and help Fletch launch his comeback as an international tennis star based in Hong Kong. For the last month the now unused rail line to Paris had beckoned me every morning while I lay in bed. But now it was Arch's turn in the front bedroom.

I had already told Max Schofield of my European plans, without mentioning Red China, while we were walking on Lantau. Knowing he was first and foremost a Pom, I emphasised that I wanted to visit what we in Australia called "the Mother Country". But, at the same time, I said I didn't want to let him down.

"Good show, Lunn," Max said, to my relief, as we walked back down Rotten Head Peak. "A bit of civilisation never did you people from the antipodes any harm. Make sure you have a Double Diamond for me: that's a beer my boy! And stay out of Soho, the only sights you will see there after dark are all banned in Australia."

But, like all employers, he wasn't letting me off completely.

"All I ask is that you get that first damned edition of the *Far East Medical Journal* ready before you go. Think of all the *Playboy Magazines* we can send to frustrated doctors in Australia," and at this Max laughed so outrageously that it echoed off the Dog Teeth Hills and he held on to his moustache as if he were afraid it would fall off.

So here I was again, walking past the pistol-packing guard inside the front door of the Bank of China Building to the woman at the desk, the same woman I had spoken to before Christmas. The one who said we Australians were renegades.

"I wish to see your comrades," I said, choosing the words carefully as I showed her the letter from Russia.

"This is from the authorities in Moscow," I said, pointing at the official red chop.

It worked. She took the letter and my passport, and ushered me into a lift without saying anything. Compared with the fast lifts in the rest of Hong Kong, we went ever so slowly to the top floor — or at least as far as the lift would go. Knowing the Chicoms, they probably had a secret floor on top.

I imagined I would see oceans of people in China, some of the 750 million Red Chinese who swarmed above Hong Kong like bees: one-quarter of all humanity. So many that, although you never saw them, you knew they were there. I could see all these people, who to the Australian government didn't exist, in my mind: marching around twenty-five abreast and multiplying at a rate too fast to chalk up. No wonder they had the Americans scared: the United States didn't recognise the world's most populous nation either.

Catholics feared Communists no end. To a Catholic the doors to this building were the equivalent of the Gates of Hell: and I had to hope that, as in the Catholic prayer, "the Gates of Hell do not prevail against us". Especially as Olive had again urged me not to go in to Communist China, saying I might never get out: "I've always said that if you love someone you ought to tell them. I love you, so I don't want you to take this foolish risk. Just because Kenny Fletcher puts his head in a fire, it doesn't mean you have to."

Mum couldn't imagine that this journey was my own idea, my own plan. It was the first time I had ever made my own decision on where to go. Up until now I had always gone on holidays with the Lunn family, or with my older brother Jack, or down the South Coast with Jim, or to the Victorian tennis championships with Ken. But, now that I was 23 and living on my own, I could go wherever I liked: even to places where I wasn't supposed to.

One of the things that interested me about the Chicoms was that they had such an exaggerated way of abusing people, just like my good mate Jim Egoroff. While Jim would say "You are a wretch who, having seen the consequences of a thousand errors, continues still to blunder", the Red Chinese were always being quoted in the Hong

135

Kong papers saying things like: "The United States is a paper tiger which, like a rat crossing the street, is being chased by every passer-by". And, while Jim would say "You blocks, you stones, you worse than senseless things", the Chicoms accused countries like Australia of being "double-dealing, running-dog, puppet lackeys of the Yankee imperialists".

The unending supply of Red Chinese insults poured forth from their New China Newsagency, or were quoted from their official paper, the *Peoples Daily*. It was almost as if the Chinese Communists had written a new brand of the English language to use on those who did not share their revolutionary vision.

While Jim still stuck to "are you a perverted little agent or something?", the Chinese came up with new ones every week like: "ideological disdaining deviationist self-indulgent bourgeois experts". This, I knew, would make them interesting to deal with: how could you argue with people who talked like that?

We emerged from the tiny lift to front a long polished wood counter. Side-on behind the counter, on brown lino, were three long rows of Chinese men and women working keenly in neat lines of old varnished timber desks piled high with pieces of paper in wire trays. These clerks used staples and chops and red wax and pencils and paper that wasn't quite white — like the Moscow letter. As they toiled, the scene reminded me of the Mobilgas office in Brisbane where I worked when I first left school, even down to the man walking through the rows keeping an eye out to see that everyone was hard at it.

Except, that is, for the clothes. This office looked nothing like the rest of Hong Kong. There were no colourful cheongsams in greens and reds and pale blues. Everyone, man and woman, was in dark trousers and white cotton shirts. Only the longer hair marked out female from male. It was just what I had always imagined a Communist office would look like. Lots of people, all looking the same, doing the same repetitive things.

A tall, thin man, much taller than any Chinese I had seen in Hong Kong, emerged from a nearby office carrying the Moscow letter and my passport. He stood out from all the others on this floor, not just because of his height, but because he wore a dark blue jacket done up to the neck. He was clearly in charge, but he didn't look that much older than me.

The tall man stood back from the other side of the counter as if I had bad breath and said: "Ne hoi bien doa?" which I knew meant something like "where are you going?"

"To Red China," I said.

"So, Hu Lun, you speak Chinese!" he said in English, as if he had tricked me.

"Ne home ma?" I said, greeting him politely in Cantonese to show my interest in his country. "No, I don't speak your language. I have heard that phrase a lot since I came to Hong Kong five months ago. You Chinese say it all the time."

"Your passport says you are a journalist, Hu Lun, so you must know your country is a renegade," he said.

"Yes, I have heard that," I agreed.

"Australia has not recognised that China exists. So, although we would like to help you visit the Socialist World and our great friends in the Soviet Union, your passport is not valid."

So Steve Dunleavy was right again. Back in Brisbane, I had listed "journalist" in my passport application because I was proud to have made it through my four-year newspaper cadetship. But one day in Nathan Road Steve warned me that this had not been a good idea.

"Hughie, most countries, most people even, don't like journalists," Steve said. "That's an unpleasant fact we have to face mate. It's not that they don't think that the public should know everything. Most people don't think the public should know *anything*. So why advertise the fact that you're a journalist when you don't have to? Mate, the smart journalist lists himself in his passport as a Librarian, or a History Teacher, or a Lawyer, or something else innocuous." And Steve gave me a friendly punch in the bicep to emphasise that he was just being helpful, and not interfering.

Having made the mistake, it was a problem I was going to have to overcome. No wonder Fletch was always quoting from his book of sayings: "Travel makes a wise man wiser, and a fool worse."

Knowing that the Brits, in order to keep Hong Kong safe from attack, had — unlike Australia and the United States — continued to recognise China, and kept plumping for it to be admitted to the UN instead of Formosa, I said: "But this is a *British Passport*."

The tall official looked surprised, studied the blue cover and frowned. At the top the passport said "AUSTRALIA", but at the bottom it said "BRITISH PASSPORT". I pointed to the gold Royal Crown above "AUSTRALIA" as further evidence. Then I read out from the inside cover: "In the name of Her Majesty Elizabeth the Second, Queen of the United Kingdom *and* of Australia, I request all those whom it may concern to allow the bearer to pass freely without let or hindrance ..."

He was surprised, but unfazed. Advancing, as if he had a good idea, he moved towards the counter and leaned against it.

"So Britain is your Capitalist Landlord, Hu Lun. Do Australians live under Colonial Extortion with an Unequal Treaty like Hong Kong?"

I assured him that was not the case. We were not a Colony. England was known to Australians as the "Mother Country" purely because that was where our ancestors came from in the eighteenth century. "They sent all their criminals to Australia as punishment in sailing ships, and these convicts, and their guards, went on and built up a new nation from there with the help of new migrants from Britain and elsewhere in Europe," I replied. "But their English Queen continued on as our Queen as well. And that's why Australians travel on British Passports like this one here."

"Imperialist Oppression, Hu Lun," he said, unimpressed by my country's colonial history. "China suffered this Capitalist Outrage for hundreds and hundreds of years until the Revolution."

Since he kept using my name, I asked for his.

"Kiat," he said.

"Ho," I replied, which was like saying "fine".

"So, Hu Lun, why do you wish to see somewhere that does not exist?"

Kiat smiled at his trick question, revealing teeth crushed together like a woman's toes.

"Look Mr Kiat I just want to have a look at your country because I've been living in Hong Kong and now I've seen China across the border from the New Territories; I've seen China from on top of Lantau Peak; and I've seen it from Macau. In this part of the world Red China seems omnipotent. It has made me interested in China. It's that simple."

"Who do you represent?"

"I represent myself."

"Are you taking part in idle individualism?"

It was like the Third Degree. In all this time, none of the Chinese at their desks looked our way. But they must surely have been listening. Why didn't Mr Kiat take me into his big corner office. I guessed he was showing off to his staff.

"My father, Fred, would love to meet you, Mr Kiat," I said, knowing how much Dad hated what he called "isms and osims".

Strangely enough, Mr Kiat took this as a huge compliment, bowed his head, and thanked me generously.

"Nothing is simple, Hu Lun," he said, apparently sympathetically. "You are a journalist. Western journalists are poisonous weeds because they are fiction experts. Fiction experts who dwell on negativism. If we let you into China, you will write bad stories about our struggle, instead of telling of the success of the Great Proletarian Revolution."

"That's not true Mr Kiat," I said honestly. "China is a place of much interest to me."

"What interest, Hu Lun?" he said, raising his front lip in a sneer. "Are you a bourgeois idealist?"

As he said this, Mr Kiat placed the passport and Moscow letter on the counter and pushed them back across. Being a Dragon on a Pillar, or even having red cheeks, didn't seem to go over with the Chinese Communists as I had hoped.

The only thing I could think of on the spur of the moment was the magazine in my hand which had just come out that day.

"Architecture," I said. "Peking Architecture is one interest. I like the way your roofs curl up at the points, and the unusual tiling system where you use U-shaped clay tiles alternately up and down across a roof."

I showed him the *Far East Architect and Builder*, which included my piece on an Australian architect who had recently set up an office in Hong Kong. To my surprise, Mr Kiat took the magazine and read from it, as if to show the staff how well he could read English. Standing very erect, and reading slowly and correctly, he half-faced the staff who looked around like waiters in a busy restaurant: their eyes flitting on everything, but seeing nothing.

"Alan R. Gilbert was an assistant lecturer in the Faculty of Architecture, University of New South Wales, who decided to go to those parts of the world that *nurtured great civilisations*. Thus he came to Hong Kong."

Mr Kiat looked up from the article: "Dai Yut! Very bold story, Hu Lun."

He put the magazine inside his coat and invited me into his office, saying there was a question he wanted me to answer which would be better done in private.

The office was in a corner of the building with million dollar views overlooking Hong Kong harbour, the City Hall, and the Hong Kong Cricket Club. But I didn't say anything about having played cricket there. His office was too high to break a window anyway.

We sat down on furniture which went more with a view of Ekibin Creek. A man brought us each a hot tea as Mr Kiat warned: "You should not feel denunciation."

Having a clear conscience about my reasons for wanting to travel through China I was up front about the question he wanted to ask: "Sure. Fire away."

Mr Kiat didn't know what I meant.

"It is an Australian expression: it means 'go ahead, ask me anything you like. I don't mind'."

Mr Kiat hesitated, as my mind raced ahead as it always did: I just hoped he wasn't going to ask if I was anti-Communist.

"What happened to your left ear, may I inquire, Hu Lun?" he said finally.

I almost burst out laughing. What a question for a Chicom to worry about asking.

Next to "journalist" in my passport, under the heading "Visible Peculiarities", it said (in red type): *"Scar L ear"*.

I told Mr Kiat how I set my mosquito net on fire when I was six years old, because I needed dead matches for school. "We used dead matches to learn to count because, after the War against the Japanese, everything in Australia had been used up and there was nothing else for teachers to use in classrooms. No one in our family smoked, so I was trying to turn live matches into dead ones."

Mr Kiat expressed unguarded surprise that Australia had also fought against the Japanese who, he said, were defeated "in the Great Socialist Struggle of World War II".

"The Australians stopped them dead in the New Guinea jungles," I said.

Since Mr Kiat had asked me a personal question I asked if he would mind telling me his age. He said he was thirty-two, nine years older than me. So I knew he had spent only half his life under Communism.

Mr Kiat stood up.

"Come back in a month — if you are still interested in Chinese architecture, Hu Lun," he said, leaning over the desk as he spoke in what I read as a gesture of friendliness.

I raced back to the office to check what else my article on the Australian architect said, since I had written it two months earlier. I hoped it didn't say anything that could be interpreted as anti-Red China.

My luck was in.

Mr Gilbert had said: "I want to gather information by talking, reading, drawing, and taking pictures of architecture in China and other countries for a thesis on 'architectural symbolism'. The thing that distinguishes Architecture from simply building is that Architecture is an art, an art akin to music. In traditional societies the principles which pervaded all the arts were defined by the society's philosophic structure, which formed the 'Grand Theme'. Hong Kong has given too little recognition to the Colony's unique environment, both geographically *and in its proximity to one of the great traditions of the past.*"

My magazine article could not have worked better, even if I had known it was going to fall into Communist hands.

One of Mr Kiat's magazines had conversely fallen into my hands. A Chicom magazine showing pictures of destroyed American planes, blown-up hotels, and wounded US troops on the cover. The heading, translated, read: "Strike crushing blows at the U.S. aggressors."

The article said: "The U.S. aggressors cannot escape final defeat in South Vietnam. If the U.S. dares to continue its intrusions into the Democratic Republic of Vietnam and expands the war in Indo-China its defeat will be so much the speedier and more disastrous."

The magazine revealed that even Chinese literature was now devoted entirely to attacking the Americans. Two volumes called "Letters from South Vietnam", it claimed, had sold four million copies in six months. A Chinese critic and poet who reviewed the two books in the magazine wrote:

"In spite of myself, tears of sorrow and indignation came. What tortures our brothers and sisters of South Vietnam are enduring! The U.S. imperialists and their stooges have committed indescribable crimes ... they have cut out the livers of hundreds of our own people, gouged out their eyes ... even put our people into jars, pouring boiling water over them, skinning them, and then eating their flesh. A Vietnamese wife was given 'the crucifixion Maria' — tied to a cross and raped. They then cut her open, tore out her liver, cooked it, and ate it."

How could they believe such lies? The Red Chinese had to be totally indoctrinated if they believed Americans would tear human livers out of live people and eat them. Or skin people for a meal. What was it that made people always think other races were the cannibals? What hatred made the Chicoms believe these stories about the Yanks who had saved us from the Zombie-making Japs?

Nor could I believe what the Chinese said about American soldiers.

One "letter from South Vietnam" was quoted as saying: *"The Yankee soldiers run in disorder and panic when yelled at furiously."*

Then it occurred to me. The Red Chinese had their own fiction experts.

Now the Chinese Communists were surely going to say the same things about Australians if we sent troops to Vietnam. My older brother, Jack, who was a political reporter on the *Courier-Mail*, wrote to say that Mr Menzies had re-introduced conscription, and was planning to send Australian troops to the Vietnam "struggle", as it was always called back home. So, when next the Red Chinese talked about "Yankee stooges", they were going to be talking about Australians.

I wrote a story and sent it home to the *Courier-Mail* saying we would become a target for just such unmitigated Red Chinese hatred if we went into Vietnam. And I quoted all the stuff about eating people's livers, and skinning Vietnamese peasants alive. I posted it off and was surprised that they ran every word almost immediately. So it must have been news to them, as it was to me. The headline, across the top of the feature page, read "Chinese HATE attack" and the story, with my name on top, followed:

"A tremendous 'hate' campaign is being carried out by the Red Chinese against America and to date the U.S. has been bearing these Chinese threats and propaganda attacks alone.

"Now Australia has placed herself in the shadow of that awakening giant, Red China."

This success augured well for any stories I might write once inside China. So, on receipt of the *Courier-Mail* clipping from Olive, I hurried back around to the Bank of China Building to see Mr Kiat again, even though it was only a fortnight since my last visit. Naturally, I didn't take the clipping of my story.

But I picked a bad time.

Upstairs, the rows of Chinese workers were all asleep on their hands at their desks, and there was no one serving the counter. I coughed politely, but none would look up. Perhaps they'd all come down with something.

Then, Mr Kiat — who acted as if he was exempt from all office rules — appeared from around a corner.

"This is a compulsory rest session for the masses, Hu Lun," he said. "So that we can strengthen our assiduity. Joy Geen."

11   "Flashy Fletcher" for Wimbledon

Fletch was making three times as much money as me, playing doubles with rich Chinese businessmen who gambled on their tennis. So he always had pockets full of money, which he splashed around. Before he left Australia, Ken's doubles partners were Roy Emerson and John Newcombe. Now he had one elderly Chinese partner who owned a battery factory, and another who owned a chain of language schools.

These old men, Ken said, enjoyed life because although they lost their fortunes when China went Communist, they had become multi-millionaires all over again in less than 15 years in Hong Kong.

I sometimes went to watch them play. While an ageing Chinese man staggered around the baseline, Fletch was a white flash at the net, hammering the white ball for winner after winner: often straight through the lime line. Usually his partner had nothing to do at all because, once Fletch stepped onto a tennis court, his usual friendly demeanour changed. He became haughty and aggressive and never went easy on the opposition.

"Why should I but," he said. "That would be insulting them."

Ken took all the overheads, smashing the ball at such pace that it was dangerous to stand anywhere but behind the fence. His opponents spent most of the time applauding.

His reputation was enhanced when our mate Victor Sun played the new young Chinese gun player, Gerry Sung, in a local championship final. I joined the crowd to watch the match on the yellowish granite courts cut into a slope next to the Queen Elizabeth Hospital. Young Gerry had just returned from representing his university in the US where, it was said, he was coached by former world champion Pancho Gonzales. It was important for Ken that Victor win, but Victor kept saying how good Gerry looked in early rounds.

"You'll be surprised how much worse he looks when you pressure him," Ken said. "We're here, on your side, Victor. I can tell you, and I know: you are better than him. But don't look at him: tennis is a game that's played in the mind."

It was a real Chinese shoot-out with a lot of face at stake. The Sungs were one of the richest Chinese families in the Far East, while Victor's family were famous for being relatives of Sun Yat-sen. Gerry's father, Mr Sung, chose to watch from a Rolls Royce parked up on the hill above the courts, while Mr Sun watched from the back of the clubhouse.

Victor won the match and the championship. After the Suns had left, the Rolls Royce pulled up and Mr Sung emerged: a thick-set man in a long, rich, vicuna overcoat, dark glasses, and small-brimmed black hat with the brim turned up all the way around.

"Mr Fletcher," he said. "I want you to coach my son for next year's championship. State what you require."

"Struth," said Ken. "I'm off to Manila tomorrow."

"Then I will enjoy meeting you on your return," said Mr Sung, and stepped back into his Rolls and left.

There was just no doubt about it, Hong Kong had never seen a tennis player up close even a quarter as good as Fletch. People gathered alongside the court every time he played, marvelling at his topspin forehand: a stroke which Australian Davis Cup coach Harry Hopman said was the best in the world. Hong Kong papers wrote about him every week. He was invited to all the important functions. Because, for the first time, the Colony had its own world-ranked sportsman.

Ken had been in an Australian team that won the Davis Cup. He was a Wimbledon doubles finalist; a French doubles champion; and had recently won the first-ever Grand Slam of Mixed Doubles with Margaret Smith: the Australian, the French, Wimbledon, plus the United States title at Forest Hills in New York. In singles, Ken had been seeded number three at Wimbledon, had made the final of the Australian, and had won the New Zealand, Philippines, and Czechoslovakian titles in the one year. Even as an 18-year-old in 1959, he had been a member of the six-man squad that went to America and brought back the Davis Cup.

Fletch was popular in America, where he had made the quarter-finals of the singles at Forest Hills. He had also played in places like Boston, and he and Wimbledon women's champion Maria Bueno were given a personal tour of Warner Brothers studios in the San Fernando Valley when they played in the Pacific Southwest championships in Los Angeles. Fletch even got to meet Efren Zimbalist Jnr of *77 Sunset Strip* and Ed "Cookie" Byrnes, and saw Anthony Perkins and Jane Fonda in the shower making a film. Plus he met Charlton Heston "*Ben Hur* himself," as Ken called him, in New York.

It was a sad series of events which had banished Fletch from Australia and led him to hold court in Hong Kong.

In December 1963, Ken had taken me with him to a secret meeting of Australia's leading tennis players in Melbourne at the home of a wealthy industrialist known as "the mystery man of Australian tennis". The players were upset that the Australian association had decreed they could not leave the country before the end of March. Whereas the mystery man said they were free citizens and, like everyone else, could leave whenever they liked.

"This isn't East Germany," he told them.

With international champions Roy Emerson, Fred Stolle, Bob Hewitt, and Martin Mulligan there, I felt embarrassed to be listening. But Ken told them I was his best mate. We were shown through a large brick mansion to a barbeque on the backyard-sized tiled rear patio around the mystery man's swimming pool where some of Australia's top female tennis players cooked steaks and served drinks as the men talked.

The five champions agreed that Australia was better served by them winning tournaments around the world than playing exhibitions at home. Thus they all agreed to break the deadline: "because it is much harder to break five sticks at once than five sticks one at a time".

In February 1964, before the deadline, Fletch and Emerson flew off to play tournaments in the Caribbean and South America. Fred Stolle and Bob Hewitt flew to South Africa. And Martin Mulligan went to play in Italy. As it turned out, two of the five, Emerson and Stolle, reached the final of Wimbledon that year, so Australian tennis — desperately in need of two champions to hold on to the precious Davis Cup — forgave, and selected them.

But they did not select, or forgive, the other three. The Davis Cup career Ken had planned since he was a six-year-old was over. To be a member of an Australian team which won the imposing chalice-like Davis Cup was to be a national hero. Fans queued for tickets, large temporary grandstands were built around the courts, and almost everyone in Australia listened on their wireless to the fast and furious commentary that could not keep up. No one could escape hearing the result.

Now, all Ken had to remind him of it all was the team photo of him standing with Rod Laver, Neale Fraser, Roy Emerson and Harry Hopman around the Davis Cup that they won in 1962 in front of 18,700 people at Milton stadium. Plus the menu he kept from the victory dinner: Canapes Mexicane, Queensland Iced Oysters, Barrier Reef Coral Trout Meuniere, Roast Tom Turkey and Victory Bombe Glacee. The menu boasted that Brisbane's Milton Clubhouse was "the only air-conditioned tennis headquarters in the world".

This was why Fletch wanted me to go to England with him — so he could win Wimbledon's singles crown and prove the Australian selectors wrong. He had played Wimbledon five times, and had recently got within a point or two of making the semi-finals. He was now 24 years old, the right age for his best chance: and his old Queensland nemesis, Rod Laver, had left the amateur ranks and turned professional.

As we sat in the Bayside for a farewell drink the night before he left for Manila, I told him of my visit to Mr Kiat.

"Going into Communist China would be a very foolish act but," Ken said as he downed another cold beer. "Your mother and father knew you were coming overseas with me. So I feel a bit responsible for you, and now you want to piss off into Red China and yet you don't even know a bloody prostitute when you see one, let alone a Commo."

Ken and I hadn't had an argument since we were kids, and even then it was over who owned some marbles. But I quickly recognised the same signs of aggression in us both.

"Instead of stuffing around with the Commos, come to Wimbledon with me. It will be too difficult to win alone."

I said I doubted my presence would make any difference.

"All the champion desperates are at Wimbledon from every corner of the world," Ken said. "The married ones are hard to beat because when they win a point they look up and see someone on their side. Instead of battling alone they play for the little lady. Others look up and see their Mum, or their girlfriend, or their coach, or team manager. But if my sandshoe falls off in the final, I haven't even got someone to get me another one."

They should concentrate on their tennis, I said.

"I've told you before Hughie that you're the world's greatest off-court tennis player. Every human being needs someone to hang on to," Ken replied, sinking a beer. "You can see them all, every player, looking up into the Wimbledon stand at someone. On the Centre Court most people admire you, but, as my book says, 'all that glisters is not gold'. You need a friend there who you know is with you, come what may. Otherwise your dreams all go to pot."

Ken said leaving Australian tennis had made it more difficult. "I'll need my best mate there at Wimbledon to talk to before I go out to play so I can say 'shit I'm nervous today' and you can say: 'you can beat this mug, I saw you clean him up in Melbourne well'. Otherwise the tension gets greater and greater while you wait alone in the dressing shed. Then you walk out under that sign over the entrance to the Centre Court which says 'if you can meet with triumph and disaster' and the umpire says 'play shall be continuous. Players ready, play,' and there is no turning back."

Sometimes crowds overseas hated him for no good reason. "That's precisely the time when you need a friendly face, and how much better if it is my best mate. Those crowds bring out the mongrel in me and I start sticking it up the section barracking for the other mug."

"But don't you get to know lots of important people at these tournaments?".

"You get a few hangers-on basking in your glory, and it's nice to have them. But a real mate is another story. It's the Ivory Tower Syndrome that I hate about tennis. The way it is now, if I win Wimbledon in July I'll go back and sit in a lounge chair in some hotel room in Kensington and say to myself: 'Shit hey. I just won Wimbledon'."

As Ken ordered another round, I said I was still going into Red China if I could. I was the journalist. He was the tennis player. I was sick of people telling me what to do. I said I was going to Red China and Red Russia and Red anywhere-else even if I missed Wimbledon.

"You're a grown up now, Hughie, so I won't tell you what to do. I'm telling you but, there's a danger you'll end up in prison, or worse. You think you can fool the Chinese. Events can turn quickly where there is no democracy."

What made him think the Communists would worry about one Australian? They probably wouldn't even know I was there, I said over another drink.

I said I was onto a great story and had come overseas looking for adventure. I wasn't going to start complaining about leaving the comforts of home behind.

"You don't know these people," Fletch said. "They are pursuing an ideology. They are going to wonder who you are and what you're up to.

"Look, Hughie, I've been around the world five times. This is the first time you've left Brisbane. It's not as if you are being sent there by a newspaper, or Reuters, or the Australian government so they can protect you. I wouldn't have gone to Russia except that I was in the Australian team. Even then I was glad to get out of the bloody joint. Why do you think these countries are surrounded by high walls? You Lunn boys have always seen yourselves as too important. That was alright at Annerley Junction. The world doesn't revolve around the Lunn family but."

"And it doesn't revolve around your tennis matches," I said, annoyed.

Ken was born in the Year of the Dragon, and Dragon boys are stubborn and quick-tempered. He drained his beer in the dark smoke of the Bayside: "What if they torture you, you bloody big ... you never bloody ... you would ..."

"Go on, say it," I challenged him, knowing exactly what was coming. But he stopped short.

"Say it."

"... how are you going to get on in Red China well, when you nearly fainted when we went to get our injections to come here, you stupid bastard."

That was it. I hadn't nearly fainted at all. I'd just asked if I could sit down. I turned and left the Bayside and went home.

Since Ken was leaving for Manila, the next morning I dropped around to the Grand early. "A boy born in the Year of the Dragon has the potential to be the ruler", I read out from a Chinese book of proverbs I had bought for him. "This augurs well for Wimbledon, Fletch." I knew that would make him smile, and it did. He always said that no one ever won Wimbledon without a touch of luck. Or, as he put it: "without God on your side".

The rest of the proverb, which I did not read out, said: "Dragon boys are wonderful workers, but at times they display a willingness to lose their way."

Ken had lost his way for six months in Hong Kong. Now, in March 1965, he faced three months of championship tennis, hopefully leading to the Wimbledon final. No wonder he was a bit on edge.

The first step was the Philippines championship. Then the Egyptian. Not that Fletch wanted to play in Egypt, but, no longer in the Australian team, he had to pay his own travel expenses and the Egyptians had offered him a free round-the-world air ticket. The Philippines title would be difficult, because it was played on ultra-slow courts made of crushed coral on which the locals were expert. Three people could beat him: Raymundo Deyro, who had beaten Bob Hewitt in 1962; Felicisimo Ampon, ten-time winner; and Dutch champion Tom Okker, who had such speed that newspapers christened him "the Flying Dutchman". Okker had a last start victory over Fred Stolle.

I was worried Ken might not be able to repeat his 1962 victory: were the Bayside and the Firecracker Bar an ideal preparation? So every day for two weeks I rushed down out of Alexandra House at lunch time to buy the *Manila Times* and the *Philippines Herald* as soon as they arrived in Hong Kong, to see how he went. Fletch was, surprisingly, seeded number two behind the Flying Dutchman because Australia refused to list him as a ranked player now he had rebelled.

In the semi-finals, the Flying Dutchman crash-landed, suffering the usual fate of European champs in the humid Orient: losing to Deyro 6-1, 6-2, 6-2. Ken, who had played all the world's surfaces, including the slow cow dung courts in India, beat Felicisimo Ampon in straight sets. Once again he would play Deyro in the final.

I was surprised to see the huge newspaper coverage tennis got in the Philippines, but then I found out that they were the country which had donated the Davis Cup trophy. Every day there were front page picture stories under headings like: "Flashy Fletcher", "Fumbling Fletcher", and "Fletcher put to Test" — each accompanied by long match reports. I loved the uninhibited way the Filipinos wrote. They didn't just give scores: they captured the character of the player, and even his philosophy of life. It was a much more interesting way to write.

"The crowd rooted so boisterously for Deyro that it had to be hushed by the umpire at the request of the nettled Fletcher who lost the first set 2-6," said the *Herald*. "But the temperamental Australian relieved the tension with his clowning, and earned some big ovations for his occasional gems when he overcame his own temper to save several set points to win the second set 9-7."

Ken lost the third set 0-6, and appeared well beaten.

"But those who had expected spectacular displays of temper on the part of the erstwhile *enfant terrible* Fletcher were disappointed," said the *Herald* writer. "Fletcher kept his volatile spirit in check, though he occasionally went through some mild antics which amused the gallery. His favourite pose was to stare at the offending ball dribbling back from the net and give it a mock kick which would be short by a few inches. Another crowd-pleaser was his cutie motion with the arm, to show contempt for the sissy shot he had just made. The hustling Australian put on a fluid finishing kick and the local netter found no answer to Fletcher's crackling forehand that punctuated his incisive game."

The sports editor, Eddie Lachua, wrote in a column: "Fletcher had to come from behind four times — against Delfin Contreras, Mike Dungo, Johny Jose, and Raymundo Deyro, but the Aussie always had the grit and the cussedness to prevail."

Deyro said after the match: "I would have won without that forehand of his."

I found it strange that Filipinos got to know so much more about Australian tennis rebels than people in Sydney or Melbourne. Eddie Lachua reported: "This was yet another major prize won by Fletcher without the help of the Lawn Tennis Association of Australia. He is still showing no signs of contrition as far as his quarrel with them is concerned, and he will have to continue to tour the Middle East and Europe on his own." And Antonio Siddayao in the *Manila Times*: "The five Australian rebels agreed to stick together ... but verbal pacts, like success, are a short-lived thing in the sports jungle ... swallowing its pride for the sake of exigency, the Lawn Tennis Association of Australia took back two of the rebels to its bosom, and in two months the world's most coveted piece of tin was back down under. But, by winning here, Fletcher has scored in his feud with Australian Tennis. He will soon hop to Cairo to resume the long hard road back to full respectability at home — if he can succeed at Wimbledon."

Siddayao was so right.

As Eddie Lachua said: "While they still have Roy Emerson and Fred Stolle around to defend the Davis Cup, Australia couldn't care less if it didn't have Fletcher's services. Aged 24, Fletcher still has a big tennis future, if only Australia will have him back."

Ken's only chance of absolution was to win Wimbledon. It was important I get to London.

12   Spies Like Us

I never realised how famous Fletch was until I got up one morning and read in the *South China Morning Post* that the Americans were in Hong Kong to make a TV series about us. It was to be filmed in full colour and called "I Spy".

The *Post* said the TV series was to be about an international tennis champion who goes to live in Hong Kong, and brings his best mate along with him. Well, Ken was the only international tennis star who had ever shifted to Hong Kong to make it his world touring base. Plus he had brought his best mate with him.

Naturally, the American producers changed Ken's nationality and made him into an American tennis player, to suit their audience. Handsome Hollywood actor Robert Culp — who did not look unlike Fletch — was chosen to play the part. They couldn't call the tennis player "Kenny Fletcher", so they called him "Kelly Robinson": with exactly the same number of letters in each name.

Kelly's sidekick and buddy in the series was "Scottie", whereas Fletch always called me "Hughie".

According to the article, Scottie was to be played by an unknown American comedian who had never acted before in his life, a bloke called Bill Cosby.

In the series, the producers said, Scottie would travel overseas to live with his tennis champion mate in Hong Kong: just like us. Then the pair would tour the world together, as we planned to do. And, just like me, Scottie didn't play tennis at all, and wasn't the star of the duo. While Kelly, his famous tennis buddy, was out wooing the girls in the stands, Scottie generally stayed in his room and, like me, read poetry.

I wondered how they knew so much about us.

The paper said the two "I Spy" jetsetters would spend very little time on the tennis court. Which was pretty spot-on too. But still, it showed just what a popular sport tennis was in America these days: even though we had all the champions.

"Most of the time Kelly and Scottie chase beautiful girls, drink in nightclubs, gamble at exotic casinos, dress in dinner suits for millionaires' parties, and catch aeroplanes, ferries and rickshaws," the story said.

They would get into scrapes in bars, and mix with tough international blokes: who I imagined would be just like Steve Dunleavy, or John Ball, or even our tall, handsome, debonair Pakistani mate, Farid Khan, who was not only an Olympic hockey player and Colony squash champion but also boss of more than 150 Pakistani watchmen.

The only extra dimension added by the TV show was that, unlike us, they were both spies. I knew for sure that Kelly, I mean Kenny, wasn't a spy. But that was showbusiness. After all, such a series would have to compete with James Bond films for popularity, and our lives did get a bit dreary every now and then. But Fletch had always said a champion tennis player was a great cover for a spy. "Tennis is played in every country in the world, so you can go anywhere you like without arousing suspicion. Plus you always get to meet all the right people," he said, long before the Yanks even thought of "I Spy".

Kenny had played tennis behind the Iron Curtain in Moscow, had met the Shah of Persia, had had dinner at 10 Downing Street with the British Prime Minister, and had even shaken hands with royalty in England: all because he had played in several Wimbledon finals on television. He had even played tennis in Saigon in the midst of the Vietnam War. Just about the only place he hadn't been invited was Red China. But they never put on tournaments.

The *Post* said Culp and Cosby were arriving in the Colony in a couple of weeks to film outdoor scenes on Hong Kong's famous harbour and up on Victoria Peak. It was thrilling to think Ken's move to Hong Kong had excited interest in far-away Hollywood: even if no one at home in Australia gave a damn. Fletch didn't seem to mind that the American producers hadn't bothered to tell him about the show.

When I picked him up at the airport on his return from his triumph in the Philippines and told him that he was about to become an international TV star, Ken said: "Anyway, I'm the original. At least that bloke Culp has a good-looking dial. They'll have to get a stand-in to play the tennis scenes for him but."

"The only difference is, Fletch," I said, "the producers have turned us both into a couple of spies."

"You mean," said Ken, "the only difference is that they've made you black."

Ken was right. It turned out that Bill Cosby was black. But I was very pleased to hear that he was the comedian of the duo.

Everyone in Hong Kong was talking about "I Spy" because the only other Western TV series ever set in the Colony was "Hong Kong", made five years ago in 1960. Coincidentally, Australia had a starring role in that series too because the main actor, Rod Taylor, was an Australian: but he was made into a Yank as well. Instead of being about tennis and spies, "Hong Kong" was about dope-peddlers and smugglers, and every scene took place behind a beaded curtain. Which showed just how wrong Hollywood could be, because there were no beaded curtains in Hong Kong.

Rod Taylor played an American newspaper correspondent who hung out in a place a bit like the Firecracker Bar — "Tully's Bar" — and helped the British fight crime in the Orient. Everyone in Australia liked the theme song "Honourable Hong Kong Rock" which mixed Chinese gongs and electric guitars, conducted by Lionel Newman. The Lunn family, except Fred, used to watch it every week because Rod Taylor drove around in the same type of sports car that I owned, a Sunbeam Alpine. Fletch, of course, knew Rod Taylor, and had once gone out on the town with him in the south of France. Tennis players often mixed with film stars for some reason.

An even more important event had happened in the week Ken was away: a rumour had gone around that Hong Kong's banks were all going to go bust. Chinese had formed mile-long queues outside banks throughout the Colony to try to get their money out. Of course, pretty soon the banks ran out of cash and shut their doors.

People wept in the streets despite assurances from the British Governor that their money was safe. At one stage the bigger banks tried to restore confidence by taking bars of gold out of their vaults and putting them on display on the front counter, but nothing could convince the Chinese that the rumours were wrong and that the banks had enough money to pay everybody back. The fact that some banks printed their own Hong Kong dollar notes added to the confusion.

A top British financial expert had been hurriedly flown out from the Bank of England to try to stem the run: and it turned out that he was one of Arch's best mates. So he had dinner at our flat on arrival. And was Ah Ping glad to meet this balding middle-aged banker that night. She had disappeared for the previous two days, queueing with everyone else to try to get her money out. Then, when her bank closed its doors, poor Ah Ping came home in tears.

"Ah Ping lose money Dragon Master. Ah Ping lose life money. Life money gone Master."

Suddenly she looked old and grey and broken. It was hard to imagine that she could go downhill so quickly. Arch and I knew nothing about the situation, but we tried unsuccessfully to comfort Ah Ping, assuring her that everything would work out alright.

But Ah Ping was convinced it was the end of the world as she knew it: "No more money. All gone," she said, crying her eyes out into a tea towel.

Then Arch told Ah Ping how he had this mate, a banker, who had arrived to fix everything up. Ah Ping put on a feast for that banker the like of which had never been seen before. For once she acted the servant and waited on him hand and foot, forgetting about her two Masters. He was presented with shark's fin soup, steamed fried rice in lotus leaf, rice dumpling filled with duck and wrapped in bamboo leaves, steamed spare ribs with red pepper sauce, and, her speciality, curried king prawns. All were served on the Communist Chinese store blue plates I bought which had bits of rice embedded inside the china.

"Bank Master dai yut. Big Bank Master save Ah Ping money," she said, as she served the banker lashings of Chinese food.

Bemused by all the attention from this small old Chinese lady wearing her hair in a grey bun — and not knowing that we had promised he would rescue her from an old age of poverty — he kept remarking on what wonderful lives we lived in the Colonies.

I felt particularly sorry for Ah Ping because Fred was always quoting his old man, Grandpa Hugh Lunn, as saying: "Age and want are an ill-matched pair".

Over the Daan tarts with coconut pudding, Arch's British mate — they were in the same hockey club in London — said the only way out of the run on the banks was for the Hong Kong tellers to stand at their counters and pay every last customer in the Colony back their money.

To the last Hong Kong cent.

Ah Ping nodded enthusiastic agreement, and I noted that after a while the banker began addressing her rather than us: "They must keep paying until there isn't one person left in a queue. Once that is done, the population will regain confidence and they will all queue up again to put their money back," he said.

This would require astronomical amounts of cash, and there were not enough Hong Kong dollars in print.

"Pay money back. Cash," said Ah Ping. "Bank Master brave Master, good Master."

"Yes, you can't pay people back with the assets that make a bank rich," he said, as Ah Ping took a seat on the fourth chair. "Gold bars, promissory notes, lease agreements, buildings, bills of exchange, business stock, mortgages, share certificates, houses: none of these are of any use in this situation. It has to be cash. So, today, I have ordered seven Boeing 707 loads of British bank bills flown out from London. It's almost all British five-pound notes. It's the only way to end the crisis."

The first of the seven plane loads of money was at that moment winging its way over India: and we were the only people in Hong Kong to know. Ah Ping waved her arms up and down like a bird as she flew back down the hall for the tea.

Late that night a group of us gathered at Steve Dunleavy's new nightclub overlooking Prince Edward Road to farewell Fletch as he prepared to fly off to Cairo on the next stage of his journey to Wimbledon. Everyone was talking about the run on the banks and about "I Spy". They laughed and said how the secret was out: that we were really a couple of spies.

Ken played along. "I keep my telescopic camera in the handle of my tennis racquet," he explained to his girlfriend Pamela loudly enough for all to hear. "I'll show it to you one night. And one of my tennis balls is a James Bond type of ball: when you open it up, it's a phone: the dial just fits perfectly inside."

Just as he had started his own newspaper, Steve Dunleavy now had his own club. Which wasn't surprising: it was hard to imagine anyone ordering him around. It wasn't really a nightclub, just a long room on the first floor where Steve acted as host to the sort of people he liked: people interested in what was going on. It was a place where you could meet and talk and have a drink or a cup of coffee.

Built-in padded seats stretched along each side of the long narrow room with some armchairs in the corners, coffee tables, a bar, and small dim lamps. There were no girls available like in a bar, and no band playing *I Left My Heart in San Francisco* like in a regular nightclub. In fact, the only attraction at Steve's club was Steve himself. Probably because he was just so Australian.

I noticed how we had all become much more Australian now we were overseas.

Many at the club were what locals called "China Watchers". China Watchers were journalists, or Embassy political secretaries, who were sent to Hong Kong to find out and report back on what was happening inside Red China — since this was as close to Red China as they could get. They were from the many countries which were not allowed to send any representatives, or enough representatives, to Peking. Yet, because China was the most populous country in the world, they wanted to know what it was up to.

Mostly they were Americans since, like Australia, the US had no diplomatic relations with Red China. Also, the Chinese were supporting the Vietnamese Communists in the war in nearby Vietnam. These Americans were interested in everything: they were even keen to hear about the cocktail party that was put on for Ken and the Aussie tennis team at the Continental Hotel in Saigon to reward them for turning up to play in the middle of a war. They thought it was a strange place for a tennis team to go.

Australians, Canadians and Britons were also prominent among these China Watchers who were sort of like espionage agents. They monitored Chinese radio broadcasts, grabbed hold of any newspapers that made their way out, or any books or magazines smuggled out of the mainland, interviewed escaped refugees, even studied the text of new Chinese plays to see what scraps of information they could pick up. But mainly they monitored the official New China Newsagency and the *People's Daily* to see what might be happening.

Not being there, they could never be sure how accurate these reports were. Because of the round-about way the Red Chinese said things, and the peculiar language they used, China Watchers had to be experts to work out what the Chicoms really meant. One had made his reputation by realising that a one-line reference in the New China Newsagency — "the Russians and the Americans are bed-fellows" — meant China and Russia had split and this would lead to the withdrawal of Russian technical aid, setting China back a decade.

They were required to interpret what went on in China, and some of the American China Watchers saw the run on the banks as a Communist-inspired plot to ruin the British Colony's fragile economy by "rumour-mongering": thus ending British rule three decades early.

Were these China Watchers surprised when I happened to mention that seven plane loads of five-pound notes were on their way from England. They demanded to know how I knew. But I couldn't say. All I could reveal was that I had dinner that night with the man who ordered the money flown out.

Since I was trying to get into Communist China — though I didn't tell anybody at the club — I had become a bit of a China Watcher myself, and thus listened intently to all their stories. So I thought I should contribute a bit of information.

"The first plane load is right now winging its way over India," I said. "The British plan is for the tellers to stand at their counters and pay every last cent back — then the local Chinese will all come and put their money back, and the crisis will be over. It's got nothing to do with the Communists."

For the first time, the China Watchers were asking me questions.

"Why do they have to fly English pounds in?" asked an American.

"You can't pay depositors back with the assets that make a bank rich — buildings, promissory notes, gold bars. There aren't enough Hong Kong bank notes in existence to do that. It's a question of economics," I said. "I can't say any more."

The China Watchers were all surprised at my knowledge and I saw them look at each other and raise their eyebrows. Luckily we were interrupted by Steve Dunleavy before I could give away any more secrets. Steve brought over a slender man who was just starting to get flecks of grey in his short dark hair.

"Now that you two are television stars," Steve said, "there's an Aussie here I'd like you to meet."

This Australian was an international television cinematographer who just laughed when I said the American "I Spy" TV series was based on us. He seemed to think I was kidding myself. So I asked him why we Australians didn't make TV shows like "I Spy" and "Hong Kong" about ourselves, instead of always leaving our stories for the Yanks to make as their stories.

"No chance," the cinematographer said emphatically, with a slightly American accent.

"Filmatic research shows that the United States would never accept our Aussie accent. They can't stand it. It grates. It's far too rough, and experience has shown that, except in a few cases like Rod Taylor, it cannot be modified enough. We just have to accept our role in the world: we plough the ground and grow the food; the English write our books; and the Americans make our films and TV shows. It's our image — not only in the eyes of others, but in the eyes of Australians themselves. Ask any Australian, and they will tell you that writers and film makers are important people who live overseas."

I was surprised, and disappointed. It sounded like he was calling us a nation of peasants. But he seemed to know what he was talking about, and Ken agreed that the Australian accent could sound pretty rough around the edges, if you hadn't heard one for quite a while.

Steve would soon put this guy in his place. But he wasn't with me on this one: "If you want to make films or television

163

shows or write best-sellers and you're an Australian, then you're in the right place, Hughie: overseas," he said emphatically.

Steve was laughing about a front-page picture-story in the *South China Morning Post*. An English engineer, addressing a Hong Kong business luncheon, had suggested a possible solution to the problem of not being able to grow enough food in the Colony because of the land shortage.

"Instead of importing food," he told the Hong Kong businessmen, "you should build a giant pipeline from Red China all the way down to Kowloon's New Territories. Then you could pipe vast amounts of human waste from China down to Hong Kong to be used as fertiliser to grow more food," he said.

Everyone with a nose knew that the farmers in Hong Kong's New Territories already used shit for fertiliser, and therefore knew that this bloke was kidding. But the *South China Morning Post* printed the story straight: as if he really meant a shit pipeline should be built.

"Pipe all the crap down from China. Those people at the *Post* must have shit for brains," Steve said in between laughing his guts out. "They just wouldn't bloody know."

Fletch laughed along with Steve and everyone else, and as usual kept the joke going by saying: "They made a meal of it! Of course, we Aussies are above all that. There are no flies on us. You can see where they've been but."

Ken said he had his own export scheme lined up. He asked Pamela to stand up and spin around and, as she did, he pointed out her sequinned, beaded, fluffy jumper, saying he was taking a port-full on his tennis tour: "You don't have to be a rocket scientist to work out that these beaded jumpers will catch on in Africa. They are so cheap the African women will think I'm the Fairy Godmother," Ken said.

We agreed Fletch was onto something. But one China Watcher, who had been to Oxford University, no less, said: "They might keep the ladies warm, Fletch, but tennis is a far classier cover for your nefarious activities on behalf of your country."

That got a laugh.

I wanted Ken to buy a movie camera so I could film him from the stands when I got to Wimbledon, but he wasn't interested, saying: "Tennis is all down to scores on the board. People only want to know if you were the champion or not. That's all."

"A pity you didn't buy a movie camera instead of all those jumpers Fletch," I said.

"Yes. That would come in handy in your line of business," said the Oxford bloke. He seemed convinced we really were a pair of spies.

To change the subject, I said Jeanette had told me an American had asked her out just before I came along.

"There's another thing," Fletch said, laughing as though he had just had a brainwave. "Pamela had an American after her when I came along! We're getting some of our own back on the Yanks for racing off our Australian girls while the men were away at the last war."

As Fletch left the club to fly out for the six-month international tennis circuit, Steve Dunleavy handed out some advice at the front door.

"Fletch," Steve said, shaking hands warmly, "if you want to be a winner, always come out fighting."

Ken didn't like advice on how to play tennis.

"Everyone wants to be a winner, Steve," Ken replied, "and everyone's a fighter or else they wouldn't be there. It's all down to how you play on the day but."

"But in your case, and Kelly Robinson's," Steve said, winking at me, "it's how well you've played the night before!"

13 Just Not Cricket

Mr Kiat had no news from Peking when I dropped in to the Bank of China Building at lunch time.

"Your struggle, Hu Lun, has not yet received leniency," he said in that weird dictionary-derived English of the Red Chinese, while looking down at me almost sympathetically from behind the wide counter. "Do not be in a hurry, Hu Lun."

"But Mr Kiat, I first came around before Christmas last year. Now it's already April," I told him, saying I had arranged to see some people in Paris next month, and if I missed them the trip would be a waste of time. So I had to know.

"You are joining your clique in Paris?"

"No. I'm meeting Kenny Fletcher. He's a tennis player, and he's playing in the French Championships which are held in May every year. Then Wimbledon. You play tennis in China don't you?"

"No. Tennis is a bourgeois game."

"Not in Australia it isn't Mr Kiat. Anybody who wants to, can play tennis in Australia. Kenny Fletcher learnt to play in his backyard on a court made of crushed ants' nests. Beat that. And his father is from the labouring masses. He drives trains for Queensland Railways and used to take Kenny with him to help stoke the fire with coal. Yet now Ken plays at Wimbledon."

"Nevertheless, Hu Lun, I have no news."

"Well I have news for you Mr Kiat," I said. "I know your name means 'brave man' in your language so I am confident you will struggle for me."

I proudly plopped a magazine down on the counter, and opened it at the double-page spread displaying my article on Peking Opera faces. Mr Kiat hesitated, momentarily, and then held the magazine up in his hands. He read, but gave no hint of the effect it must have had.

Using my collection of painted faces I had tried to write an article that might help me get in to Red China: how Peking Opera actors learned both the words and gestures, and never improvised; how they played the same role for life: "This entertainment for the largest group of humans on earth is the antithesis of the Hollywood film," my article now in Mr Kiat's hands said.

"While Hollywood strives for realism, Chinese Opera is all symbolic. A conspicuously white face represents nothing else but treachery, whereas a white nose could mean a clown. A red face shows loyalty, courage and straight-forwardness; blue ferocity and fearlessness; and green could signify an evil spirit. Every design, every stroke of colour on the face is a rich metaphor, and people well-versed in Chinese operas will instantly recognise the character of a role from the lines and the colour of the painted face, or the length of the beard. Some can denote a 'good young bloke' or a 'good old bloke'. When embellished with magnificent head-dresses, variously coloured robes, moustaches and beards (reaching below the waist for an important character) the last traits of these personages are revealed. A blood red robe embroidered with gold would mean the character had supernatural powers."

I had hoped Mr Kiat would read the whole article, but he quickly closed the magazine and left, saying: "I will send this up to Canton, Hu Lun. Joy Geen."

At least he kept my story. But why Canton and not Peking?

Mr Kiat, I knew, would have to be impressed by a Westerner writing about China's greatest tradition. Sort of like a Chicom writing about Don Bradman and Test cricket, I supposed, and explaining terms for the Communists like "square leg", "block hole", "silly mid on", and "leg before wicket".

So many good things were happening in Hong Kong that I had recently dropped my old Brisbane sayings: "As one door slams in your face, another door slams in your face," and "so far, so bad". For the first time in my life I had won a Cup. And, of all things, for cricket.

On one weekend a year, Hong Kong played a championship in a strange game of cricket they had invented called "six-a-side". Each side batted for six overs, so only twelve overs, or less, decided a match. Thus lots of teams could be eliminated in the one weekend. This six-a-side game suited cricketers like me who could bat a bit, bowl a bit, and field well. Each team member had to bowl one six-ball over, no matter how bad, and, with only six fielders, it was easy for the opposition to score off a weak bowler. And, since there were only thirty-six balls in an innings, batsmen had to be good enough to score off almost every ball.

To benefit attacking batsmen, and because there were so few balls to score off, a four was worth six runs; and a six was worth an amazing ten.

My team was one of several from the Kowloon Cricket Club. The captain picked me because, like him, I was an Australian. He probably thought I'd be outstanding. But, although my grandfather Jack Duncan was a champion cricketer for Nerang — Olive said a man on a pony patrolled outside the ground to collect the ball whenever he was batting — I had never managed to succeed at the game. My speciality was fielding, plus batting brilliantly in the nets at practice. Batting out in the middle I always seized up like a zombie just as the ripe red cherry arched menacingly through the shadowy air that always seemed to surround it: like the pitch blackness around the red flash of menace on a redback spider.

One nick and you knew you were out. Forever. Thus, instead of attacking the ball and risking failure, I always froze up. No one in Hong Kong knew, but my last seven innings in Australia were ducks, though I made some good scores in Hong Kong because I batted nervelessly, since nobody knew me from Adam. My only duck was when a left-arm Portuguese fast bowler clean bowled me first ball. I didn't even see it.

Our captain was a tall man, his face cracked here and there like concrete: which was appropriate, because he worked for a concrete construction company. He was one of the Colony's best cricketers and, it was said, was also a squash champion. Because of his all-round brilliance, we made it through to the Sunday afternoon final against the favourites.

All of the players and spectators from the dozens of other matches arrived to watch the final as our Kowloon Cricket Club captain called us together under a tree and said we had a problem: "They've got this bloody giant fast bowler who took four wickets for just two runs against the touring English county champions last year, including clean bowling an English Test batsman! He will only get to bowl six bloody balls, but that's all he bloody needed to get his whole bloody team through to this final." He looked around at his by now terrified team. "Let me tell you, this bastard is the Keith Miller of Hong Kong. Frankly, he's too good for me. And he's too good for George here. Now I'm talking tactics here. George and me have to be protected from this bloody bastard so we can score a lot of runs against the other bowlers. What we need is someone to open the innings against him and last as many bloody balls as possible. Three or four would be very, very nice."

The Australian captain was looking at me.

"You're young, Hughie, you're a left-hander — which might put him off a bit — and you're an Aussie, which'll worry the bastard."

Not if he somehow knew about my seven ducks in a row for the *Courier-Mail* journalists.

"Go out there and blunt the bugger. Don't play at anything you don't have to. Don't take any singles or threes to expose George here."

I was scared but, at the same time, amazed the captain had chosen me for the job. All my life I had been volunteering for jobs on the cricket field, yet never got any of the important ones. Never got to open the bowling (hardly got to bowl at all). Never got to field in slips (always on the fence). Never got to be opening batsman (always down in the tail). Never captain, or vice-captain, or even fielded at silly mid-on.

Yet now I had been chosen for the toughest, most dangerous job of all. I just hoped I could do it. I said a silent prayer to Saint Anthony, my favourite saint. Saint Anthony was the finder of lost things, so I asked him to help me find the middle of the bat.

A couple of hundred people sat in groups around the ground to watch the final. I could see the fast bowler out in the field because he was too big to miss. In fact he looked a bit overweight to me. Perhaps too heavy to be that fast?

The captain called me over alone before I went to the wicket. He produced a special cricketer's box with a pad attached to the top to protect the lower stomach as well as my wedding gear below. I had never seen one like that before. Maybe this bowler was that fast.

"Now remember, Hughie, if you go out first bloody ball we could all be out in the first bloody over," the captain said, patting me on the back.

As I took guard centre-to-leg in my whites I adjusted the uncomfortable padded box, which wouldn't fit unless I left my fly zipper down. I turned and lifted the right pad for more protection for my exposed right thigh, and scraped a batting mark in the hard black soil with the metal studs of what were once my older brother Jack's cricket boots.

The only thing I knew as I faced up was that I had to watch that red cherry like mad: and hold the bat perpendicular. Grandpa Duncan had told me that much when he carved my first cricket bat with his pocket-knife when I was three-years-old — the same knife he used to cut his plugs of tobacco. In the 20 years since, I had played a million games of backyard cricket, practised for hours hitting a ball in Olive's stocking hung from the clothes line, watched the technique of famous batsmen at the Gabba: all for noughts.

This famous Colonial bowler ran towards me in a very strange way. Hundreds of fast bowlers had run my way, and they all jerked and moved around like broken dolls in a cyclone. But this one glided towards the wicket like a ghost. At every pace he bounced, and his outstretched white-clothed legs seemed to be suspended momentarily above the ground. It was like seeing a man doing aerial splits across a green stage while showing his white socks, and with one arm dangling way, way behind him.

I kept transferring my weight backwards and forwards from one foot to the other, so as not to be standing still when the projectile was loosed. If it was short, I would step back. If it was full, I would go forward. If it was between the two, I knew from experience I would be in trouble.

He was taking a long time to reach the wicket. Or was my concentration slowing him down?

As this man of pace reached the opposite crease his socks both disappeared. The dragging arm went, only to re-appear pointed straight at me. A white hand behind a bright red ball with six white stitch stripes down the centre. I could see each stitch. It took some time to leave his hand but when, finally, it did it was suddenly at my end: as if somehow foiling the speed of light to reappear fifteen yards further on without any time elapsing.

The red ball was moving sideways as it accelerated out of its own jet stream, coming at me low on the full but moving sharply from left to right.

It turned me swiftly around so that my legs were as wide apart as a huntsman spider's. The cherry fizzed past, ripping black dirt out with its raised stitching next to my right ankle as I followed, too late, with the white willow bat. But, as the ball cut and reared to leave, I caught up to it underneath from behind. Up, up, up and away the cherry went, though I had barely felt the hit.

Up, still up, carried by the speedster's stifling speed — guided by my bat — it landed among my team mates on the long grassy slope at fine leg for a ten.

They yelled for joy. My captain yahooed and danced around a small tree, bending and straightening in the sun like a Red Indian doing a war dance and yelling out "you little bloody beauty".

I had never hit a six in my life, but now — of a sudden — I had hit a ten.

There was a large red dot right in the middle of the meat of my bat. Now I was looking forward to the challenge of the next deliveries coming my way.

The English County cricket champions, Worcester, came to Hong Kong as their reward and, as a member of the Hong Kong champion six-a-side team, I got a free invite to their welcome dinner at the Mandarin hotel. I could hardly believe it when JJJ and I were shown to the main table and placed exactly opposite English Test batsman Tom Graveney, one of the all-time great batsmen in the world. Many was the night in Brisbane Jack and I listened on the wireless to the Aussies trying to bowl Graveney out.

Now I got to call him "Tom".

You could tell his occupation just by looking at him. Tom's left shoulder was held up close to his neck, and his right shoulder sloped downwards — from thousands and thousands of hours facing up side-on as a right-handed batsman. But Tom didn't seem like a Test cricket star. He talked to us as if he was just anybody, and even congratulated me on our six-a-side victory.

At the dinner, our winning six-a-side team was presented with a bottle of Scotch about two feet high. I had never seen — or imagined — bottles that big, and I told Tom I would hate to be the bloke who had to sort the empty ones under the hotels. This bottle was about ten times as big as the largest bottle of Tristrams lemonade. Instead of keeping the bottle for ourselves, the captain suggested that the following weekend we put it on the bloody bar for the members at the Kowloon Cricket Club: so all the bloody bastards could partake of our victory.

As a hundred glasses of scotch poured forth for club members that Saturday afternoon at the Club, I leant against the bar as close as I could get to the victory bottle, briefly re-living for different elderly members how I lined up that big fast bowler and hit him for ten. All the Poms were saying I'd done it because I was Australian. One elderly gentleman confided: "As you walked out to the wicket I said to those around me 'this Aussie lad'll win cup for club'."

The club president — no less — came and listened and, when I finished, shook my hand saying how proud he was of me, of Australia, and of the team. I was amazed at the power of victory: I had never got to meet the president before.

"Congratulations," he said in an English upper-class accent. "Tell me, Hugh, where are you from in Australia?"

"Brisbane," I said innocently.

"Brisbane!" he said. "I've got three sisters who emigrated to Australia years ago, and they all live in Brisbane. I'm sure I would have noticed your membership application when it came in ... when was it you say you joined the Club?"

For the first time in six months I remembered that I had never joined the Kowloon Cricket Club. I had merely wandered in to the dressing sheds and got in a cricket team. Slowly, over the last six months, I had begun to believe I actually was a member. I knew all the cricketers personally, and they were all members: so far as I knew.

"I came in about six months ago," I said, trying not to lie straight out.

"That's funny," he said, trying to understand. "I'm sure I would have noticed a nomination if the person was from Brisbane."

"Perhaps you were away," I said, turning for support towards the group of members to whom I had been explaining about the ten.

"No. I haven't left the Colony for two years," he said. "No it couldn't be. I see all the nominations."

The president was now looking at me with different eyes. Well, I couldn't tell him that his fees were far too high. In Brisbane I had never once paid for the right to play cricket, or tennis, or footy. Let alone hundreds and hundreds of dollars. Sport was free in Australia.

Luckily, I was tugged away to once more demonstrate how I hit that ball for ten, and to again tell the story of how my grandfather hit six sixes in one over with a broken finger on the Nerang Cricket Ground.

Then I saw the president drifting off determinedly towards his office, so I decided it was time I left too: even though the presentation of the Cup — and the six small replica Cups for each player — was yet to be made.

I headed for the lavatories, veered right out of the front door: never to return to collect my one and only Cup.

14 Almost a Man of the World

Olive always said Fred had a "cast iron constitution" because of his days in the West Australian orphanage. So it was a real shock to get her letter saying he had had a heart attack.

Fred was in the Mater hospital, and — though he had been in to Pikes to get his first new suit in 30 years — he wouldn't be well enough to attend Gay's wedding.

Dad never got a cold like the rest of us Lunns. But in the years before I left, his black hair had started to go grey and he often had long nose bleeds. When this happened, Mum would use her great capacity for cheerful understatement and say: "Freddie's a bit off colour today". And Fred would say to me: "You'll get all this sort of thing, if you live long enough."

Dad also suffered from what he called "arthur-itis" which made lifting the heavy black trays in and out of the oven difficult. So he would invariably ask anyone standing around in the cake shop to help out, saying: "here, lend me a pound".

Fred had been the biggest surprise package of my six months overseas, just by writing letters. More letters than anyone else. Up until then I didn't even know he could write, except on the top of cakes with icing. I knew Mum and Jack and Gay, and even Sheryl, would write — but Fred didn't seem the type to stop cooking and doing his homework long enough to write to his number two son. Yet his letters — written with a fountain pen — were the best, and so was his long flowing hand-writing. They must have had good teachers at his orphanage because Fred never spelt a word wrong, though occasionally he mixed up his tenses a bit, like Jim.

He always started a letter by saying: "I am now going to give you my undivided attention", and he sprinkled the letters with bits of his philosophy and asked lots of questions about food like: "do those other fellas eat tapioca pudding?"

A week after his heart attack, I received a very short letter from Fred apologising for "disturbing the peace". Reminding me that when he first met Olive he already had his boat ticket to New York, and his tax clearance as well, he said: "Stick to your guns and don't take any notice of the women. But when dealing with those other fellas I reckon you'll have to use your discretion. Keep going, and you can get to New York."

I never could understand why Fred was always on about New York. It didn't interest me at all. I wanted to go to Peking, which at least would be different as well as a good story. I was sure Red China was no more dangerous than anywhere else: didn't Fred himself say of all countries and nationalities (including Australians): "They'll all shoot you, quick."

It was almost May, so I had just about given up hope of joining Fletch in Paris in time for the French Championships, which were due to start soon. Fletch had written from Cairo to say he could get me a very cheap airfare on Egyptian Airlines, because he had won their tournament. Poor Ken still couldn't understand why I wanted to travel via Red China: "It's like going steerage," he wrote. "When you travel you have to think of the general wear and tear."

Ken was suffering some of that himself. He had got into a fight with some Egyptians at his Cairo Hotel because they demanded he remove a Japanese girl from his room, even though it was the middle of the day. Maybe they had heard about "I Spy" and thought Fletch was up to something. As a result, he was kicked out of this luxury hotel overlooking the Nile and had to carry his luggage and his brown port full of jumpers half a mile to another hotel.

"The jumpers were a big hit down in Uganda among the black women, but few could afford them." he wrote.

Several days later, Max Schofield came around and leaned across my desk laughing, so that he looked like a circus clown without his makeup. He was shouting loudly enough for everyone in the building to hear: "There's a Mr Keee-at been on the blower looking for you. Reckons he knows you. He's from the Bank of China Building. It's the first time we've ever had a ring from Mao Tse-tung's lot. What's going on my boy? Have the Communists capitulated?"

And Max roared at his own joke.

I leapt up and raced the two blocks to the Bank of China Building. Mr Kiat had a message from Canton: if I caught the train to the border the following Monday morning there might be a visa waiting there for me.

Might? I would have to move out of my flat, pack all my things, resign, say goodbye to all my friends including the lovely Jeanette, and go to the border — all on the off chance that there *might* be a visa there. I wanted something more definite.

"Nothing in life is definite, Hu Lun," Mr Kiat said. He wanted my passport, so I handed it over.

At least I was ready to leave: I had finally got the first edition of the *Far East Medical Journal* out — thanks to the advice of an old *Brisbane Telegraph* sub-editor, Mr McKeirnan, who I wrote to for help. He said to buy a dozen similiar magazines and copy their layouts and typefaces.

This journal was such a big deal that Max Schofield's boss flew out from London for the launch. On his second day, the UK boss walked in with some page proofs and said: "There's something wrong with the typesetting here." I had deliberately set this story in "hanging indent": the first line of each paragraph set left and the other lines set one pica in from the left-hand side: the opposite of the usual typesetting. Mr McKeirnan, who had six beautiful daughters, said it was especially useful when the story wasn't quite long enough to fill the space. When I explained this, the boss offered me a job in London: if I could get there.

That night JJJ took me shopping for the long trip. The one thing I knew about Siberia was that it was cold, but it was hard to find a suitable warm jacket in tropical Hong Kong, and there wasn't time to have one tailor-made. Eventually I purchased an artificial sheep-skin jacket.

Because I was going to write for newspapers about the trip, I bought a brand new silver portable Olivetti typewriter in its own case, a packet of typing paper and some carbon paper. Plus a Thermos flask, six notebooks, half a dozen colour films, and — most important of all — a moneybelt to ensure I wasn't robbed and left stranded in the middle of Communist China with nothing. It was a shiny black plastic Chinese moneybelt with four separate compartments, two of them secured by press-studs (so you'd hear if anyone was opening it), one zippered, plus a secret pocket slit which was hard to find. The belt had a large brass buckle.

I was careful not to buy too much because I had to carry everything a long way right across Asia and Europe, including my portable National "dual-speed" tape-recorder in its special black plastic carrying case. Being the latest model tape-recorder it was even smaller than the portable typewriter.

I bought the tape-recorder and a tape of French lessons so I could hit Paris already talking the language. Since it was far too complicated to remove the tape and replace it with another one, I didn't bother buying a spare spool of tape to use for interviews.

For the same reason, I didn't record any music for the trip.

The National was the smallest and best tape-recorder around because, being dual-speed, you could record and play back at the fast speed: using more tape for quality

178

sound like music. While for ordinary speech you used slow speed, so you could capture nearly three times as much: but of a lower quality. Slowing the tape down was done by screwing a shiny round steel bolt into the mechanism, so that the tape had to travel an extra distance around it.

Because Ken wouldn't buy a movie camera, I bought an Asahi Pentax 35mm camera with a 200mm long-range lens to take photos of him at Wimbledon so he would have a close-up memento of his days on the Centre Court to show his kids. Plus I could perhaps sell some photos of inside Red China. The lens itself was a foot long, and heavy, but the camera was easy to sling across one shoulder. Since I wasn't going to be wearing either of my two suits, or my tailor-made shirts with my initials on the pockets, I locked them in the small blue port Gay had given me when I left Brisbane.

My plan was to travel rough, not shave, and to wear old clothes since I would be travelling incognito and wouldn't be seeing anyone important.

I held no fear of the Red Chinese and was confident they wouldn't worry about one small person like me. I suspected most of what we heard in Australia was just propaganda. At Catholic schools we learned to worry what the Protestants were up to: but when I went to work it turned out that they were just the same as us, if less forgiving of themselves.

I wrote a quick note to Gay, telling her not to expect a telegram for the wedding, because I would be on a train somewhere deep in Communist China. I told her to look at my journey from Hong Kong to Moscow on an atlas: "About as far as from Cairns to Melbourne and back — three times."

Gay worked as a medical secretary, going into operations and taking notes from the surgeons, so I told her how the Chinese had a totally different attitude to medicine. "For example, they say the discovery of anaesthetic put doctors one hundred years behind: because it stopped them concentrating on learning how the human mind and body work as a unit."

179

Luckily, I had already sent her a present. I got Olive to supply Gay's exact measurements (waist seventeen inches) and had H.W. Allen and Co., "Tailors to Film Stars", make a cheongsam, matching cape and handbag for her going-away outfit. I chose a white material with an embossed golden pattern that looked every bit as real as the bars of gold they sold in Hong Kong shops. Plus I sent enough material to cover her shoes.

Gay's husband-to-be, Vic, was an engineer with several job offers and Gay wrote to say he didn't know whether or not to resign. I wrote back saying to forget the question of high wages and free flats: "Is Vic happy where he is now? If he likes it he should stay. If not leave. And if not again, leave again. There is nothing worse — I'm glad I found out at Mobilgas — than working in a job you don't like. Time goes slowly and it drives you mad until you hate everyone around you."

When I brought the brocade dress home from the tailor Ah Ping was amazed.

"Gold dress, Master," she said. "Master plenty money. Big big money Master buy missy gold dress."

Once again I tried to explain to Ah Ping that I was definitely not rich.

"Yes, oooh very rich Master. Too much money. Spend plenty money."

Exasperated, I brought Ah Ping back down to earth.

"Hold on, Ah Ping," I said, folding my arms. "Who was doing all the crying when the Hong Kong banks shut. Not me. You were the one shedding the tears all over the place. Ah Ping plenty money in bank: Master spend money — no money in bank."

That stopped her in her tracks. Instead of clattering around, Ah Ping made no noise and stood very still.

"Ah Ping never buy gold dress," she said sadly.

Now Ah Ping was sad again. This time because I was leaving. "Dragon Master good house, good girl, good Amah, big job. Go why?"

Knowing it would make Ah Ping feel better about my leaving, I said I could earn much, much more money in Europe. "Double wages. Like Chinese New Year every month," I explained.

To my surprise, she turned to Jeanette: "Then Missy go with Master." I wondered what JJJ would say to that.

"Yes, he must go," she said. "But he will come back." They were talking as if I wasn't even in the room.

On possibly my last night in the Colony, Jeanette and I, and Arch and his American girlfriend, caught a ferry and tram to Wanchai on Hong Kong side: to have a last look at Suzie Wong territory. The Wanchai bars were lit up inside, unlike the Kowloon nightclubs. The bars were full of beautiful Chinese prostitutes in cheongsams who danced with American sailors from the several US ships that always seemed to be in port, or with each other while they waited for more American sailors to arrive. But the bars didn't mind having European couples along.

We sat at one of the many small round tables and ordered drinks. Jeanette and I danced rock-and-roll to the Beatles, and Arch and the American girl took over the floor for *I Left My Heart in San Francisco*. Every now and then a couple of giant American Naval Police in white sailor's uniforms blustered in and looked around nervously while hitting their left hands with their wooden truncheons. They were on the lookout for drunken or brawling Yank sailors, so the Chinese owner made sure he looked after them.

I peeked around the corner on their seventh raid to see what went on. There was the broad white back of the bigger naval policeman. A white-sleeved arm reached out towards the Chinese owner, greedily grabbed a large glass mug of beer, the head tipped back, the empty glass was handed back. The other arm went up and moved across the mouth and the Military Policeman turned around and once again marched out of the bar to watch out for drunken sailors.

Nothing much was happening in Wanchai so we headed back Kowloon-side to the opening of a new nightclub called

The Gaslight. On the way, the American girl caught one of her white stiletto-heeled shoes in a steel grate and it came off. She hobbled on a few paces and then stopped still and looked at poor Arch. I wondered why she hadn't collected her shoe.

"Well?" she said imperiously.

"Let her get it herself, Arch," I said. I didn't think she should think she was so important to be ordering other people to pick up her shoe.

But Arch was always a gentleman. He said he didn't mind helping out, and he even carefully fitted the shoe back on her foot as she stood on one leg, beaming.

The only thing different about The Gaslight was that there were lots of pretty Chinese waitresses instead of bar girls, and they all wore black fishnet stockings and pink satin bloomer suits instead of cheongsams, which was the big surprise. However, I wasn't surprised to see Steve Dunleavy in the crowd, looking very suave in a brand spanking new double-breasted blue-grey suit.

I told Steve I was off to Red China first thing in the morning to write some feature articles and break back into newspapers. It was the only way I could get a big story.

He didn't believe me at first. "It's a bloody miracle. No one goes *in* there Hughie, they only come *out*," Steve said. "You could end up in more trouble than Ned Kelly. I hope you've got yourself a Mao suit, or the bastards just might lock you up."

I was taken aback by Steve's reaction. I had imagined he would think going into Red China was all in a day's work. If it worried Steve Dunleavy what was I doing?

Steve must have seen my mood change: "Boy, the China Watchers are all going to be pissed right off with you: they'll think they're a bunch of real no-hopers. You'll see all the things they only ever get to dream about: like concubines, and Communists, and eunuchs."

Since Steve was such an experienced journalist I asked what angle he thought I should take for my stories.

"Well Hughie, put it this way. What do you know about Communist China?"

"When Red China sneezes the whole of Asia catches a cold," I said. "It's the 'awakening giant' of the world — the implication being: don't be the one to wake it up. The Chinese Communists are said to be inscrutable, unfathomable, very polite, impenetrable, and to have designs on the rest of Asia, and Australia. In the 'Domino Theory' China is the first black piece on the board."

"Good," said Steve. "Now, if you remember not to use any of that, you'll write some interesting stories."

It seemed a strange thing to say. Later, as I left The Gaslight after midnight to walk Jeanette home, Steve shook hands and wished me luck.

"By the way, Steve," I said. "What's the Going Rate for Chinese Communists?"

"Can't say," said Steve. "You'll have to let me know. When you get out."

It was pouring rain so I hailed a taxi and said: "Wei un dai ha. Austin Do mai Guangdong Do" and took Jeanette home. We had a cup of coffee in Jeanette's mother's kitchen until after one o'clock, and said goodbye next to the sliding steel grills at the entrance to the building. I was pleased by the rain. It was warm and meant that I didn't have to step over, or around, the usual scores of sleeping Chinese bodies all the way up the long, wide cement footpath of Austin Road. It made me wonder where all the tramps and homeless went in the Colony on such a woeful night.

As I walked up Austin Road the little boys were still there despite the hour and the rain, still urging and pestering white people like me to accept their offer of "young girl". It really annoyed me, because they were so persistent. They acted as if they thought I would eventually give in.

Exhilarated by my China breakthrough I had a bright idea. I wondered why I hadn't thought of it before. I would put one over on them.

"No. Not young girl," I shouted through the storm. "I want old woman. Old woman do you hear? I want very, very old woman. Old woman dai yut," — and I held up my right thumb for the "number one" sign.

It worked. The boys took off straight away, and, as they ran up the road, it made me smile to know that I had straightened out these wayward Chinese boys with a brilliant bit of repartee. I could see now that I was learning to think fast here in the old Far East. I was becoming a man of the Globe, just like John Ball, and Steve Dunleavy, and Max Schofield, and, of course, Fletch. I now knew how to gamble in casinos, speak Chinese, climb mountains, write feature stories and columns for magazines, and even how to get into forbidden China. All learnt in just seven months away from Brisbane. I had even read a book on sex called *Kama Sutra*, but I couldn't make head nor tail of it.

No wonder sex was a sin. Max Schofield said that "of course" *Kama Sutra* was banned "like everything else" in Australia. But I couldn't see why. It was written by an Indian using lots of words I had never heard before and in a strange rambling, crazy way. No one in Australia would have bothered to read it.

In the chapter on how to get a girlfriend it advised: "At parties and assemblies of his caste he should sit near her ... and having placed his foot upon hers he should slowly touch each of her toes, and press the end of the nails ... he should press a finger of her hand between his toes when she happens to be washing his feet ... he should sprinkle upon her the water brought from rinsing his mouth.'

If none of this worked "the bone of a camel is dipped into the juice of the plant eclipta prostata and then burnt, and the black pigment produced is placed in a box also made of the bone of a camel and applied with antimony to the eyelashes with a pencil, also made of the bone of a camel, then that serves as a means of subjugating others."

I had learned a lot in the Orient about things unheard of, or banned, back home where most things were forbid-

184

den. One of Ken's friends said you could buy a tube of cream in Hong Kong "to keep it up" for hours; a Thai woman at a nightclub boasted of her "electric glove"; and I now understood that "being good in bed" had a totally different meaning for most people from the one the nuns had taught us.

It was said you could never put one over on the Chinese, but I had done a pretty good job on these young boys. Now I didn't mind a single bit that I was soaking wet, or that it was nearly two in the morning.

The whole of Kowloon was deserted, which was unusual at any time of night. As I waited at Nathan Road for a taxi I saw some shadowy movements through the dark rainy mist. As the movements came closer I could see it was the two Chinese boys again. My heart sank. Normally I never saw them this close to the main road. They appeared to have someone with them. An adult with an umbrella. Had a parent, at last, caught up with them?

A small adult dressed all in black, she looked like an Amah. Why would an Amah be out on the streets of Hong Kong with these kids at this time of the night and in this weather? Maybe she had come to get them in off the streets.

"Old Lady. You want Old Lady," said one of the boys, and the shrunken woman shuffled forward and looked up at me. Under the streetlight her eyes were so small, her mouth so sunken and creased, that it was impossible to tell what she was thinking as she held out a wizened hand.

The world was much worse than I had ever imagined.

15 Clean through the Bamboo Curtain

That morning I stood alone on the colonnaded railway station at the tip of the Kowloon peninsula beneath the white domed clock tower, loaded and ready to go into Red China. I had a port, portable typewriter, new National portable tape-recorder, camera, 200mm lens, and a bag banging against my black moneybelt. There was no room in my port for the fake sheep-skin coat, so I had seven items to remember at every stop.

I had insisted no one come to see me off because I fully expected to be back in Kowloon in a couple of hours. Who knew what game Mr Kiat and the Reds were playing?

The train was crowded, but with each stop closer to the border fewer and fewer people remained. At the final stop — Lo Wu station — I was the only one who got off and stood on the bare cement platform. The long narrow wooden station-house was deserted, except for a few people in railway uniform. Up ahead, way past the station, Chinese Colonial police guarded a narrow wooden single track railway bridge.

This was the only split in the Bamboo Curtain between the West and China.

There didn't appear to be a place to ask questions. I walked fifty yards back to the other end of the railway office and poked around, but there was no one there either. I approached some railway workers but, as I did, they boarded the train as it took off back to Kowloon.

Just as I decided Mr Kiat had let me down, I heard a voice from directly behind. I swung around and there was a short, fat Chinese man in a single-breasted suit. He was holding my passport. I opened it up, but there was no visa inside. Just a signed stamped entry saying: "Lo Wu Immigration Control OUTGOING".

"You can go. You can go," he said and pointed towards the small wooden bridge.

I was sort of hoping for something official and Red Chinese in my passport before going in. Not just something saying that I was leaving Hong Kong. But the man insisted a visa awaited on the other side.

As I approached the bridge, two Hong Kong Chinese police in starched and ironed khaki shorts with black revolver holsters stood on the British end, their hands clasped behind their backs below diagonal black gun belts. They walked around in circles in shiny black boots and knee-high black gaiters, as if not allowed to leave their end of the bridge.

Not much more than a cricket pitch length across the bridge stood two Chicom soldiers in shabby un-ironed khaki pyjamas with khaki caps bearing small red stars. There was no shining leather on them. They didn't have their hands clasped behind their backs either, but around Chinese AK-47 automatic rifles held diagonally across the chest.

I expected the Hong Kong police at the nearby border post to stop me for questioning, but they did nothing as I approached the bridge, loaded down with my gear and trying to stop the artifical sheepskin jacket from dragging in the dust. To keep in good with them, I nodded: but they wouldn't look at me.

It was another twenty yards to the bridge, then past the two Hong Kong guards. In a month, the sun would pass directly over nearby Canton: the guards threw very short thick black shadows in the hot midday sun. This really was *High Noon in Hong Kong*. Here I was walking a narrow path, caught between ideologically opposed armed guards, alone: much like Gary Cooper in the film.

On into the middle of the bridge, walking slowly between the two lines of parallel steel under the weight of much cultural baggage. Now exactly halfway between the two warring camps of the world. Slowly bending open the Bamboo Curtain. I really was getting in. The Peking Opera story must have worked. So I wouldn't be catching the next train back to Kowloon after all. Arch and JJJ and Ah Ping would be surprised.

When we were kids digging holes under the house in Brisbane we always said we were digging through the earth "all the way to China". Now, after six months of trying, I had dug my way to China. Of course, I knew that everyone outside Communist China was very grateful to be outside: "better dead than Red". But I was very grateful to be going in.

A few yards from the Red Chinese guards, who held the menacingly-curved black steel magazines of their rifles pressed against flat stomachs, I suddenly realised I was getting my first sight of the feared Commos. I studied their faces carefully, but they squinted past, never taking their eyes off their British Chinese revolutionary class enemy cousins at the other end of the bridge.

I stopped to look at one Chicom soldier. I was a Catholic. He was anti-Christian, anti-religion even. What the Church would call a heathen. When these pagans talked about impure thoughts, they were talking politics. I drew level with him, but still he didn't look at me. Back in Australia, I suddenly recalled, if something really hurt it was called "Chinese torture".

The other soldier walked forward, took my passport, and led me onto Red Chinese soil. There would be no chance of making a long-distance trunk call home from here. When the Chinese took Tibet no country was game enough to do anything about it. Not even America. Being Australian couldn't help me now. "You'll be stuck there for the duration," was Olive's final warning. But I suspected Mum was really worried because, when I was born, Grandpa Hugh Lunn wrote from Mt Isa predicting that I would become a famous Communist and would one day lead a People's

Army "when the people of Australia have had a bellyful of what is being dished out to them". But the people back in Australia loved what was being dished out to them.

Up ahead, a large black steam engine with a red star covering the whole of the front pulled into the terminus. A score of young Chinese men and women sat on the front cow guard, or ran beside the engine, cheering: as if the arrival of a train at the border of the most Capitalist city in the world was itself a revolutionary act. As the train came to a stop the steam of the engine engulfed them all.

Whenever we wouldn't eat our tripe and white sauce for tea, Olive would admonish us Lunn kids saying: "Think of the starving millions in China." These youths were them, except they weren't starving. They were the "Yellow Peril" the St Joseph's nuns had told us about at the Convent at Mary Immaculate Church, Annerley, when we were four years old — the nuns waving their hands across a brown paper and ink map of the world. I felt alone in hostile territory. Like the man from Snowy River when he started that terrible descent.

The only thing to be seen on the other side of the muddy creek that served as the Bamboo Curtain was a large, flat-roofed single-storey modern building with no obvious windows. The soldier steered me inside to one of several uniformed Red Chinese officials standing behind a long, low counter.

I handed over my passport. Expected problems. As he examined it, the official grimaced — probably at the sight of the British gold crown on the front. Then he ever-so-slowly turned over every last one of the 32 pages, only to find that 31 were blank: since the only other place I had ever been to in the world was Hong Kong. The Communist official examined my black and white photo, with its overlaid imprint of a British Crown inside a star. He looked up at me. Then back again. Several times. He seemed to doubt it was really me. Had a specially close look at my burnt left ear.

189

The official then leaned with both brown knuckles on the counter and, in good English, asked: "Do you ever plan to visit the United States of America?"

It wasn't a question I was expecting. My first instinct was to lie. I knew the United States was a class enemy of what they called here "the People's Republic of China". These Communist Chinese saw the United States, backed up by Australia, as the nation that was keeping them out of the UN, and thus exiled from the world community. But I decided it was wiser not to lie. I didn't want to tempt the Chinese Gods.

"Yes, I might go to the US one day," I said. "My father, Fred, had his ticket, but never got to New York because he got married and had four children. He's sick in hospital right now and he wants me to go to New York on his behalf, if I ever get the chance."

The official nodded politely and reached into a drawer. He pulled out a small slip of white paper covered in Chinese printing on the shiny side. Ever so carefully, he attached this piece of white paper to a page of my passport with a paperclip, filled in my passport and visa details, then stamped the white paper a couple of times with a red chop. I was getting in for my chop.

He looked up and smiled.

"Because you wish to visit the United States of America we will not put our chops in your passport so the Americans will never know you have been here. This is an Aliens Permit issued by the Guangdong Province People's Committee Security Department: in Peking you will need another Permit. You must carry it and please show it when asked. We have very strict control on the street. Once you leave the People's Republic you can remove this and any other papers: otherwise the United States of America will think you are a spy, and they will not let you visit New York."

He passed the passport back across the counter while shaking his head sideways and saying, as if we were both on the same side: "Well, you know how strange the Americans are."

190

I nearly started laughing.

As I moved on I checked the paper. There wasn't a word of English — not even my name.

Two more uniformed Chinese waited at the next counter. They seemed happy to see me as well. One spoke English and, indicating a waist-high wire basket, said I should throw any propaganda, exposed film, newspapers, or magazines into it. Mr Kiat warned me not to take any newspapers into China, but I did have an old *Philippines Herald* weekly magazine. Not wanting to get into trouble, I showed it, saying I really only wished to keep one article: "Dashing Men Somewhere Overseas". About Foreign Correspondents, since I was thinking of becoming one when I got to London by joining Reuters, if I couldn't get something better.

"A more energetic and interesting, if not always amiable, breed of the human species could hardly be imagined than the Foreign Correspondent," the article said. According to Fletch, who had been to just about every country in the world, the first person he always ran into on some isolated strange shore was the Reuter Correspondent. Ken used to imitate the radio news, saying: "Reuter says the Queen today had eggs for breakfast."

The English-speaking Chinese studied the article for a moment, and then asked me to read aloud the second paragraph: "In their most celebrated moments, Foreign Correspondents have wielded enormous influence. Their writings have moved peoples, caused statesmen to fall. At least four wars can be said to have been in part or whole fomented by their journalistic activity."

Didn't sound too good. He ripped the double-page out of the Filipino magazine and threw the rest in the bin. I hoped he might give me the article, but it was folded tightly and disappeared into his jacket pocket. The pair then started on my luggage, heading straight for the new-fangled National portable tape-recorder. The English-speaker picked it up carefully in both hands and held it like an expensive dinner plate:

"Is this propaganda for broadcast?" he asked.

"No. There's nothing for broadcast," I said, exasperated by the question. "It's just French lessons. I play the French lessons on the recorder and listen to learn the language for when I get to Europe."

The Customs man pulled out the batteries, had a look, and then put them back in their slots. He pressed the play button. I was just as surprised as the Chinese by what came out of the recorder's ash-tray sized speaker. It sounded like an Adolph Hitler speech. Fast and furious high-pitched language in some tongue no one could recognise filled the huge Red Chinese Customs Hall. You couldn't tell if the voice was male or female. Even the Immigration officer I had just seen came running across to join the throng of interpreters and bureaucrats who gathered around the black recorder.

I quickly realised what was wrong. The chrome insert which diverted the reel-to-reel tape to slow it down was not in place. So the recorder was playing the French lessons at three times normal speed: the speed used when playing quality music on this brand new device which the backward Communists would never have seen before. I whipped the round chrome piece out of my black money belt, opened the top of the recorder — despite an attempt to stop me — and screwed it in to divert the tape on its longer journey through the mysterious Japanese workings.

"*Voulez-vous un taxi?*" it said.

"Do you want a taxi?" I said, and we all laughed at the unfortunate misunderstanding.

Of all the things I wasn't expecting, the English-speaking Customs man picked out two of my three books: *Collected Verse of Paterson* and *Poetical Works of Lawson*, both published by Angus and Robertson with red linen covers.

He ignored *Seven Centuries of Poetry*, a blue-covered book.

"Red books!" he said.

"Yes. They contain the stories and events on which our Australian heritage is based."

"We have only one Red Book in the People's Republic: Chairman Mao's Red Book," he said, and looked upwards.

So Mao Tse-tung had a red book. It couldn't possibly be remotely like these. I piped up: "They're just Australian poetry books my mother gave me to remind me of home." And I showed Olive's inscriptions on the inside of the two covers, and read out the one from the Paterson book: "This will be a piece of Australia to cherish".

"They are political books?" the Customs man said.

"No," I said. "Poetical books. They are about horses, and swagmen, and ringers. They are no use as propaganda because no one outside Australia would relate to them."

I offered to recite *The Man From Snowy River* to show how well known these stories were in Australia, but the official confiscated both books. He said they would be returned on my way out of Red China, which I knew would never happen. Meanwhile, one of the other crack Customs men gathered to the fray, searching for further subversive propaganda. They examined my cheap imitation-gold cuff-links sculptured in Chinese writing, the crocodile-skin belt I had picked up at the Hong Kong markets, and paid particular attention to the lining of the imitation sheep-skin jacket. But they left my moneybelt, with its secret compartment, alone.

A form to be filled in: how much money did I have on me. List "objects of value". I nearly burst out laughing when their check-list included "fountain pen" and "clock". You could buy those for nothing in Hong Kong.

"Typewriter, camera, lens, tape-recorder, watch, cuff-links, and crocodile-skin belt." Then I handed over all my US dollar travellers cheques and asked that $100 be changed into Chinese money, called Yuan. Fletch said to always carry Yankee dollars as these were sought-after in every country in the world. He warned that overseas countries had never heard of Australian pounds.

For $US100 I received a stack of reddish-brown five Yuan notes, not unlike the ten shilling notes back home, and coins which hardly seemed like money at all. These Communist Chinese coins were made, of all things, from aluminium, so they lacked the solid feel of real money. Australian coins were made of copper or a precious metal, silver, and thus were very heavy. Particularly our two-bob bits. Even a threepence was heavier than the largest of these Chinese coins, though threepences were as tiny as the end of a little finger. Our Australian coins also had deeply etched sides, and carved images of sheep's heads, and British Kings and Queens, and our coat of arms. The main thing on these aluminium coins was a pattern of stars: one large star inside a semi-circle of four small stars. I couldn't help feeling the Chinese people were being ripped off. If the coins had no intrinsic value as precious metal then the People's Republic could just manufacture as many coins as they liked. They might as well make their money out of plastic.

But I didn't say anything. Though I was inclined to speak out when the Bank of China teller issued a stern warning to make sure I changed any Chinese money back to US dollars before I left the country — saying it was forbidden to take China's precious Yuan out of the Republic. Yet I knew from living in Hong Kong that the Communist Chinese weren't supposed to have any US dollars. That was the whole idea of the American trade embargo. The reason for those Certificates of Origin in Hong Kong.

Lastly, they checked my vaccinations for typhoid, cholera, and smallpox.

At the railway station, as I lined up to buy the train ticket to Peking, there was a choice of travelling "hard" or "soft" class.

I chose "soft".

16   Putting on the Biff in Goat Town

The steam train to Canton with the red star up front was as comfortable in soft class as any Australian train. Waitresses in clean white coats poured tall glasses of boiling green tea for every passenger as the driver blew the steam whistle over and over as if it were a toy.

Chinese men stood drinking tea at both ends of the carriage and chatted happily. They could have been from Hong Kong, except that they were poorly dressed. It was as if there was no colour allowed in their lives: other than dark blue or khaki. As far as I could see I was the only European. We sat in comfortable cloth-covered seats with starched white head covers.

I had two seats, and settled in next to the left window. No one seemed to take any particular notice of me. The waitresses didn't give my pink cheeks a second glance.

Rice fields and green paddocks stretched to both horizons and almost touched the edge of the train line. There was no machinery in the fields, just people with conical straw hats, white shirts, and trousers rolled to the knees. Sometimes fields looked like mirrors.

The most surprising thing was that every railway bridge was guarded at both ends by armed People's Republic soldiers in their loose-fitting untidy uniforms. If they needed to guard every bridge in Red China, then Chairman Mao was in trouble.

Did the Australian government know of this internal security problem in China? Still, I had to remember I was a guest, and so resolved to say nothing about the guarded bridges until I got out. Since she couldn't stop me from going in, Olive had made me promise not to argue with anyone in Communist China.

"Remember, we can't send a search party out looking for you," she wrote.

I had to be extra careful because, only a few days before, Sir Robert Menzies had announced Australia was sending a battalion of our best troops to fight alongside the Americans in Vietnam. Prime Minister Menzies said it was a "grave" situation. He said Australia was threatened because the war was part of a thrust south by these Chinese Communists.

So now I could easily be classed as an enemy. The Asiatics were always fighting us Australians: the Japanese fought us in Singapore, and in New Guinea in the '40s; the Koreans and the Red Chinese fought us in Korea in the '50s; then the Indonesians fought us in Borneo and Malaysia; and now, in May 1965, the Vietnamese were going to fight us in Vietnam. These Chinese Communists would probably be next. I wondered why they didn't just leave us alone.

After two-and-a-half hours we hit Canton. Southern China's biggest city was a shock after the traffic and skyscrapers of Hong Kong. Three million people, no building much more than a few storeys tall, and hardly any cars. Instead of trucks, old wooden platform carts with wooden wheels moved the goods. Sometimes the wheels of these carts had wooden spokes, other times they were discs made of wood bolted together — like in the Middle Ages. Even as kids in Brisbane our billy-carts had steel wheels, though the steering was done with a bit of old rope. These Canton carts were loaded, pulled, and pushed by up to five Chinese men and women at the same time.

The only trucks I saw that first day were both army vehicles, each carrying three times as many soldiers as an Australian army truck. Soldiers stacked upright like soft drink bottles in a box. A Zephyr Six would have looked as out of place in Canton as the Queen of England on a tram. The only cars were a few black taxis, made in Poland.

Although they looked fairly new they had the sloping-back appearance of pre-war Fords, or the Standard Vanguards which in Australia had competed unsuccessfully for sales against the more modern look of the Holdens and Zephyrs in the 1950s.

Thousands of men rode through the streets on old bikes, many with rifles, and some with their targets too — bullseyes, inners and outers in black and grey — slung over their backs. The Chinese were definitely readying for a fight.

I was met at Canton Station by a slim Chinese student called Chen who wore steel-rimmed glasses and had a strange habit of blinking every time he spoke, as if synchronised with his speech. He carried a black umbrella, even though it didn't look remotely like rain. With a distinct accent Chen said I had been "allocated" to him by the People's Republic Ministry of Culture: not the local Guangdong Province. I suspected he was just there to spy, so I told him I could find my way around perfectly well by myself.

"Chinese towns are not open places," he said, blinking more quickly than usual. "I have come from Peking to look after you. It is a high honour for me, and it is my job. I have volunteered so I can practise my English."

"Your English is perfect already, Chen."

I thought he must have learnt in England, but he said he had never before spoken English with a native speaker like me.

"I have only learned at University in Peking and spoken with other Chinese," he claimed.

How could he learn to speak English so well without leaving this alienated country? Probably with tape-recorded lessons like mine, I reckoned. He seemed a bit older than me, though he claimed he was still a student. I could tell I was stuck with him.

Chen followed me out of the station, ordered a taxi, told me how many Yuan to pay the woman driver, carried my imitation sheep-skin coat, camera, lens, and National tape-recorder up to my room in the hotel, and said he would show me the view from the roof — as the hotel, though not at all high by Hong Kong standards, overlooked the city and the river.

From the top, Canton looked like a big city that had been bombed out. For as far as I could see, except for parks, there were one or two storey decaying old brick buildings in various colours from dirty red to dark brown. To me it looked like a brick factory, and I couldn't help comparing it with Brisbane, where the timber and lattice homes were painted various colours, with red or silver tin roofs over wide verandahs, and large green backyards containing trees: mango, persimmon, gum, Queensland nut, hibiscus, jacaranda, Moreton Bay fig, silky oak, cascara bean … Except in the parks, there were almost no trees in this tropical city of Canton, which was about the same distance from the equator as Rockhampton.

I didn't express my thoughts. They would go straight back to Peking via Chen. Instead, I admired the large open grassed square in front of the hotel with its sparsely planted small trees and the white statue of a revolutionary figure on a high pillar, with a rifle of course. He faced south towards a huge iron bridge over the Pearl River. Although used mainly by people on bicycles, this bridge was shaped like Brisbane's Grey Street bridge and constructed of webs of steel like the Story Bridge.

In the distance, in what looked like a park, was a gleaming blue roof that stood out from the brown-red brick of the town like Wordsworth's violet by a mossy stone. This was the Sun Yat-sen Memorial Hall which, Chen said, was located here because Canton was China's "revolutionary city".

"He removed the hereditary monarch long before monarchs were removed in Europe," Chen said proudly. "And this was his home town." I thought of telling him Sun Yat-sen's relatives were friends of mine, but decided against it. It would make me seem more important than I was.

Mao Tse-tung and Chou En Lai had started their political careers from this city too, according to Chen.

Chen seemed to think I was very interested in Chinese culture and history. He said there were forty million people in this one province. The Cantonese Chinese were considered barbaric in far-away Peking, and there was no doubt they were the roughest and toughest people in China: probably because of the heat. They had kept their own language here, and always wanted to go it alone against the rest of the nation.

"It sounds a bit like Queensland," I said. But Chen had never heard of our states.

"Right at this moment in Queensland the entire population will be getting ready for the biggest event of the year," I said, since Chen kept asking what was happening in Australia. "It's the one thing I regret missing out on. Every year in mid-May, Queensland plays New South Wales in a game of football called 'rugby league' in Brisbane at night under lights. We usually lose the match, but everyone goes to see us win the fight which starts seven minutes into the game."

Chen wanted to know why a fist-fight started every year at exactly the same time, and only in the first of the four-match series.

"It's part of our Australian culture," I explained.

"What do Australian people call this ideology?"

"It's called 'putting on the biff'."

That night Chen took me to the Canton Cultural Centre after dinner. When I asked what we were going to see he said, without blinking: "Putting on the biff".

So I was no wiser.

Anti-American banners and billboards hung at every main intersection in Canton, and the Cultural Centre was no different. On either side of the entrance were two building-sized posters: one depicted an Asian soldier pointing a giant automatic rifle into a tiny President Johnson's mouth; the other showed Asian soldiers hurling grenades, while women in the background fired rifles at American GIs. The one common denominator of all these signs was that the Chinese workers and the Asian soldiers always had slightly pink cheeks and gigantic brown forearms. Like Jim's. Not that I had seen any large forearms among the slender Chinese in Canton.

As gongs sounded, acrobats bounced brilliantly through the air on to the deep timber stage and leapt on top of each other like in a circus. The hundreds of Chinese in the audience enjoyed it far more than I did. Probably because they didn't have access to films like *Lawrence of Arabia* and *Jedda*, or to TV shows like *The Untouchables* and *Palladin* "have gun, will travel". In fact, they didn't even have television.

After a series of acrobatic displays there was a long break, and then out onto the stage stumbled several drunk "American" soldiers in uniform, followed by three men and three women acrobats who danced and spun around the stage, weapons in hand, bravely searching out the GIs. When the acrobats landed, the GIs walked backwards. They bumped into one another, jumping with fright.

Later that night, when writing home to Fred and Olive, I said the evening of cultural entertainment "made my stomach go cold" because I could see the position Australia was getting itself into by sending soldiers to Vietnam. But the next morning I decided against posting the letter, in case it was opened by the Chinese: or frightened Olive.

I ripped it up into a million pieces and, instead, sent a black-and-white postcard depicting Wu Ling, "Five Mountain Range", in the northern part of Canton province: saying I had arrived in China safe and sound, but tired from the two train trips. But I doubted the postcard would ever see Annerley Junction.

The hotel manager at reception seemed to think I was in Canton for some annual export International Fair in an Exhibition Hall across the square. He kept asking if I was buying ivory, or silk.

Chen arrived under hot blue skies with his black umbrella and I soon found out why: he liked to point things out with it. We walked up Liberation Avenue just near the Hotel. I kept seeing the same banner in Chinese over and over again: always a red sign with eleven symbols.

Chen read it aloud for me: "Americans get out of Vietnam".

Down Sun Yat-sen Avenue, and Red China was starting to look like one large military camp. Everywhere we went we passed groups of young people in red scarves, not yet teenagers, marching along in military platoon formation. Most Chinese youngsters seemed to march everywhere, as did groups of labourers — "work parties going about their revolutionary tasks" — when moving from one site to another. But these little people with red scarves sang loudly as they marched. Chen said they were the future political leaders known as "Young Pioneers".

Chen said they were singing *We are the sons of Communism* as they marched. These Young Pioneers looked like trouble to me.

"How old are they?"

"Young Pioneers start at nine-years-old," Chen said proudly. "They are the Socialist Vanguard. They practise frugality, and fight against excesses," he added in the peculiar English the Chinese had invented, and were now, apparently, all learning by heart at their universities so they could all repeat the right phrases: and be judged accordingly.

In one way Canton was a very Catholic city because it was filled with memorials to martyrs. Except, in this case, they had died for the *Glorious Socialist Revolution*, rather than the *One True Church*. But they didn't keep relics like we Catholics did. In fact, Chen didn't know what a relic was.

Unlike Hong Kong, there were no people sleeping on the footpaths, or prostitutes. The whole city was very clean with no beggars. Canton was parks, tombs, museums, statues and bricks, bricks, bricks.

Although I seemed to be the only European wandering around, the people in the streets took no notice. There was no aggression and — again unlike Hong Kong — no Colonial deference to the white man or his money. After Hong Kong, where I was always pestered in the streets for something, it was strange to be ignored. As if I were invisible. Maybe it was because they didn't have anything to sell. Or was it because, like Australians, they had never received a tip? Perhaps their isolation had made the Reds scared of strangers. But Chen assured me over and over again: "China has friends all over the world."

Chen showed me a famous white statue of five goats, one of them an old bearded billy goat standing high above the others, his huge curved horns sticking into the sky above. In ancient myth, Canton was created by five celestial genies who arrived on the site of the city riding, of all things, goats. So it was known colloquially as "Goat Town".

"That name wouldn't attract any tourists from Australia," I said. "Goat is a term of abuse back home: as in 'you silly old goat'."

Chen was amazed: "This is also a term of abuse in China."

"What, goat?" I said, amazed.

"No, I thought you said 'ghost'," Chen replied. "In China it can be an insult to call someone a ghost."

For the next two hours he repeated "silly old goat" over and over. Laughed each time. Chen loved to learn new ways of saying things in English. When I said Canton struck me as a "pretty ordinary" place, he wanted to know how it could be both "pretty" and "ordinary" at the same time. I explained that this was an Australian phrase for something that wasn't much chop.

He took me to a small building where the first Communist school started in the 1920s — leading inexorably to Red China. When I complained about the lack of greenery, we visited a beautiful park of lawn and flowers with a lake and a tiny curved bridge. I liked it so much I got him to take my photo. But he wouldn't be in a photo himself. Which showed he was scared of something.

There was no one else in that tranquil park. And there was something else odd about this town that I couldn't quite put my finger on. I didn't work out what it was until we stopped off at a local cafe for some tea. It was a large cafe, appropriately enough beneath the Chinese symbol for "big", open to the street on two sides, with ceiling fans and male waiters in white coats: a bit subservient for Commos. When we sat down I remembered the scores of beautiful waitresses in Hong Kong and realised what was missing: there were no pretty girls. Hong Kong seemed to burst with girls, all done up in various coloured and multi-patterned body-hugging cheongsams. But inside China there were no cheongsams.

That was it. Every girl here wore the same blue-cloth loose-fitting trousers, white shirt, and no make-up at all. Usually they had their hair in plaits. The one certain way of telling them from the blokes. I mentioned this noticeable lack of dolled-up girls to Chen in the cafe, where we had been joined by a student mate of his who was down from Peking for something called a "struggle meeting".

Chen's mate took immediate exception. "Perhaps you have not yet thought keenly enough. Female fashion is a form of bourgeois ruffian oppression, an exploitation of women which must be denounced."

"What's wrong with a girl trying to look her best?" I countered. "Australian girls carry small mirrors with powder inside so they can keep checking up on their appearance. And Hong Kong girls look much, much prettier than the girls here."

"You have only just arrived," Chen's friend said. "You are yet to learn that we are not a decadent nation of fashion-conscious coffee shop-dwellers." Girls wore blue trousers to "protect their modesty".

Even though I had sworn not to argue, I could see, as Fred would say, that I would have to pay attention. So I told the two of them a few home truths: I was surprised they continually referred to their country as "Socialist" when they were Communists; "ruffians" was an English word used only in Phantom comics; and Australians were definitely not "coffee shop-dwellers".

"That's Americans," I said. "Beer, tea and milkshakes are the national drinks in Australia. The men drink beer in the pubs, which are in every suburb, and the women drink tea at home. In the whole of Brisbane there would only be one coffee shop: the Piccadilly Coffee Lounge. And the only person I know who spends a lot of time there is my Russian mate Jim Egoroff: and he was born here in China, in Harbin."

"I can understand your perversity," Chen said sympathetically. "Don't worry about my friend, he is pretty ordinary today."

We both laughed.

Then Chen turned towards his mate: "Silly old goat!"

His mate had no idea what we were talking about.

Chen continued to stick up for me: "We in this ancient Socialist Republic understand that Australians are the product of recalcitrant Imperialism and chaos in Europe, and are not the real culprits," he said generously.

But his friend would not accept this, saying we had long since been unmasked: "You Australians have chosen to become a uniform Anglo-Saxon feudal Kingdom."

I could see he was leading up to the usual attack on Australia's White Australia Policy. It was difficult to explain that the policy wasn't there for racist reasons — but historical reasons. That we were a proud, independent, democratic country on the edge of the Far East, but with families in England and Ireland: both white countries. We elected our own governments, although it was true that — standing above each of our elected Parliaments — were seven unelected Governors representing the Queen of England. I had learnt this in Political Science 1 at university.

"For example, in Queensland our Governor is Captain Henry Abel Smith," I explained. "He was sent out from the

Queen's own Royal Horse Guards because his wife, Her Serene Highness Princess May Helen Emma of Teck, is a cousin of the Queen. Having an hereditary monarch in England gives us an unelected balance to the elected Parliaments."

"This is the same system as the Emperors," said Chen's mate in disbelief. "Emperors imposed from a distant land."

I explained that we had very close ties with English royalty.

"Only last month the Duke and the Duchess of Gloucester visited Australia for our most important celebration: Anzac Day, to commemorate the landing of Australian forces in Turkey exactly 50 years ago."

"You Australians fight wars in Europe, and you call Asia the Far East? Far from where and east of what?" said Chen's mate aggressively.

I kept thinking of Fred telling me to use my discretion. So I agreed that Australia was basically a part of England, rather than a part of Asia. Chen could see my discomfort and interrupted on my behalf:

"Your countrymen were sent to Asia by your Capitalist Landlords as retribution on the laboring masses. So we have blurred feelings towards you. But you have made a mistake sending your soldiers to drown in the quagmire of Vietnam."

I explained we Australians felt we owed the Americans one for stopping the Japs in World War II. "We are the last ones to turn our backs on a friend in need."

"You mean Australians are always warring," said Chen's mate sourly. "You will regret this arbitrary decision to interfere in the struggle in Vietnam."

Trying to end the conversation, I said the People's Republic had no idea of the military might of the US: "The Yanks can wipe the floor with them in Vietnam any time they want."

Chen was not angry. He merely stared ahead, and ordered more tea. When he wasn't talking he could stare without blinking for half and hour, as if he were dead.

"Putting on the biff will not make victory in Vietnam," he said when the tea arrived. "The felicity of the people. The felicity of all the people of the world is important. Chairman Mao says that when the people swim among their enemy like fish in water they cannot be defeated. When the people are close to war they can overcome all obstacles and tendencies to achieve retribution."

"The Yanks haven't even tried yet," I said. "So far in Vietnam they have not even used jet fighters. They are only using old propellor-driven planes."

"But the Americans are a divided people."

I couldn't put up with that. "China is so divided that you don't even all speak the same language," I said.

"Yes we do speak with one tongue. We are one nation," said Chen, blinking fiercely.

"Then would you order me an orange juice please?"

Chen called over the waiter and spoke in Mandarin.

"Huh?" said the waiter.

Chen's mate repeated the order, but the waiter shook his head.

"There you are," I said. "A divided nation. Divided by language."

"Mandarin is our national language, but not everyone yet speaks it. That is our number one aim. Meanwhile, we celebrate diversity," Chen said.

"We all read the same writing," said Chen's mate, and wrote a short column of Chinese letters on my notebook and held it up to the waiter.

The waiter couldn't read.

Then I spoke one of my most used Cantonese phrases: "Mmm goi ne chang jup," and the waiter smiled broadly and went and got me an orange juice.

17 An Ear-bashing on the Peking Express

On the train to Peking, and rid of Chen, there was time to think instead of talk. Perhaps I had gone too far arguing the toss with him and his mad mate, losing my cool and breaking all the promises to keep my trap shut once inside Red China. Still, it was hard to be pessimistic now that I was finally on my way, across the top of the world to Paris.

I was feeling proud. While Hong Kong was overflowing with Western journalists locked out of Communist China for sixteen years and desperate to know what went on inside — but only able to watch and listen from a distance — here I was travelling 1400 miles north through the heart of the country.

At the back of my mind I was hoping to see the "Forbidden City" in Peking. Being a Catholic, I was attracted by the name.

Now, for 43 hours, there was nothing to do but sit back and observe. No employer to tell me what to do; no one relying on me; and, for the first time since I was three years old, no examinations to do at the end of the year. Totally anonymous among 750 million people. More people than the United States, England, France, Germany, Italy, Australia, New Zealand, and even Russia too — plus a dozen other nations — put together.

Every year, enough babies to make another Australia. Another 23 Australian nations had been born to Red China in my lifetime. No wonder the Chicoms claimed "the East is Red". Yet still Australia wouldn't recognise them. We were helping to exclude them from the United Nations: which,

I learnt at school, was formed to get nations together and stop wars.

The train was surprisingly modern inside. It had a canteen carriage with waiters in white coats serving meals on thick white tablecloths with red napkins and ivory chopsticks. I scored my own double sleeper cabin with wine-red flower-patterned cloth seats and a large picture window looking out to the east. From here, the East really was Red.

For the first few hours I locked myself in and looked out at China as if dreaming, my eyes lazily out of focus until a lone man ploughed through a rice field or herded hundreds of ducks along a dirt road with an elongated fishing rod.

No buildings. Anywhere. Few trees, no tractors, no horses. Everything done by humans, every square inch of low-lying ground cultivated. I was surprised how few people there were. I thought China would have crowds crushed together, but the hot rice fields were practically deserted.

The only distraction was a noisy loudspeaker under my picture window which continually broadcast someone speaking in Chinese. I guessed it was the local wireless station. I could turn the volume down, but there was no knob to turn it off or change the station. After a while, the constant, strident, shouting, repetitious voice got on my works. It was enough to make me leave the cabin and go looking for someone to fix the problem. However, as I walked through the carriage, I could hear the same demanding voice echoed from all the cabins. Even from above the doorway inside the eating carriage. The only phrase I could pick up from the screeching voice — which reminded me of old newsreels of Adolph Hitler, or the intensity of George Lovejoy's rugby league broadcasts in Brisbane — was something like "may gwar".

This was used in almost every sentence; every thirty seconds or so. There was nothing to do but turn the loudspeaker down as far as it would go. Then after a while I didn't notice it. Feet up on the red seat opposite, I pondered my position. This was the country that had kicked out my old mate, Jim Egoroff, when he was nine-years-old. Which was why he ended up sitting next to me at school in Australia for eight years.

Jim's home-town of Harbin was on the rail line in northern China. They survived the Japanese occupation of China during World War II. But when the Communists won the civil war in 1949 the Egoroffs, and the other Russians, were kicked out because the Communist Chinese said they were "nothing but radishes". Even though Russia was the home of Communism, and the Chinese were always quoting "Marxism-Leninism", the Russians in China weren't trusted: probably because they had built the railways and power stations for the previous non-Communist government.

When Jim and I finally became friends at Mary Immaculate, Annerley, he told me what had happened back in his China days: "Cutting a long story short Lunn, you Bastard Boy, my family had of been very well known in China because Grandpapa loved Grandmama's eyes. Grandpapa's transport company had hundreds of horses which could of have been recognised all over China because the yokes over all his horses' heads had of been painted light blue to match Grandmama's blue eyes. But, Lord and behold, one of those couple of last days, the Chinese said we were all 'radishes', that while we had of been Red on the outside, we were totally White on the inside. That is why we are called 'White Russians'."

Jim was explaining why I was wrong when, a few days after he arrived at Mary Immaculate, I called him a "Communist Pig" just because he was a Russky, causing him to grab me and rub my ears with the palms of his hands.

But Jim got his own back on the Chicoms before being kicked out, with the aid of his older brother, George. Because their father worked for a large engineering firm near Harbin, they were able to secretly use the workshop to make a small cannon with a steam pipe, some steel ball bearings, and gunpowder from shotgun bullets. Jim was always inventing things.

"In any case," Jim said, "we went with our dog to the top of a hill and fired at the Hi La railway bridge over the Amur river while it was being guarded by a platoon of Communist Chinese soldiers. Lord and behold, when those steel balls have of had hit the iron bridge the Chinese threw themselves down, and George and me, fair dinkum Lunn, we were rolling ourselves."

Jim wouldn't be the only one surprised when he found out that I was inside the land of his birth. Peter Thompson had written to Hong Kong: "Do you realise old chap that you are the first Third Man to go overseas? The rest of us have talked about it, and made vague plans at drunken parties, but we've never done anything so progressive. There's no doubt in my mind that a journalist has to get himself overseas, and, if he waits around hoping for a posting to some exotic clime, the chances are he will never get there."

That evening the only people in the canteen on the train were, to my surprise, a Western family having their dinner: a middle-aged couple, two children, and a tall twenty-something-year-old blonde English girl whom they had brought along to look after the children. She was the one I noticed first because of her translucent ivory skin which was completely without wrinkles.

This family was equally surprised to see me. So we had dinner together. The father was a British Diplomat returning for his second term in Peking, so he knew a lot about Red China. The family was to do another two years, which was why they brought the maid along to help look after, and teach, the children.

The Diplomat knew far more about the Chinese than I did. It was difficult to talk above the clatter of the train, the shrill steam whistle, and the screaming roar of the loudspeaker above the canteen door, so I asked the waiter to turn it off. He laughed to think I would even suggest such a thing, and pulled his hand across his neck while widening his eyes. He wouldn't even turn it down.

The speech, the Diplomat said, was coming from an "audio centre" on board our train, which was normal in Communist China. The voice was over and over again condemning the USA for its actions around the globe: "US Imperialism is headed for total collapse"; "America get out of Vietnam"; "Running dog US Imperialists". The "may gwar" I kept hearing was "mei guo": which meant "American".

"Actually, because the Chinese used to like the Americans, mei guo literally translated means 'beautiful people'," the Diplomat said. "But now, of course, the meaning of the words has totally changed. In effect, though the translation is still the same, mei guo now means anything in the range from hooligans to traitors."

"But the Chinese government can't just change the meaning of the words," I said.

"Oh yes. Every country does," said the Diplomat. "Not overnight, but over time. Words have their own life, and then slowly, ever so slowly, the time zone they were useful in passes and they become something else. They begin to mean what ruling authorities want them to mean. As Orwell wrote, 'love' becomes 'hate' and 'peace' becomes 'war'. In my game, the meaning of words is vital, so that almost nothing is as it seems. Usually it pays to use words which are the opposite of what you mean. Like when two governments say 'we have had full and frank discussions', they actually mean that neither side brought up anything contentious." He burst out laughing. So did the maid.

So what I was hearing day and night on the train was the good old US of A being called a nation of "culprits", "betrayers", and "tyrants". The hatred in Red China was even worse than I thought. I had to get out and write about it soon before someone else got the story.

I could see World War III starting at any time. After all, we hadn't had a World War for 20 years. There had been

211

only 21 years between World War I and World War II, so I reckoned another World War was about due anytime.

The English Diplomat said nothing to allay this fear as he translated the broadcast: "America fights wars of aggression". I said I thought all wars were agressive. "Only other people's wars," said my friend.

"The worrying thing is that China has now become the world's fifth nuclear power," he said. "The Americans and the Australians are underestimating the Chinese, and are trying to ignore them. But, in the end, you can't ignore any nation with nuclear power: particularly not if it is the biggest nation on earth."

But rather than being scared of the Red Chinese, this Diplomat seemed to admire them.

"They are a brilliant people," he told us over Peking duck and soft, puffy white rice like you could never buy in Australia, even if you wanted to eat rice instead of potatoes, which nobody at home did.

The Chinese had invented paper, dynamite, printing, the cannon — and had made iron a thousand years before Europe.

"And don't worry if you fall ill while you are here," he said. "You will get better medical treatment in China than anywhere else in the world."

I told him I already had an inkling of this. Mr Kiat had shown me an article on a Chinese man whose arm had been completely severed halfway between the elbow and the shoulder. Chinese surgeons had sewn it back on, and there were pictures of him playing table tennis with the arm to prove it: you could see the deep circular scar right around the muscle.

The Diplomat also pointed out that we were in a completely non-Christian country. It seemed hard to believe that the message of Jesus Christ and his ten commandments, his miracles, his saints, the Virgin Mary and the Crucifixon, and the Pope, and Easter, and Original Sin hadn't penetrated these closed borders. Thus the average

Red Chinese knew nothing of the concept of Sin, apparently, let alone Purgatory, or Hell, or Confession, or even the nine First Fridays.

Back in my cabin, after choosing the top bunk, there was plenty of time in the dark to contemplate the fact that these Chinese would not make very good enemies if they knew nothing of damnation for all time, or even the benefits of Contrition.

Catholics were supposed to say an "Act of Contrition" every night before going to sleep, just in case.

Contrition was a complex subject because, in order to achieve God's forgiveness for breaking his commandments (like "Thou shalt not Kill"), you had not only to be genuinely sorry, but to promise faithfully that you would not commit that sin again. Plus, beyond that, there was "Perfect Contrition" and "Imperfect Contrition": a difficult concept, even for Catholics. Jim Egoroff, even though he was Russian Orthodox, still knew the difference. He had a fantastic memory for detail, so his favourite party trick was to challenge Catholics to come up with the answer: something we had all long since forgotten.

Then Jim would say: "This is really, really honestly true. 'Perfect Contrition' is when you should of have been sorry because your sin offended God; and 'Imperfect Contrition' is when you had sorrow only because you had of been dead scared of going to Hell forever."

The next morning I awoke to another surprise. By now we were nearly 500 miles inland, yet the country was still as green as it was near the coast. I had covered the Charleville Show in Australia, a similiar distance inland, and all was straw and brown, and dead and dry. Dust and stunted trees. Here everything was deep green and wet and growing. No wonder China was able to feed so many people.

At breakfast, the Diplomat pointed through the canteen window at workers in the boiling fields: "Nowhere else in the world will you find people willing to work all day and all evening. That's why they are now selling rice to the rest of Asia after feeding themselves. That's why we in Britain are going to try to start selling to them: before they start selling to us."

He said that, unlike Australia, Britain had recognised Red China right from the Communist Revolution in 1949, but had not yet been able to establish full diplomatic relations as the French had done the year before. "This has put the French a big jump ahead of Great Britain. So my job is to try to catch up."

The major stumbling block for Britain was Hong Kong. The Chinese argued that Britain had annexed the Colony by force of arms, and they wanted it back.

Travelling through China was like passing through one big green rice field tended by some strange, incomplete civilisation. Every time we pulled into a railway station, or passed through a town, it was dwarfed somewhere by a rusting steel skeleton that had been deserted by its workforce before completion as a building. Now the sole use for these structures was as picture rails for huge painted signs.

What I was seeing, apparently, was the failure of Mao Tse-tung's so-called "Great Leap Forward", better known to the head waiter as "the disastrous Leap", and to the Diplomat as "GLF". These incomplete buildings had been part of Mao's 1958 plan for the Chinese to form village Communes and turn Red China from an agricultural nation of peasants to an industrial power of blue collar workers. To become the equal of the United States in 15 years.

Hundreds of thousands of peasants were put to work on these vast construction projects, and attempts were made to create small rural industries in every town: with peasants moved from farms to factories. Chairman Mao renounced all foreign help, thus the huge number of Soviet experts who had been sent to help China after the Revolution a decade before had suddenly shot through.

"The peasants no longer tended their fields," the Diplomat said. "There was crop failure, and five years ago famine struck. Millions of Chinese died in the next two years, until at last the peasants were sent back to their fields."

These ubiquitous steel shells of buildings were the unfinished factories the peasants left behind.

"You can understand it," he said sympathetically. "The Communists were hiding in caves less than ten years before coming up with this plan. They were totally isolated from the modern world."

But the population didn't blame Chairman Mao. He was smart enough to apply the diplomatic theory of opposites: saying his GLF successfully steered China through "the Socialist transition". Thus he became known as "The Helmsman".

Ironically, from atop many see-through GLF structures, Mao's round red-painted face shined like a sun from the top of advertising posters on to the crowds painted below: his black tufts of hair sticking out at the sides like Dagwood's. He was like their God.

Surprisingly, the English girl seemed to know a lot about Chairman Mao. She said that while Mao had failed economically, he had succeeded completely in getting the support of the people for his ideals: which made GLF an economic failure but a political success. One of the ways he did this was to remind everyone how terrible it was under the Japanese with the slogan: "Remember the Bitter Past".

"One thing the Red Chinese are experts at are slogans," the Diplomat said, and we all laughed and retired happily to our cabins. I could see that once you are only allowed to say things in a certain way, you are soon reduced to slogans.

A few hours later, an armed guard with a revolver attached by a piece of cord to his military jacket, and held in a thick leather holster on his right hip, stepped into my cabin without knocking. He didn't look at me, just quietly shut my window. Then left without saying anything.

I followed the armed guard softly down the corridor from cabin to cabin to the canteen where, unaware of my presence, he shut all the windows next to the tables while the waiters smiled at his actions. My waiter friend said this was because we were approaching the Yangtze River. This river was so sacred that no one was allowed to throw anything into it: not like the Brisbane River where everyone threw the things they didn't want, from prawn shells wrapped in newspaper to kittens in weighted sugar bags.

The Yangtze meant we were arriving at Hanyang in Central China. Looking out the window I saw the bridge as we approached around a long curve of steel. As a child, I thought God had made the Story Bridge because it was such a massive structure. Later, aged 13, I saw the even bigger Sydney Harbour Bridge. But this bridge made them both seem like toys.

I would have taken a photo, but I had been warned by the Chinese not to take any pictures of bridges, airports, or soldiers. And I couldn't get away with it anyway, because no one was allowed to take exposed film out of Red China.

There were massive six-storey stone towers topped with high red claws on either side holding up the bridge, which took a dozen steel spans to cross the wide Yangtze. This was not merely one bridge, it was two bridges in one — with a road across the top, two hundred-and-sixty feet above the water, and a railway line through the middle of the bridge girders. It was like entering a tunnel of patterned steel which magnified the noise of the train. I peered down through the moving, curved black steel at the sacred river below: catching only glimpses through the glass.

It seemed the Chinese treated this river in the same way Catholics did Holy Water. The waiter said it was seen as the river that had spawned the Chinese race, and that every year it re-claimed thousands of them in floods. It was as long as Australia was wide, cutting Red China in two halves — north and south. A river from Brisbane to Perth.

On and on we rattled for more than a mile before emerging on the other side into the bright sunlight on the northern side of China, and pulled in to Hanyang station: considered the halfway point between Hong Kong and

Peking. Near the station was a sprawling, partially completed steel works, as silent as the aftermath of any failed jump.

The women who sold food from stalls wore white surgical masks covering their faces, except for the eyes and forehead: the waiter said it was to stop the spread of germs. Instead of the usual advertisements in railway stations, red slogans said: "Americans are hooligans to be struggled against," "Down with Reaction," and "Americans get out of Vietnam". Anti-American hatred was everywhere. This time Mao wore a cap, and his red cheeks looked down on a painted Chinese landscape: river, stone bridge, trees, mountains, and what looked like a tall pagoda.

I was running well behind schedule to meet Ken in Paris for the French championships. We had arranged to meet at 1 p.m. on the corner of the Champs Elysees and the Rue De Colisse on the first day of the tournament. I wasn't going to make that. There was no way of telling Ken, but I wasn't late yet. I hated running early and I was getting closer to Paris every day.

Even though Fletch was great company, travelling alone was better. I could do what I liked without him there to tell me I needed a haircut, or a shave. Instead, I was growing a beard, which was coming out red. To think that I had failed all those exams at school, and got to go to secondary school by only half a mark. Had God lifted the black scum off my brain that I used to think was holding me back when I was thirteen?

The Diplomat sought me out for conversation; even the waiter sat down to talk to me, and the English maid trusted me enough to pass on the name of a friend in Moscow: a correspondent for a Fleet Street newspaper no less. I thought I might become an actor in films in London, since they didn't make pictures any more in Australia.

As the train pushed on through the night towards Peking, the maid stayed up talking, while the Chinese waiter sat at our table. He undid the buttons of his white jacket and listened and laughed. When I asked her if she liked her

217

job as a maid, her eyes narrowed in anger. She said she was "an au pair".

"An au pair is not a servant, just an assistant," she said.

The waiter liked it when the au pair said Chinese trains always, but always, ran on time. And that the population had virtually wiped out flies by getting everyone to kill as many as possible each day.

"Five flies each, and that's three thousand seven hundred million flies gone in a day, you see!" she said.

And dogs. Pet dogs were banned.

"Anyone who keeps a dog is considered a Capitalist roader. So no one wants one, you see."

I had always thought this Communist Chinese term of denigration was "Capitalist roadster" — thinking that they were referring to the Western predeliction for sports cars. The maid and the waiter cacked themselves laughing at that one.

"No roadster in China," the head waiter said.

The maid said "Capitalist roader" was a term applied to any Chinese who were "taking the Capitalist road".

We were having such a wonderful time, with the maid telling me to be extremely careful of the Russians, who were much, much more dangerous customers than the Chicoms, that I begged the ageing waiter to turn the loudspeaker off. Just this once. To my surprise, he climbed up on a chair and did just that. The au pair and I stood up and cheered and clapped him and we all laughed, probably with relief that the 24-hour-a-day haranguing was finally over. She said the Chinese were obsessed with ensuring the population listened to the correct broadcasts: thus listening to foreign broadcasts was banned, even for foreigners.

Within seconds, the armed guard in military jacket appeared with his hand on his holster. He shouted angrily at the cowering waiter who was in the poo because of me. The waiter buttoned up his jacket as he leapt in panic back up on the chair and turned the hysterical voice back on, and up. It never shut up until late the next morning when we pulled noisily into Peking station in a cloud of coal dust.

18 Spies from the old Gold Coast

There was no Chinese official to meet me in Peking and the railway station was nearly deserted. After hanging around the station for an hour the thought occurred: had the Communists forgotten I was in China? Eventually, I picked up my many parcels and hailed one of the old, unmarked black taxis at the station. As in Canton, the back door opened from the centre pillar backwards towards the boot and the woman driver insisted on also acting as porter.

Since Cantonese was useless in Peking, I wasn't able to ask the driver to take me to a hotel. She drove off without speaking, or bothering to look back through the football-sized rear-view mirror.

She seemed to know where she was going. A few minutes later we pulled in to a parking area outside an elegant old ornate stone-fronted building several storeys high which could have come straight off a European postcard. There were several other taxis parked outside, and, except for the women drivers, it looked like the set for an old black-and-white American film.

The man at reception was not at all fazed when I walked up, unshaven and wearing a black money belt. He was obviously familiar with Europeans. Then I noticed several European men in suits talking in groups around the foyer. The man at reception spoke English and said this was the hotel where all overseas visitors stayed: which was why the driver knew where to take me. Peking obviously didn't get very many foreign visitors.

It was a surprisingly classy hotel with a large restaurant on the top floor. From the small window in my room I could see an old stone wall thicker than the biggest car. It must have been nearly twenty feet high and ran past the side of the hotel, where there was an archway over the road big enough to drive a truck through. I assumed it was part of an old wall that once protected Peking from the Mongol hordes.

After waiting to see if any government official, like Chen, turned up, I went for a walk. There was no one around this area at all. The houses, or offices, were low and unobtrusive. Everything was very clean, and the road surfaces were smooth all the way to the gutters, unlike in Brisbane where there was nearly always dirt between the bitumen and the gutter.

I soon came to what was certainly the principal thoroughfare in Peking, a busy avenue called Tranquility Boulevard. It was quite beautiful: a straight road wide enough for eight rows of cars side-by-side (had there been enough cars), and lined with trees smothered in large new green leaves. It was a silkworm's paradise.

The road stretched to my left for as far as the eye could see. The thing that impressed me most, however, were the lamp posts. They weren't just a single light bulb stuck high on an old tree stump. The hundreds of lamp posts along both sides of this road were cream-painted sculptured steel rising up to five round white lights like on a candlestick holder on a Catholic altar.

But there was something else. Around the top of each pole, just below the lights, was a circular enclosed box. I couldn't imagine what these were for.

It was sunny, cool, clear spring weather. I had never seen our Australian capital, Canberra, but I imagined it probably looked something like this, except for the paucity of cars. Canberra would have had lots of cars of all makes and colours: not only Holdens and Ford Falcons, but Humber Super Snipes, MGs, Morris Minors, Rovers, VWs, Wolseleys,

Armstrong Siddley Sapphires, Plymouth Belvederes, Hill-mans, Peugeots, Triumphs, Austins, Chevrolets, Vauxhalls, Humber Hawks, Studebakers, Vanguards … whereas here the roads were crowded with men and women riding thou-sands of the oldest bicycles I had ever seen, dodging in and out of the mule-drawn wagons and old carts pulled by bicycles which wended their way slowly and almost silently through the city. There were so many bicycles that there was practically a bicycle traffic jam at one intersection. From all the squeaks, I could tell that these bikes were poorly maintained.

And then something truly amazing: an electric trolley-bus. As well as trams and diesel buses, Brisbane had a couple of these silent trolley-buses. They ran from the Gabba to the General Hospital past the Museum; and from Wickham Terrace down to the Botanical Gardens and back. They were like a cross between a bus and a tram. They looked like buses, but had two poles sticking up from the roof to touch electric overhead wires just like a tram. In Brisbane they were considered ultra-modern. So it was a surprise to see them in Peking.

Using just picks and shovels, a few road and building workers toiled. There were no advertising signs for soft drinks and ice creams and beer, but instead inspirational posters the size of mango trees dominated nearly every corner. Huge crude paintings of hard-working men with unmarked pink faces, red cheeks, and forearms as thick as large soft drink bottles. Sometimes they wore cloth caps with red stars, and scarves tied jauntily around pink necks. The men invariably looked towards the sky, while pink-faced women dressed like European peasants danced hap-pily around, holding out the edges of long colourful skirts.

Of course none of the people down at ground level looked or dressed remotely like this. It reminded me of the Diplomatic theory of opposites I heard about on the train. Peking women didn't wear skirts, as far as I could see: almost exclusively they wore blue trousers and white shirts.

And they didn't wear large coloured scarves. They mostly sported plaits.

Beneath their caps, the men of Peking showed brown, lined faces without a hint of red anywhere. A few Chinese officials at the hotel were in Mao suits, which were like a Beatle suit without the thin tie. Everyone looked happy and passive enough, despite living under the iron heel of Communism. Obviously they had all been indoctrinated to believe that this was the best of all possible worlds and no one was allowed to tell them any different.

But there was no one playing games in the streets. Or loafing, or just standing around enjoying themselves. A squad of youngsters in red scarves marched down the street chanting slogans as they went off on work parties: more of the dreaded Young Pioneers. I understood them better now that I knew from the Diplomat that half of the Chinese population was under twenty-one.

It was true, as the maid said, that there were no flies. Or dogs. Even on a lead. That much I liked. Brisbane was a city of large backyards, falling down fences, and loose dogs. It was very rare in Brisbane not to hear a dog barking somewhere nearby, unless it was midday. The only time Chen's mate had laughed was when I described how Fred would get our Boxer dog, Droopy, to sit on a chair at the dinner table with the rest of the family.

That evening at dinner on the top floor of the hotel the restaurant was filled with dozens of Europeans, including a couple of women: but no one was speaking English. I felt a bit out of place in trousers, shirt and moneybelt because the furniture was all antique, and the men all wore suits and ties. But luckily for me there was one other bloke, a tall, handsome middle-aged man with a bit of a belly, who not only wore no suit or tie: he wore a cloth cap like an English sports car driver, plus a lairy multi-coloured shirt with painted hibiscus flowers all the way down the long, long sleeves.

We were the only two who sat and ate alone. However, that wasn't why I noticed him so quickly. He was black, and I certainly hadn't expected to see any black men inside the closed borders of post-Colonial China.

When he finished dinner this black chappie walked off into a room to the side of the restaurant next to the bar. I could see him walking around looking down all the time, showing the top of his grey cloth cap, which was pulled forward over his forehead. But I couldn't work out what he was up to.

I changed position, and saw he was playing snooker. All by himself.

My father Fred had been something of a snooker champion in the 1930s in Mt Isa, so he reckoned, and he taught me to play at the Irish Club: though I never did manage to make the white ball spin left or right or backwards after it hit a coloured ball the way Fred could. So I watched from a distance to see how well this gentleman could play.

The gaudy African was unlikely ever to finish a game. He didn't bend low enough over the cue to sink many reds. Not that I could talk. Just a month before, I missed the pink ball from three feet away as it sat invitingly in front of a side pocket, and Fletch and I lost lunch to two Englishmen. Ken was annoyed and kept bringing it up: "You would have to get the elbow on the pink." He didn't even like losing a social game of snooker to some friends in Hong Kong, let alone a tennis match at Wimbledon.

"He who aims high never falls low," Ken said, quoting his book of proverbs, when I made this observation.

Although he wasn't a class player, the African was pleasant to watch purely because his large frame slid silently and quickly, backwards or forwards, around the large rectangular table as if he was on rollers. The way he moved he looked like a tall, black version of Minnesota Fats.

It wasn't much fun playing snooker alone so — not hopeful that he would be able to speak good English — I asked the African if he wanted a game.

A light suddenly turned on inside his head.

"That would be absolutely, truly delightful, stranger," he said, in suspiciously perfect Queen's English, sticking out a long, soft hand that completely enveloped my white one.

"I have become far too dedicated to seclusion here in Peking. And tell me, my friend, where might you be from? And to whom do you report?"

He was as English as you could get, and his name was even the same as our late King's, "George". His full name was George Kitson Mills, and he said he was from "somewhere west of Suez".

"Actually, to be more precise, I hail from James Town, Accra, in Ghana. That's north-west Africa to you. By way of an unwise and an untimely decision, I have been ensconced in China for nine months since."

I told him I too had left my homeland getting on close enough to nine months ago, so I knew what he was going through.

George lived fulltime in this international hotel, which meant he was important: and obviously very, very well paid. But by whom?

How come he spoke such good English?

"I have travelled expensively," George said, laughing at his own play-on-words. "But really Hugo, English is the main language spoken in Ghana and taught in our schools, since my country was a British Colony for nigh on 90 years."

"You did better than us," I said. "We were a British Colony for more than a century."

I had to admit to George that I had never heard of Ghana.

"Methinks that's not surprising really," he said, accidentally sinking a red in-off the blue. "Until eight years ago my country was called the Colony of 'Gold Coast'."

"So you're from the Gold Coast?" I said. "Well, George, so am I!"

I told him how my mother, Olive, was from the Gold Coast, Australia. "It used to be called the 'South Coast', but soon after you changed your name from 'Gold Coast', we changed ours to 'Gold Coast'. So we must have taken the name from you."

"Your tale, Hugo, would cure deafness," said George in astonishment as he missed the blue. "A most auspicious star. It has been otherwise ordained that you and my crying self are countrymen." And he shook my hand again as if we had been friends for life.

George didn't seem to know anything much about Australia, except that it was a place to which Britain had shipped its convicts, and that he couldn't live there because he was black.

"It is my bountiful misfortune to be banished from that magical isle," he said.

"We Aussies like to ban things," I told him. "My English boss in Hong Kong, Max Schofield, reckons Australia bans everything because we are afraid of being tempted back into committing the sins and crimes of our convict ancestors."

George was more interested in the fact that I was a journalist than an Australian.

"Journalists can go where fancy leads. But they must avoid falsehood and crediting lies," he said. "Wherefore I will help you in Peking. But, since you are a journalist, it could be difficult, and we needs must be discreet."

Even though I told him why I was in Peking, George wouldn't tell me what he was doing in China.

"You are the journalist, Hugo. You must work it out for yourself. That is the role the journalist plays in the modern world."

"Can't you give me a clue, George?"

"I already have," he said, smiling through his large teeth, made whiter by his skin, "but you must yet see it."

What clue had he given to his work in China?

I was getting so mixed up searching back through our conversation that, having nominated the black ball for my next shot, I discovered it wasn't where I thought it was just a moment before. Instead, I found myself aiming down the other end of the full-sized snooker table at nothing but the cush.

"I spy with my little eye … the blacks are both up here," said George, standing and pointing helpfully behind me and in front of him.

Not only was the black ball up the other end, but somehow I had inadvertently snookered myself behind the pink with my previous shot. So I nominated the yellow.

Having given away four points by missing completely, I asked George why he liked playing snooker so much that he played by himself.

"Forsooth, you have to eliminate the reds before you can score," George replied, shutting his dexter eyelid. "And because the object of the game is to hide the colours from view."

He had me thinking now. Was he an anti-Red. Or did he have something to do with the demand for Civil Rights in America? He said not.

"In a way Hugo," George said, as he bent to line up a red across the wide expanse of green baize, "I am nothing but a professional liar. I have come here to the East solely to make things appear as they are not."

Was George an English-speaking African CIA spy in Peking? Or, worse, an agent provocateur? I resolved to hold my peace, just like I promised Olive.

After a few long games — because we had such trouble sinking all the reds — the restaurant and bar closed: and George opened up.

"I guess you could say," he said, as he chalked his cue, "that my darker purposes are to eliminate."

"Eliminate what?"

"Things," he said. "Or people, if need be."

So he was a black James Bond. If he was, he certainly wasn't travelling incognito. There was no way George could blend in with the crowd in Peking. Not in that orange hibiscus shirt.

"Who are you working for then George," I whispered, standing cue to cue as we shared the same cube of blue chalk: long since worn down to the thin red paper that surrounded it.

"By the very nature of my work," he said behind his left palm, "only two or three people East of Suez have ever seen what I do: though most of the world would dearly love to. But that will never be. The only people to whom I divulge my secrets are a small chosen group of Red Chinese."

"So that's why you're here?"

"Yes. I tell the Chinese Communists everything I know. Well, nearly everything, but not quite."

Why was he telling me all this?

"Do you steal documents, George?" I asked tentatively.

"I pray you, let us just say that on many an occasion I have conjured some document to re-appear: in the right place, at the right time."

Here I had been thinking the English maid on the train knew a little too much, and all the time the biggest spy in all of Red China was an African. The trouble was that, just by knowing this, I was now involved.

"What happens to the people you make disappear?"

"Oh, they bob up somewhere else later on," he said.

Like in the ocean?

My mind was racing so fast that I had done it again. I had nominated the blue ball, lined it up, and now it wasn't even on the table.

I checked all six table pockets, but no blue anywhere.

Then I felt it. The blue was in my left trouser pocket, and George was laughing at me.

As I looked across the wide snooker table he picked up two empty rice bowls off the bar and asked whether I knew how to solve the world's food shortages.

George tipped the empty bowls on their side and tapped the tops together and, as he sat them down in the middle of the snooker table, both bowls overflowed with rice. It scattered white across the dark green baize just a yard from my own eyes.

George wasn't a spy at all.

He was a magician.

19 Magical Mystery Tour

George advised me to buy something warmer than my artificial sheep-skin jacket for the week-long train trip across Siberia to Moscow. The train was leaving in three days, so I had to quickly buy supplies and organise the visa the Russians had promised to give me if I ever got to Peking.

It turned out that George was being paid by the Red Chinese government to teach them how to do magic tricks. He was supplied with his own official interpreter, given full board and lodging in the best hotel in town, as well as a substantial salary. It seemed hard to believe that, while other world super powers were pouring money into space travel, Red China was hiring magicians.

George was quite a celebrity. Every Chinese who walked past him in the hotel smiled upwards at him, showing by their giggles that he had tricked them all at some stage of his stay.

"These mean fellows drop their sour-eyed disdain when they see my charms work," George said, throwing a breakfast cup into the air with his long black fingers. His very speech had a floating air of magic about it.

"Their barren hate melts into thin air," he said, as the cup disappeared into the ether and waiters gaped.

George couldn't come shopping, because he was performing at a Chinese Magicians Conference, but he invited me along for the post-conference concert that afternoon.

I found the trolley-bus a few streets away and, to my surprise, it pulled up. Every seat was taken, so I took up my usual stance on a bus: holding the vertical bar next to the back stairs. As we moved silently off there was a loud commotion. The conductor yelled and screamed and stamped her tiny foot, while swinging around on a leather strap like a trapeze artist. She was addressing the whole bus. As she did so her bag of aluminium money clattered hollowly, lacking the rich Australian conductor sound of real silver colliding.

She showed a large set of front teeth, and talked loudly and constantly, reminding me of those non-stop broadcasts on the train. She must have been important, because most of the people on the bus stood up as she spoke.

The conductor then headed for me, reached out and pushed me gently backwards into a soft seat. Straightening up, she again aggressively addressed the passengers. Then all but one young woman sat back down.

George explained it later: the conductor had abused the passengers for not standing up for a foreigner, which reminded me of my schooldays when we were required to stand up for adults on trams or buses. If you didn't stand, the conductor didn't care, but as sure as eggs some nosey parker would dob you in to the Brothers.

It seemed a strange deference to stand up for a "white Devil" like me, but George said I was a foreign visitor and that "white ghost" was a better translation of the Chinese term for a Westerner than Hong Kong's "white Devil": the Chinese not being familiar with the Christian's Lucifer anyway.

According to Chen, "ghost" was also a term of abuse in China, but George said an even better translation was "white shadow" because, unlike a ghost, white Europeans were not seen as something "to be entirely feared".

As instructed in Canton, I reported to the Peking City Ministry of Security and a second piece of white paper with red Chinese chops was stuck in my passport.

I was surprised how free I was, and looked around for something interesting. Quite a crowd had gathered four or five deep along one side of a wall that stood alone in a street.

They were reading the pages of a broadsheet Chinese newspaper stuck up a double-page at a time just above eye level.

Since no Western newspapers were allowed in Peking, I pushed through to see if I could make out what had been happening in the outside world. Just like in Australia the paper had large headlines, photos, and a cartoon. Of all things, the cartoon was a drawing of a kangaroo. Slowly I worked close enough to see that the kangaroo had some figures in its pouch, each feebly holding on to rifles. They were wearing slouch hats with the side turned up, and peeked nervously out: some very apprehensive-looking Australian soldiers.

The smiling, ingenuous kangaroo was bounding happily off across a map of southeast Asia carrying the Australian soldiers, as if not knowing that disaster lay ahead as it island-hopped north: bouncing on New Guinea, hopping across the islands of Indonesia, springing on Singapore, skipping up through Malaya, re-bounding across Thailand, onto Cambodia, and into Vietnam: a country which bordered Red China.

It looked awfully like the Domino Theory in reverse.

I couldn't read the cartoon's caption, but I could see enough to realise that I was now behind enemy lines.

The few Peking shops had little to sell besides food. There was no jewellery that I could see, no gold bars in all shapes and sizes like in Hong Kong, no gramophones, no washing-machines, no lace, no TVs, and no chocolates — which I wanted as back-up food for the journey. But there were no queues anywhere for food either, as I had expected in a state-run country. And no old people working, like in Hong Kong.

The people and their children wore fresh, ironed clothes.

The only large department store I could find had no chairs for customers. Just like the stores in Australia they wanted customers to keep moving. But that didn't work here. Whole families just sat down on the floor between the counters when they felt tired. They chatted away, laughed, played, and argued, while staff ignored them, and the other customers stepped over or around.

Having rejected embroidered silk dressing gowns and sewn padded jackets, I stumbled on to a real find: large animal skins, something I had never seen for sale in Australian shops. I had no idea what animals the skins were from, but I fell for a black-and-white skin the size of a large blanket, and bought it for practically nothing.

With the skin wrapped in brown paper under my arm, I caught a cab to the Russian Embassy using a note written by George's translator. Although he was a sophisticated, educated man, George couldn't speak Chinese. He said he could never learn all the tones.

The Soviet Embassy was a sprawling, beautiful old building with a shining ribbed silver dome on the roof which could be seen from afar. For some reason I had pictured a broken-down, small, dank, musty, unpainted double-storey concrete bunker.

The Russian official was an even bigger surprise. Rather than big and strong like Jim, he was short and dapper. He looked like a tiny version of an Italian male mannequin in his cute zoot suit, shiny black leather pumps, black receding hair oiled straight back, and beautiful white teeth. This suave Russian had the best office I had ever seen: a ceiling as high as a squash court, a green dado of appropriate raptors around the walls, and a polished antique timber desk bigger than a three-quarter sized bed. He spoke perfect English, with only the slightest hint of a foreign accent.

I passed across my faded, unsigned, unassigned letter from Moscow which sort-of promised a visa, should I ever get to Peking. The well-dressed Commie official held it out at arm's length by the tip of one corner as if it were unclean.

Once again I had to explain who I represented.

"I'm writing a story on travelling through China and Russia to London which I hope to sell to newspapers in

Australia," I said. "I'm calling the story *Through two Curtains and a Wall* — the Bamboo Curtain, the Iron Curtain, and the Berlin Wall."

The Russian feigned disinterest by reading papers on his desk.

"You're probably wondering how I got into Red China, since Australia doesn't recognise this country. Well I wrote a feature about Peking Opera faces, and what the various colours and patterns mean."

That got him to look up.

"Passport?"

Before he could issue me with a Soviet visa, I would have to go and get one from the Polish Embassy: to make certain that, once inside the Soviet Union, I wouldn't be stuck there and become their responsibilty. You couldn't get into most countries, he said, unless you first had a visa for the next country.

"Yet the Chinese have let you in here, and now we are under pressure to give you a visa to get you out again."

He was right. The Polish Embassy wouldn't give me a visa — until I got one from the Democratic Republic of East Germany: so that I wouldn't be stuck in Poland and become a drain on their Communist society as well. Back at the Soviet Embassy, and armed with an array of visas, the official was about to stamp my passport when he said I needed a visa to travel on the train through Mongolia.

This was news to me: "I thought the Chinese ran Mongolia."

"Did the Chinese tell you that?" the smooth Russian said, for the first time interested in my situation. He seemed relieved by my answer. He said it would take weeks, possibly months, to get a visa for Mongolia. I was getting sick of this: the East certainly was Red — red tape.

In the end, I only just made it to the magic concert in time. George saved a front row seat next to him in the open-air theatre which held about five hundred. As with all things Communist Chinese, much of the show was acrobatics. Geese disappeared somewhere, people were suspended in thin air, and a young Chinese man who was locked securely in a wardrobe on stage came into the back of the hall a few seconds later and ran down the aisle to the stage ringing a school bell. But the performances were not nearly as impressive as George's two empty bowls that suddenly, and inexplicably, over-flowed with rice when hit together.

"It is rough magic," George said disdainfully of his pupils. "The wizards are wizened."

That night I went to see a play which had set box office records in China, but it turned out to be just more anti-American propaganda. Chinese actors dressed as American troops and wearing white face make-up captured a young Vietnamese girl. But she triumphed in the end, saying: "The enemy provides our weapons."

The best things were the stage props which transported the audience with a single tree, or a lonely light. The capture of a US Colonel, for example, occurred in an eerie yellow light cast from floor-board level. Clearly it was dawn: and the actress addressed the enraptured crowd: "It is the dawn of a new era. I will write to our dear ones in the north (i.e. the Red Chinese) to tell them of our glorious victory."

The audience was silent as the curtain was pulled across by four people.

Thank God George was waiting at the snooker table when I got back to the hotel. I needed some light relaxation, and you could play snooker all night at the hotel if you wanted.

After a while we were joined by a Pakistan Airlines official who introduced himself as Siddiq Masjid, from Karachi, West Pakistan. Siddiq seemed incredibly lonely, even though he had been in Peking just a week. He said he was preparing the way for Pakistan Airlines which was about to start weekly flights from Pakistan to Peking: "These will be the first direct flights from the West into Peking. It is an important mission because it is vital for Pakistan that this works."

It was the first time I heard anyone say Pakistan was part of the West. Other than that it was hard to concentrate on our shots because Siddiq talked incessantly about his longing for his wife and family back in Khori Garden, Karachi. After midnight George walked to the wall, shelved his cue and announced: "I invite you both to my cell for some discourse. Methinks this night is so far not right for both of you. You need a minute's mirth."

Siddiq was very large, like George, so we only just fitted around a rectangular trunk used as a table, squeezed in between books and magical props.

"It's very small," I said, thinking of the nine months poor George had lived here.

"It is Dukedom large enough," he said, boiling his own little kettle and a pot of real African coffee. "After all, all I have to do here is twiddle my thumbs."

An apt description of a magician.

George was unimpressed by Siddiq's talk of homesickness. "Siddiq, I have not been near a woman these nine months since," he said. "It was made most clear by mine hosts that during this one-year I must not change eyes with a Chinese woman. A condition of the job, so-to-speak."

Nor was I impressed. "At least you have a wife, Siddiq. For five years since my redhaired girlfriend gave me up I've been looking unsuccessfully for a wife. And then, when I finally find the perfect girl in Hong Kong, Jeanette, I leave to get a job in London. Now I can't understand why I left. I won't see her again for at least a year."

"A year is a long time," said George.

Siddiq said he could understand why I was heading for London to get a job in Fleet Street to make something of myself. But he couldn't understand George. "What is it that you are doing, George," Siddiq said sadly, "letting the government tell you not to go out with any women here for a whole year. This is an atrocious arrangement."

"Well demanded, Siddiq," George said generously. "My tale provokes that question. But I have brought this bewitchment upon myself. I have come to a shore with thirty million more men than women. However, as of today, I leave ninety days hence." Then he was off to London too, to visit some old friends: Professor Agreemo, Ayeetey, Roddy and Obodia. "This is a thought I continually conjure up," he said.

All three of us became very serious as George explained to Siddiq why he was in Peking.

"Hugo here thought that I had put myself upon this land as a spy. But I landed most strangely here. The Chinese heard of my magic art, which was performed in nightclubs all over Western Europe. They somehow knew I had been taught by Britain's most famous wizard and, since they could not learn from him, they paid me most handsomely to teach them Western enchantment. They revere incantation here in the East. To them illusion is more Confucian than confusion. Magic is not seen as an insubstantial pageant in China, as in the West. Here they believe in spirits. And dead ancestors. And the powers of sorcery. This is why the Christian missionaries failed in China."

Siddiq smiled over his coffee at the foolishness of the Chinese: "My goodness me, of all the wondrous things on this earth why would the Chinese be trying to find out how the magician cuts an assistant in half or untangles some golden rings? This is too ridiculous for words. Magic is fun for children, yes, but what possible use can magic tricks be to a struggling nation like China which needs food, and technology, and industry to advance with."

But Siddiq soon stopped smiling.

George placed an empty bowl on the chest in front of him, saying "have a nut".

"But the bowl is empty," said Siddiq.

"I never have to go shopping," replied George. "Give sweets to the sweet. Have a nut" — and he handed Siddiq the bowl, which now overflowed with a variety of nuts.

George, it appeared, could conjure up anything: except a woman. He said prostitution was forbidden in Peking's revolutionary society, whereas, before the 1949 revolution, Shanghai was known as "the most sinful city East of Suez". Now there was no pornography. No nudity. Women no longer even took their husband's name. Children used either name, or both.

"The biggest thing the Communists brought to the population was an end to arranged marriages. Now people marry whomsoever they choose."

George seemed to be advocating Communism.

"So you like this system George?" I asked.

"No," he said, throwing back his head and laughing. "I would be a thrice-double ass to do that. If the Communists take over the world, all of the girls will end up wearing blue trousers!"

The three of us laughed far more than was necessary, because in one sentence George had summed up what made Red China so different from our world. Our women dressed up to attract men. Here they dressed purely to cover up.

"I'm an African," George said. "We are a colourful people. We couldn't take blue trousers on our women. Under Communism there'd be no more dwelling in coffee shops sitting around discussing erroneous ideas. There would be no coffee even. No aroma. There would be only revolutionary tea shops for revolutionary artists and revolutionary writers working for revolutionary theatres. Artists always arduously struggling to gain links with the masses."

"And no elitism. Do not forget that, please," said Siddiq, smiling.

"And we would have to love the Chairman," I found myself saying.

"And only have every second Sunday off," said George, who particularly disliked this Communist Chinese practice.

We all agreed we would prefer not to live under such regimented conditions, with no hope of owning a car, or going to the pictures every night if we wanted, or buying anything we could afford: even if we didn't need it.

"No rich peasants," I said, echoing one of Red China's favourite phrases.

"No materialism," said Siddiq.

"No adventurism," added George.

As the three of us crouched close together around the magician's trunk laughing at our jokes in the semi-darkness, it occurred to me that we were acting like an international political cell. Something I had only ever read about.

Siddiq shook his head so that his black moustache swayed at the ends and said it was much, much nicer back at home in Karachi: "The Chinese can keep their silk worms, and their excellent medical facilities, and their antibiotic factories. It's too dull here." He was laughing now, for the first time.

"Such smiling rogues as these, my friends," said George touching us both lightly on the shoulder.

I told them Peking was so dull that — according to the woman official next to the foyer at our hotel — even the world-famous Forbidden City was closed, instead of being open to all. That couldn't happen in a country like Australia. We encouraged people to see our famous places.

But George, once again, disagreed.

"The Forbidden City, by its very nature, is kept from snoopers," he said. "But this is most propitious. My high charms can work for you. Let me use my voodoo to break this taboo for you Hugo."

George smiled enigmatically: "Entrance does oft depend upon enchantment."

20   The Wizard and Chairman Mao

Next morning George woke me after breakfast for a visit to the famous Forbidden City. He was dressed in yet another bright shirt which, as usual, was not tucked into his ample waistline. It was paisley-patterned royal blue on white. Because it was a very hot day I wore my usual bone linen trousers, and one of the six light-blue cotton shirts I had picked up cheap at a sale on Nathan Road.

George wanted to know why all my shirts were the same dull blue.

"Methinks your shirts do show you have Communist tendencies, Hugo," he said as we set off laughing on our adventure. Each with a camera.

Despite his importance in Peking, in nine months George had not yet been invited inside the Forbidden City. We walked along the aptly named Tranquility Boulevard, sauntering in the shade of the trees for 20 minutes. George loped across the ground with the gait of a slow runner, lifting his knees high and taking just one step for every two of mine. He stepped out like a man on a long journey.

His translator came only as far as the walls of the Forbidden City, to read some of the city's propaganda signs and posters for me on the way. Beneath a beaming painting of Mao: "The Chairman is our Helmsman"; a painting of people happily working: "The Unity of the Great Peoples of the World"; and others like "Comrades must struggle", "Unity and Uniformity", and "Root out gangsters mercilessly …".

That one stopped me.

The translator explained: "The United States is a land of gangsters. So we equate them with gangsters."

Because of the continuous repetition of slogans I could only conclude that the Red Chinese had banned the use of alternative words and phrases as incorrect.

The eight-lane-wide Tranquility Boulevard led to a huge open square covered in large stone slabs which were clean enough to reflect ninety percent of the sun: so I had to squint hard to see clearly, as if looking into Fred's oven to see if the buns were cooked. George reckoned every one of these stone slabs was individually numbered. Though he didn't know why.

This was "Gate of Heavenly Peace Square", or "Tian an men Square" to the Chinese. Tranquility Boulevard passed through this square between it and the Forbidden City. The square was so named because it was outside the front of the Heavenly Peace Gate to the Forbidden City, one of five gates through the otherwise impenetrable wine-red wall.

In this ancient palace and its grounds at least 20 Chinese Emperors had lived, and worked, and ruled for many centuries until the Communists took control. This palace brought to mind all of those exotic words from the East: the mysterious Orient, comely concubines, emasculated eunuchs, eccentric Emperors, and meddlesome Mandarins. It was also the building where Mao Tse-tung had hoisted the Red Flag just sixteen years before — on October 1, 1949.

A prohibited zone for so long to hundreds of millions of people, here before us was the Forbidden City: the cosmic centre of China. Although this cultural icon had been closed by the Communists for much of the time since the Revolution, because of what it represented, it had not been razed by the Reds. Because this walled city was the reason Peking existed. Unlike so many other great world capitals there was no harbour here, not even a river. Peking had grown up because of the protection of this Imperial Fortress and its moat, creating what China had called for nearly seven centuries its Middle Kingdom.

Now, thanks to George's magic, I would see inside.

The roof above the City entrance was made of yellow semi-circular roof tiles laid alternately up and down to create an effect like corrugated iron. But there were no armed guards on top. No armed guards anywhere in Peking.

On the left of the square as we faced the Forbidden City was another monolithic building, its size dwarfed by the vastness of the bright square. This one was built by the Communists: the Great Hall of the People where thousands of seated Communist delegates could meet in the one hall in front of Mao. The score of sombre dark round columns along the facade created large shadowed spaces, making it look totally out of place before the majesty of the royal purple and emperor gold Forbidden City.

"They have made such a sinner of the memory," George said, shaking his head.

Inside, we could see why it had taken a quarter of a million workers to build the Forbidden City. There were a series of carved white marble bridges over a narrow stream passing through a huge stone-floored courtyard which led on to another elevated yellow-roofed palace. Then, beyond that, another large open quadrangle; and then another elevated palace. Each courtyard was much bigger than a city block. All interior balconies and staircases were edged with white marble balustrades with intricately carved post tops which rose much higher than the wall lines. Marble staircases leading up to a palace were guarded by sculptured gold lion-like creatures as big as me. These were "Qi-lins", mythical animals with huge sharp claws. They were said to be good creatures, despite their ferocious appearance. To dream of one was an omen of impending success. So I got inside the small rope barrier around one and touched it for luck. George took a photo.

Near a marble wall was a steel bird even taller than George. George said it was the sculpture of a crane. Stairs led up out of the quadrangles to interior palaces with exotic names like "Hall of Supreme Harmony". In one palace, huge golden columns surrounded a wide gold throne with a carved wall behind and a foot stool at the front. Here the Emperor sat high above interior marble steps.

The thing that struck me most in this sea of carved dragons and gold chests, and what looked like blue tea pots on curved three-legged gold stands, were the four-foot tall long-necked cranes on either side of the throne carved out of jade. George said cranes equalled long life for the Chinese. This was the "Dragon Throne" where for centuries people had kowtowed to the Emperors who were each called "Son of Heaven". So the Emperor was like a God: the hereditary God, before the political God, Mao.

These were the first centuries-old objects I had seen, and now I was surrounded by them as far as the eye could see in every direction. Strangely, no one watched, or cared, as George and I wondered at the grandeur of the Emperor's chair, looking behind and underneath, and I successfully fought the urge to touch the jade birds, or the carved dragons in nearby red pillars.

"It is as if we are God's spies," said George.

"You wouldn't want to accidentally knock over one of these birds, George," I said.

The joke was too Australian and irreverent, even for the worldly George.

"How is it this lives in your mind?" he asked, disgusted.

Except for two or three Chinese families who were also sightseeing, the Forbidden City was deserted. We were such an unusual sight for these families that they stayed far away. But whenever we took photos of each other, they all stopped to watch. In Hong Kong it was said that you shouldn't take photos of Chinese because they believed you were stealing their spirit. But these Chinese families rushed to stand in the picture fifty yards behind George.

Along an exterior wall below us were small tiled-roof buildings which George said were once the rooms that held the hundreds of concubines. "The servants had to be eunuchs, because of the concubines who were enshrined behind these walls," said George. "It had to be ensured that other men did not change eyes with His Majesty's women. Wherefore it is time I should inform you, Hugo: I am come home, here, in this place. For I am a twentieth century eunuch."

"That's a pity, George," I said, "because I could have taught you to say 'I love you' in both Cantonese and Mandarin: 'Ngoi oi ne' in Cantonese, and 'War oi knee' in Mandarin."

I told him about the beautiful cheongsams the Chinese women wore in Hong Kong, and how those dresses so suited the female form.

He wanted to know about Australian girls, so I explained how Paula Stafford on the Gold Coast had invented a tiny two-piece swimming costume, and how Australian women wouldn't be seen dead going into town without their best pair of stockings, held by tiny pink suspender hooks attached to girdles around the waist, or step-ins: and how all Australian men dreamed of seeing the area of the thigh above where the stockings stopped and the pants began.

George asked what a step-in was. I also explained about a brassiere called a "Much Ado" bra that was always advertised in the *Courier-Mail*.

"What art to enchant!" he said. "China must be the only place in the world with no such goodly creatures. As far as I am aware, the women here wear no upholstery at all."

George was surprised to hear that Australian women paid to get a permanent wave in their hair; carried gold compacts with pink face powder, a powder puff and a mirror inside; and wore narrow high heels, padded bras, and bright red nail polish and lipstick.

"Oh brave new world that has such creatures in it," he lamented.

"It's as if sex doesn't exist in China," I said. "They would all make good Catholics but."

. We made our way past some old buildings behind a palace. These were once the Imperial elephant stables, used when elephants pulled the Emperor's chariot. We paused for more photos, thinking of the elephant dung, and marvelling that there were no flies in Peking, despite the heat.

"The Chicoms really have killed all the flies, George," I said. "On a day like this in Australia the flypaper hanging from the ceiling in Dad's cake shop, and the backs of our blue shirts, would be covered with flies. Flies love blue shirts."

"Not only the dogs and flies Hugo: the very rats have quit it," George said mysteriously.

I was feeling good. Not only inside Communist China, but now inside the Middle Kingdom: the middle of China. I should stay on in Peking and keep George company for his final three months, except that I couldn't live on fresh air.

Looking around the Forbidden City we suddenly realised others had arrived unseen: thousands of them in the first quadrangle, over near the bumpy-headed Qi-lins. They were all lining up in rows. One came towards us, carrying a black umbrella. Strange, on such a fine day. Surely the unmistakeable light, easy slouch of Chen, back from Canton. I could already recognise him by the blinking, and his tendency towards bloodshot eyes.

"Mr Lunn, Mr Mills," he said, breathlessly, as if he had run some distance: "You must leave. This space is required."

"It's alright Chen," I said, "George here got us special permission."

"Yes but that is from the Ministry of Culture. Everything has changed. The Public Security Office is taking over here now. You must return to your hotel. Please go now."

Chen seemed flustered, and he looked around at the long rows of people in caps now inside the huge Forbidden City quadrangle. George tugged me by the sleeve, but I knew Chen well enough to at least ask what was going on.

"Peking is putting on the biff tomorrow," Chen said, "Everything is planned. Please go."

George was mystified, but I explained that Chen meant the Reds were getting ready for some sort of punch-up the next day. We should be ready.

The woman official at our hotel who liaised with foreigners obviously had heard nothing. She was there to arrange such things as travel within China, appointments with officials, and tickets to shows. Every day she stood unsmiling all day through the afternoon and evening writing in exercise books behind her own narrow counter next to the foyer. She wore, of course, blue trousers, a white shirt, and had long plaits.

I thought she would be impressed that I wanted a ticket to see a Peking Opera but, if anything, the question bored her. She merely asked for five yuan.

I couldn't find the theatre that night, so I walked around the middle of Peking.

Nothing was going on.

Large crowds of Chinese enjoyed a stroll up the middle of the roads beneath modern neon street lighting which lit up the traffic-free streets in a yellow tinge. I felt I was on a movie set. Lucky it was so bright, because the bike riders in Peking had no lights.

Several people noticed I was lost and — seeing the ticket in my hand — they looked at it in turns to direct me through the streets to the theatre.

It looked just like an old Brisbane suburban picture theatre — the Hollywood, the Broadway, the Rialto, the Odeon, the Crystal — in a bad state of repair. Inside, it was just like a Saturday night at the Boomerang Theatre before television: all the seats were full — reserved probably years before — and there was a buzz of anticipation like distant singing in the thick murmuring air.

My status as a foreigner had not entitled me to a better seat than anyone else, and I sat off to the right-hand side about twenty rows back.

Though the crowd loved the show, it was very disappointing for me.

The actors wore no intricate painted faces representing the masks the Chinese once wore into battle; no fresh colours, or clear-cut lines of paint, or even the tiny dots that could foretell some extra aspect; no significant long moustaches or high, rich headdresses, the more elaborate the more important; no full-length coloured costumes with long sleeves to tug to show the actor's real designs, or to signal the musicians; no dignified movements to announce that here was a scholar; no characters with obvious supernatural powers; no symbolic gestures recalling a birth place, or signifying the riding of a horse.

Instead, there were just three types of cardboard cut-out characters: strong Chinese soldiers with red faces; brave peasant women; and cowardly American soldiers with white faces, touched with blue for cruelty. Only the sparse scenery, the music, the shrill vocals, the dance, the mime — the exaggerated facial expressions and eye movements — the sword-play, and the acrobatics were traditional. But the crowd loved it. As cymbals and gongs of all sizes rang out, soldiers and peasants somersaulted and leapt bravely around the stage yelling out.

Until at last, they leapt up onto a captured American tank — as flutes fluttered, and American soldiers hid. Art had now been given a political task.

The next morning, I complained to the bored woman at the counter in the hotel that I was disappointed to find such a grand tradition had been turned into pantomime. She said traditional Opera was frowned upon as "bourgeois" and had been replaced by "Revolutionary Opera" where actors performed "real scenes" in modern dress and played modern themes.

"Socialist Realism is not just for class-conscious groups addicted to comfort and respectability," she said. "Chairman Mao says art must correctly advance the revolutionary struggle by at all times upholding proletarian ideology."

Had I known traditional Opera was dead and buried in Peking I would never have given Mr Kiat my story on Peking Opera faces. The mystery now was: why had this way-out-of-date article influenced them?

George was, of course, at the snooker table in his cap, and wearing another technicolour shirt. It was my turn to break and, as I did, George said he could have told me that the Chinese, even in his magic concerts, had banned "middle characters". These were characters who were neither good nor bad: "In China everyone must be either wholly holy, or evidently evil," George said. "There is no in between."

"So even magic shows are political?" I asked.

"All art is political, Hugo," George said. "Even mine art of enchantment."

I was about to see just how right he was. The next morning I awoke to the sound of people chanting and shouting. At first I dismissed it as a propaganda broadcast. Eventually, I realised the noise was coming from the street out the front of our hotel. A column of Chinese demonstrators, about a dozen deep, was marching past chanting slogans. These were not just Young Pioneers: they were all adults, men and women.

Other Europeans from the hotel came and stood and watched on the wide steps out the front overlooking the road, waiting for the end of the procession. The demonstrators must have been going around and around our block, because they never stopped coming.

As we waited, some French businessmen and their wives who had ignored me for two days suddenly turned and chatted. They sounded like they needed some reassurance. They were beautifully dressed in shiny suits and ties and contrasted markedly with the demonstrators. They asked what I thought was going on. France had recently re-established diplomatic ties with China, and they were there hoping to open a chemical plant: so they didn't want any political trouble in China now. No coups and killings while their wives were with them anyway.

The demonstrators seemed to be shouting the same thing over and over again.

"The only thing I can tell you is that you are safe," I told the Frenchmen. "It is not a coup or anything like that: they are condemning the Americans. It was all organised in the Forbidden City yesterday afternoon. I was there."

The businessmen and their wives relaxed when they heard it was an anti-American demonstration. They nodded their heads up and down, as if in agreement with the Chinese. They were very friendly after that, not knowing that my knowledge was limited to being able to recognise "may gwar" (or Mei Guo) from hearing the propaganda broadcasts over and over again on the train.

"They are telling the Americans to get out of Vietnam," I said. And added, to show my knowledge: "Chairman Mao says disorder and chaos is a good thing."

That got them worried.

Later, when George's translator arrived, he told us the demonstrators were, in fact, calling out four things over and over again: "America get out of Vietnam", "America get out of Latin America", "America get out of the Dominican Republic", and "America get out of the world".

"Get out of the world?" a Frenchwoman asked in English.

"Yes," the translator said.

"But there is nowhere else for them to go."

The interpreter shrugged his shoulders.

It seemed to me that World War III was upon us.

I set off alone to see where the marchers were coming from. They led me back to the ubiquitous Tranquility Boulevard, which now was anything but tranquil: another diplomatic opposite. The marchers we had seen for the last two hours were not, as we thought, the same group marching around and around our block. They were a tiny loop offshoot from the main demonstration which filled the length and breath of the Boulevard for as far as the eye could see: black haired demonstrators waving red flags and a roar of voices which filled the air like a Queensland thunderstorm.

Now I knew the significance of those strange objects high up on the lamp posts along Tranquility Boulevard. They were loudspeakers. Loudspeakers from every lamp post on both sides of the road blaring away the entire length of the boulevard above at least a million marchers.

A male voice screeched over the loudspeakers in Chinese: "Americans, get out of Vietnam!" and the million demonstrators repeated the call.

A girl's voice, even more strident: "America get out of Latin America!" and the crowd reiterated the phrase, reaching a pinnacle of passion.

"America get out of the Dominican Republic," reverberated along the six kilometre length of speakers and demonstrators, and the three rows each a dozen deep across the roadway — two moving one way, and the centre one the other — replied in a crescendo of resonated emotion.

I hadn't realised anyone in China would even know, or care, about the Dominican Republic. I wasn't sure where it was myself.

Then: "America get out of the World!" shouted all three voices in a climax of fervour — "America get out of the World!" came the raucous, rumbling reply.

This time the trees swayed. The very ground shook.

I was near one end of the march, and set out towards the Forbidden City to see if I could find the other end, and see just how big the demonstration was. Thirty minutes later I was well past the Forbidden City and still couldn't see the other end. Was this the Chinese marching twenty-five abreast and passing by forever?

Gate of Heavenly Peace Square was filled with Chinese performing plays on the flat stone area. When I tired of the marchers — who kept repeating the same old things over and over, hour after hour — I went into the Square and watched some of the scores of separate plays, each involving at least thirty actors and actresses, and each watched by an admiring crowd.

Without exception, these plays were about well-armed cowardly American soldiers being defeated by people with spears and sticks and, occasionally, modern weapons. George was right: only good and bad could survive in Communist China.

Here the actors playing American soldiers wore sharp cardboard noses as well as white face paint, plus strange little conical party hats. President Johnson was portrayed in many of the plays, mostly in a three-foot-high top hat painted with dollar signs, or the American stars and stripes, and always with a long crooked nose. He invariably carried a telescope and stayed well away from the action, while watching his troops getting killed and captured.

Many plays were based on a nuclear bomb theme. In one, American soldiers threatened advancing peasants with a black cardboard nuclear bomb. But the peasants steadfastly advanced, confident in the knowledge that, as the white-on-red cloth banners above said, they were dealing with "the American imperialist war-mongering paper tiger".

"Down with the imperialists armed invasion of Dominica," said one sign. "To the brave Dominican People — salute!" said another.

In some plays the Americans tried to hide the cardboard bomb in one of their khaki tunics, but always the vigilant people saw this and attacked: the women in European peasant dresses, colourful scarves, and black sandshoes, stomping forward and poking spears at the terrified and retreating Americans. Significantly, no cardboard H-bomb was ever thrown by the American troops, or their President.

I wished I had brought my camera along, but it was forbidden to take exposed film out of China — and I was certain that the Red Chinese wouldn't process such film and then post it on to me in London.

The marching and the plays and the shouting continued until after dark, and it was only back at the hotel that evening that I started to regret not daring to run back to the hotel and get my camera.

Up at the snooker table, I hoped George would say I did the right thing, but he seemed surprised.

"I must uneasy make you, Hugo," he said. "But how came you here? Canst thou remember?"

Yes, I could remember. I was here because I was a journalist looking for a good story and a job overseas. Then along comes the biggest story of all time and I didn't take any pictures.

How I wished I could have the time over again.

George wanted to play snooker all evening, but — because it was my last night in Peking — I wanted to see a Russian film which the Chicoms were showing for the twentieth anniversary of the defeat of Germany in World War II. The Chinese were busy claiming that the victory over what they called "German Fascism" was won by "the Socialist world". There was no mention of Australians, New Zealanders, or Americans, or British. The government announcement said merely: "The film tells how the Socialist Leninist State defeated the German Imperialists. Down with Western Imperialism."

The house was packed. The first thing I wrote in my notebook was: "the screen would fit into a small corner of a Cinemascope production".

It was a very realistic black-and-white war film in which the Russians defeated the Germans in a decisive World War II battle, but only because the badly wounded Soviet hero at the very end crawls agonisingly slowly, slowly, slowly, slowly — under withering machine-gun fire — through the mud to reach the broken wire which has stopped the Russians from blowing up the strategic bridge loaded with Germans. When he finally reaches the wire, which is right next to the tons of explosives, he is too badly wounded in both arms to thread the wires back together.

What to do? Being a solid Marxist-Leninist-Socialist-Commo he grabs each end of the severed wire with his teeth

251

and munches them together. The charge gets through, and blows the Germans, and their entire war to smithereens. Along with the hero. At least for once the Americans hadn't won the war by themselves.

After breakfast with George the next morning I said goodbye.

"Could I carry your princely trunk for you, Hugo?"

George didn't realise that, unlike him, I had no trunk. Now, with the animal skin, I had eight parcels to carry and watch.

As I packed my things, I could hear the demonstrators back again chanting in the street and calling out the same slogans over and over. Why didn't they get some new ones?

There wasn't time to go back to Tranquility Boulevard and Heavenly Peace Square and take photos — and also catch the train. Once again I stood on the front steps of the hotel watching. A middle-aged Welsh woman who had been in China three weeks said she was disgusted with what was going on. "This is a city of war," she insisted. "I visited a school yesterday and one of the games the innocent young children played was shooting pop guns at the image of an American soldier."

The three French businessmen and their wives returned again to the front steps and, gravely, they said how frightening the demonstrations were. They said they were thinking of getting out.

"Things are looking bad for the whole world," one said. "We have been told this is because Mao Tse-tung himself has made a major statement condemning United States aggression in the Dominican Republic. No one knows where it will lead"

That was it. I decided to miss the train.

Grabbing my Asahi Pentax camera and the 200mm lens I had bought to take photos of Fletch at Wimbledon, I headed off. Leaving my many pieces of baggage, and the skin still wrapped in brown paper, in the hotel foyer.

All day I expected to be stopped. When nothing happened I became more and more confident and, in the end, I sat on my haunches in among the actors in Gate of Heavenly Peace Square, taking pictures of the terrified American soldiers falling backwards and the brave young peasant women advancing. And of the waving placards and silk signs. Rather than thinking I was taking their spirit away, the Chinese were oblivious to my presence, even while tripping over me with their spears. As far as I could see I was the only non-Chinese in the square.

After dark I returned to the hotel brimming over with excitement at my story and pictures. Feeling like I had just hit another ten, I told the French about the events of the day, and, when George and Siddiq arrived I repeated the tale for them all. Just then the woman official at her counter next to the foyer called me over. She closed her exercise books. She didn't seem bored any longer.

"Mr Lunn, you did not catch the train to the Soviets today?"

"No. I decided to stay on and get the next train, on Wednesday," I said, still smiling victoriously.

"But, Mr Lunn, your visa expired today," she said.

"Yes," I said. "Please get me another one."

I turned around to acknowledge my friends again, and they were gaping at me. George took off his cap and adjusted his bright yellow shirtsleeves nervously. The French people were nowhere to be seen. Siddiq shook his head slowly from side to side. Even his moustache frowned.

"It's only a piece of paper from the Ministry of Security. It's only a red chop," I said.

As the Chinese woman picked up the heavy black telephone on her desk, George pulled me aside with Siddiq: "You are time's fool, Hugo," he said, squeezing my arm too hard. "A sweet and bitter fool. This be an error whose worth's unknown."

Siddiq said I would certainly be arrested.

"You are a strange fellow," George said.

I could explain. After all, I had stayed only to watch their demonstrations.

"Only a magician should tease the Red Chinese," George said.

Siddiq asked for phone numbers of any high-ranking officials I knew in Hong Kong and Australia. He would contact them when he got home if anything happened. I was getting pretty worried, and looked up at George for an answer. "Even I cannot make you disappear here," he said. "I would offer sanctuary in my room, Hugo, but then we would be stuck like birds singing in a cage. Visas are for brief hours and weeks."

I retired exhausted to my room which was still vacant. First I had to hide the five precious rolls of colour slide film I had taken in China. Whatever happened, the films would have to be smuggled out. This was the quickest and surest method. Since you were allowed to take only unused film out of China, I put four of the five used film rolls back inside their yellow Kodak cardboard boxes, and stuck the ends back together with glue I borrowed from George: all magicians carried glue, he said. When I finished, the boxes looked as if they had never been opened. Then I hid one roll — my personal photos in Canton and in the Forbidden City with George — inside the secret slit in my black moneybelt. After dinner I declined a game of snooker with George and Siddiq and went to bed. I was still confident the Reds would extend my visa, so much so that I pondered what I might do for the three days until the next train left. Perhaps a walk along the Great Wall of China? I could catch up with Ken later on, after Paris.

Before dawn the next morning there was loud thumping on my door. Three male Chinese officials filled the doorway. One of them said to get my things, I was leaving for Moscow — by plane.

They took me in silence through the deserted pre-dawn streets in a black limousine. There were no street lights on the long journey. At the crowded aerodrome they returned my red Paterson and Lawson poetry books, and made a straight-out swap of my rail ticket for an air ticket on a Russian Aeroflot jet that was leaving in ten minutes for Irkutzk, Omsk, and then Moscow.

21 The Party Line — Moscow Style

The interior of the Russian Aeroflot plane was like a train carriage. String luggage racks overhead, magazines and newspapers stuck up on the front walls, no limit to hand luggage. I worried that the jet might be overloaded. The central passageway was so filled with hand baggage that it looked like an airport luggage trolley.

Once again the Communists gave themselves away by separating the first class section up front, though it was empty. The rest of us were crammed in tight for the 4,000 mile, twelve-hour journey.

There wasn't a cloud in the clear pre-breakfast sky as we streaked high above Mongolia over red wasteland. In an hour I saw yesterday's train, the one I should have been on, below us in the desert. At this rate I would make up lost time and still meet Fletch in Paris.

It was just after lunch when we finally landed in Moscow. Even though it was spring in Europe, and the middle of the day, the temperature was 10 degrees Centigrade (50 degrees Fahrenheit to Australians), which meant it was as cold as a winter's night in Brisbane. The airport was unbelievably far out of town and it took more than an hour to reach the hotel.

All the way into town the Moscow horizon was lined with building cranes: something you very rarely saw in Australia. Here they even used cranes for three-storey building jobs. Scores of tall buildings were going up in Moscow, all at the one time. It was the sort of frantic economic activity I hadn't expected.

The hotel was called the Ukraine: but the stupid bus driver deposited me outside a cathedral. Or, at least, I thought it was a cathedral. But, having mounted the numerous stone stairs at the front, I found it was indeed an old hotel. A hotel that looked like a church — pointed spires and all.

The hotel was packed out with Westerners. They lined up three-deep at the reception counter to see one of several middle-aged Russian women who all towered over them because the floor behind the counter was raised. In fact, all the staff in the hotel were women. Probably the Russians trusted them more to deal with outsiders. If so, the Commos didn't trust young women. There were no women anywhere near as young as me.

I had expected Russian women to be dowdy and not fashion-conscious, just like their Communist colleagues in China. But the women in this Moscow hotel could have been working at David Jones in Sydney. All were in modern frocks, had permanent waves, perfume, and lipstick. Some even wore that most Capitalist of decorations, nail polish. They must have been well off because they wore lots of gold and silver jewellery and bright leather shoes.

Maybe the Communist world wasn't as backward as we were led to believe at home?

After filling in a form and finally getting to the front of the queue, I was offered a room — at US$60 dollars a night! That was six times what I paid in Peking, and more than three times what the Grand Hotel charged for its best room in Hong Kong. European businessmen watched as I argued that no one in Australia would ever charge that much for a hotel room.

At that rate, I said, I'd be broke well before I made Paris.

Suddenly it began to dawn on me that this was a classy hotel. I could see the restaurant from the reception counter as I argued: its polished wood and brass, the silver meat trays, the crystal glasses, and waiters in formal outfits.

I looked around for support. Every man in the queue looked at his shoes.

A middle-aged blonde Russian woman was called from another desk and appeared on my side of the counter. She looked me up and down, her eyes stopping at my animal skin, my typewriter, my moneybelt, my camera, my unshaven face, and the sagging, crumpled artificial sheep-skin jacket. Sure it looked cheap, but it was between me and the Moscow weather which, I knew from studying history, had defeated Napoleon.

"Are you a businessman?" she asked in a heavy accent just like the Russkys in the James Bond flicks. "Who do you represent?"

I was getting sick of people asking me who I represented. Ever since I'd left Australia it had been the same question over and over. For the first time I understood why Fred hated being asked: "What are ya?" He said that every time he ever filled in a form in Australia it said: "What are ya?" That was why he refused to nominate his religion on forms.

"No I'm not a businessman," I said, even though I felt that was pretty obvious.

"That is a sadness for you," she said. "Our *Intourist* organisation has a special offer for Western businessmen. It is a rate of 20 dollars a night, including two meals in the deluxe restaurant per day."

Since I was dealing with Communists, I thought I should stick with the truth.

"I'm a journalist. A freelance journalist, working for myself, and writing a series called *Through two curtains and a Wall.*"

The woman's face did not change, so I had no inkling of what was to come.

"*Da*," she said. "*Da.* Journalists are businessmen. You are a businessman."

Which wasn't what we had been taught in Journalism I and II at university.

"You shall have the businessman stay."

I was shown through some cavernous hallways on the third floor to a giant room covered in worn brown linoleum. The room made the double bed in the centre seem like a single. There were several nooks, each with a window and no curtains: but there was no building high enough outside to see in. And, anyway, the windows were at an angle to the room. A couple of locked heavy doors with large keyholes connected with other rooms.

The white tiled bathroom was almost as big as the bedroom, but there was no shower: just a stained bath on legs which was about two feet deep at the plug end. Plus several more curtainless angled windows. In Australia they would have made this room into four, and in Hong Kong it would have become eight. No wonder Russian hotel rooms were so expensive.

It seemed to me the perfect room to spy on a guest and, for the first time, I could see why the Australian Tennis Team was warned to watch what they said and did in their hotel rooms in Moscow. Even though the foyer and restaurant were so crowded, up on this floor the place was positively deserted. I walked around the wide, shadowy, labyrinthine central hallways and didn't see anyone. Not even a maid.

As I returned to my room I realised I was probably in the same hotel where Fletch, after losing to a Russian in the Moscow final, abused the Communist authorities who he believed were bugging him. The Australian team manager, Brisbane fruit and vegetable dealer and tennis writer Alf Chave, told me he had stood in just such a dim vast hallway watching Fletch in his room abusing the stone walls and the light fittings.

"Fletch didn't like the fact that the Russian was given flowers for beating him. So he was calling the Russians dingoes, and Red dopes, and drips, and 'packs of Commie mongrels'," Mr Chave said. "I don't think they would have understood a word he said." Mr Chave said he had entertained tennis officials around the world with this Moscow story, and nobody had enjoyed it more than the Poms at

Wimbledon: "They loved to think the Commies copped it from an Aussie tennis player as well."

As I set off through the wide streets, with no tail that I could see, I considered what Fletch said in Hong Kong before he left for Egypt in March: "Hughie, don't go. Russia's like one big second-hand market. No gaiety. No brightness. The churches are all museums. All of us Catholics in the Aussie Tennis Team — Margaret Smith, Madonna Schacht, and me, and even one or two non-Catholics — had to attend Mass in Moscow in a tiny apartment instead of a proper church."

Ken, as usual, was right. Moscow outside the tourist hotel was very drab. It was like watching an old black and white film. No colour at all. Everyone was dressed in black or grey overcoats and black or charcoal grey fur hats. The few shops had nothing worth buying: with goods mixed up on shelves like the jumble sale at a convent fete. I was amused by the out-of-date shapes of the black Communist cars.

Eventually, I came to a six-lane wide highway through Moscow. As I waited for a chance to cross the busy road there seemed something different about the traffic. Then I realised: the great majority of the traffic was trucks, not cars. And most of the trucks were military vehicles. There was also an absence of young men. The Russians seemed more ready for war than for living.

It was strange, too, to see women driving the trolley-buses, and the trams, and even the lifts: that job fell to limbless ex-servicemen in Australia. Most amazing of all, women worked on the building sites, carting bricks and mixing cement in their overcoats. Unlike the women in the hotel, those outside were poorly dressed. Their shoes were shapeless and worn, their overcoats old. They hardly looked like women at all. There were no high-heels, no lipstick, no coloured hats, no stockings. I decided the *Intourist* women at the hotel were allowed to dress up for propaganda purposes only.

Around a corner was a crowd of such women furtively jostling each other. They were trying to get to a young woman in the centre of the crowd who was selling imitation pearl buttons from a small tray slung around her neck, like a half-time orange juice seller at the pictures. The pearl buttons were attached four-at-a-time to playing card-sized bits of cardboard, and the Russian women were competing ferociously to buy them.

Such buttons would have cost practically nothing in Australia, and even less in Hong Kong. But here the cards of four were selling for ten bob each. The whole deal must have been illegal, because the cards of buttons were sold in minutes and the young woman hurried off with the empty tray under her arm and the money in her pocket.

That night I made contact with the London reporter recommended to me by the au pair on the Peking train. I expected he might give me the bum's rush, but instead he called by the hotel to pick me up for a journos party — even though he represented what he said was one of the biggest Fleet Street daily papers. When we jumped in a cab, the driver started shouting in Russian and holding up his fist. Most of his teeth were missing. The foreign correspondent said the driver thought we were Americans, and was boasting that the Viet Cong had just blown up some imperialist US planes in Saigon.

"It's no use trying to tell him any different," said the immaculately dressed foreign correspondent who ignored the driver and smiled back.

So cool.

The journos party was held in the smallest flat I had seen yet. Even by Hong Kong standards. The kitchen was so small only four people could stand up inside at once.

Diplomats and foreign correspondents from a dozen countries stood around with a drink in one hand and a cigarette in the other, talking. I was the only Australian, and the only outsider. When I was introduced, people seemed surprised to find an Aussie at one of these parties and wanted to know why I had come all this way from "Down Under".

They said Australia relied on English and American journalists for its news.

"You just never see Aussie journalists. Is there something going on we don't know about," asked a Yank reporter, suspiciously.

I was merely passing through Moscow on my way from Canton and Peking to Paris.

"Peking!" shouted the American, causing everyone to move slightly so that they could turn in my direction without bumping the people around them. From then on, the Americans in particular kept asking difficult questions, but always as if the answer didn't really matter:

"What's the Red Chinese attitude re Moscow's claims to Mongolia?"

"The Chinese Communists yesterday exploded their second atomic bomb, any idea how many mega-tons it was?"

"Is Red China secretly massing troops to send over the border into Vietnam like they did in Korea?"

"Is Australia worried that Russia has warned the Aussies to stay out of military conflicts in the Far East, and has pledged support for Indonesian efforts to crush Malaysia?"

I told them all I could. That the Russians in Peking were worried about China's attitude to Mongolia, and that the Chicoms saw the Domino Theory in reverse. They found that interesting. And I said honestly that I didn't think Australians were concerned about the Russians — only about the Indonesians.

When I told my Peking story about the "America get out of the world" demonstrations by a million Chinese, one of the Americans whistled. They wanted to know all about the demonstration and exactly what the loudspeakers called out. To prove what I was saying was true, I told how I successfully smuggled out the photos. An American diplomat wanted to buy them. But I said I was selling them to *Life*

Magazine when I got to London and had them developed. Or the London *Sunday Times* colour magazine.

When I said the Red Chinese were more upset about American intervention in the Dominican Republic than anything else, a US diplomat said: "Say Aussie, what are you really doing in this part of the world? We only sent our airborne to Dominica to protect our civilians and US property. Goddamn it, don't tell me the Chicoms don't know that?"

Another said: "I can understand them being upset about Vietnam and Korea, but what in tarnation have they got to do with the Caribbean? I smell Castro."

I knew these political types would be very interested in the anti-American demonstrations in Peking, but I didn't think they would get quite so excited when I mentioned Red Chinese interest in magic ahead of space travel, and George.

"So this black man is in Peking posing as a magician? Did you hear that? There's a black man spying in Peking, a friend of Hughie's here, who's posing as a magician and teaching the Chicoms how to make people disappear. I'll bet he's pulling more than a few rabbits out of his hat."

My major inquisitor pretended he wouldn't believe me that George wasn't a spy.

"I must say that we've used military attaches, missionaries, and journalists like yourselves as spies: even used Australians. But a black magician in an Hawaiian shirt is the worst cover story for a spy I've ever heard of," a British diplomat said. "What other strange contacts did you make during your sojourn in China?"

"Well there was a Pakistani snooker player called Siddiq …" But this just made everyone laugh.

"A Pakistani in a Snooker Hall in Peking? Wow," said the diplomat, "wait till the White House hears about this."

It was very much like the journo parties at Peter Thompson's house in Brisbane where everyone stood around all night drinking and laughing and boasting and smoking and arguing, with the occasional raised voice or threat. It was what the Americans aptly called "shootin' the shit".

Such parties were obviously the place to get information. I was acutely aware that Steve Dunleavy always reckoned that the best place to get stories was to listen to other journalists. "Most of the time they know good stories, but they won't write them," he told me one night late in the Firecracker Bar. "So you write the stories for them."

Steve was right. Not only had I found out about China's second atomic bomb explosion here, but I learned that the Russians had just put the first rocket on the moon. Which had thoroughly depressed the Americans. The foreign correspondents said they were all worn out because they had been following this moon story non-stop for the past 48-hours.

"Hitting the moon with a rocket puts the Russians well and truly ahead in the space race," said my English correspondent friend. "Particularly coming a couple of months after one of their astronauts walked into outer space 300 miles above earth."

"No it doesn't," argued an American correspondent, "the Russians tried for a 'soft' landing for their moon shot, and it crashed: Blam! There's a big difference between landing on the moon and hitting it! We'll still beat them to the moon. You can't land men on the moon at 500 miles an hour."

"The Russians can, if it means being first," said my English friend coolly.

At the party was an American woman architect who argued that Bangkok had the most beautiful and unusual architecture she had seen. What she said caught my ear: "Many of the old, unpainted wooden houses are expecially beautiful to the trained eye, but I doubt that the younger generation of architects in Bangkok would agree."

She said the large urban areas of the world — even Moscow — were beginning to resemble each other.

"Modern buildings may be bigger, more impressive, and more expensive, but less beautiful; and express virtually nothing of the city in which they are placed."

I told them about Brisbane, because it too was a city of wooden homes, often unpainted for decades. The architect was amazed to hear there was a whole city of wooden houses, their corrugated iron-roofs painted rust-proof red, and with sculptured verandahs and lattice and all sitting on wood stumps up to 20 feet high. To my surprise, she was even more interested in this than the others were in the Peking demonstrations. She thought Bangkok was the only city with such houses.

"Hold on to it," she said reverently. "Hold on to it whatever you do. One day you will have one of the world's only pockets of individuality. Your home town will be a shining light in an identical dull world."

No one had ever before said that Brisbane was worthwhile. It seemed I had travelled to the other end of the earth to discover that what I left behind was of greatest value. That the outside world appreciated what to me had always been ordinary.

22   From Russia with Luck

As a former tap-dancer, I decided to see the Bolshoi Ballet, since it was the one non-military thing everyone in Australia knew about Russia. But the woman at *Intourist* laughed when I asked to buy a ticket, and said the Bolshoi was always booked out for more than a year in advance. This made me keener than ever.

Wandering around town in my artificial sheep-skin, I found the Kremlin which was not just a building but another walled fortress. I had a look through an exquisite Russian church next door, surprised that the Communists kept a church open. But it seemed to be just for tourists. Then I set off across Red Square to find the Bolshoi Theatre: just in case they sold the odd left-over ticket at the door. I knew from days on the stage as a child tap-dancer that a single person could always get a seat in a theatre.

The Bolshoi Theatre was in the middle of a square by itself, there was no one around. Not even a ticket seller. All was locked and barred. No rehearsals.

While I looked around the deserted exterior of the theatre in bleak weather, three young men, all my own age, eyed me up and down. One said a cheerful "hello" in English. They were Russian students and they thought I was American. These three didn't know much about Australia, so I explained that we were pro-American and anti-Communist. To my surprise their ring leader, who wore a small-brimmed Frank Sinatra hat and a well-cut, dark blue, knee-length coat, said: "It is good."

None of these youths liked living beneath Communism's oppressive yoke, so they invited me to walk with them.

The student who couldn't speak English seemed out of place with the other two who were handsome, well-dressed and cheerful. Whereas he was none of those things. He smoked, was surly, and seemed only to know one English phrase: "You give me ..." He wanted me to give him clothes, give him US dollars, give him jewellery: even though the others kept telling him to shut up.

The ring leader said, as we strolled unnoticed through Moscow, that he was of Italian descent.

"Very unlucky me. Grandpapa left Italy in 1916 and could have went anywhere — Spain, England, America. But he chose for Russia. He wanted the Tsar. Then came the Revolution and I am trapped here forever more."

I said he looked like he was doing alright: I had noticed his thick wad of roubles.

"My parents are rich, but there is nothing to buy with money," he said.

The other well-dressed student opened his classy rain-coat and exhibited a shapeless non-wool suit underneath, which had cost 150 roubles, about 75 quid. I told them that was four times what I paid for an Anthony Squires pure wool suit at home, and seven times what a tailor-made suit cost in Hong Kong. That was why they tried to buy clothing from tourists.

"We try to buy from Americans because they have fine clothing," the ring leader Sergei said, showing me his classy black leather shoes and his watch which also cost 150 roubles.

"We want to dress like American tourists," said the other English speaker.

Fletch had told me that when he was in Moscow the local tennis players bought the sweat-soaked Fred Perry cotton tennis shirts right off his back in the dressing room. They even bought his used jock strap as soon as he took it off.

To my surprise, Sergei was able to offer a much better exchange rate than the official eight roubles for ten US dollars. He offered me thirty. This was a real boost for my budget to Paris. When I accepted, the surly one ushered me around a corner and down a laneway before we exchanged dollars for roubles. Now I could buy one of those Russian fur hats, which were very expensive.

The students walked back with me to the Hotel Ukraine, teaching me to call it "Gostinitsa Unkraina". I invited them up to my room, since they had never seen inside the hotel and were anxious to see my clothes. They were afraid to walk in together, so I took them in one at a time. Each time I had to carry the Sinatra hat back outside, and then walk in with the next student wearing it on his head — like a ticket to a show.

I showed them the imitation-gold cuff links shaped with the Chinese sign for good luck, and some with my initials, as examples of what cheap goodies were available in the non-Communist world. Sergei wanted to buy both my suits — even though they didn't fit. They wanted "anything woollen and anything that gleams". He paid two pounds ten for the gold initial cufflinks, which cost four and six in Hong Kong. For similiar cuff-links engraved with a kangaroo I got three pounds. But I wouldn't sell any clothes. I needed them.

As we bartered, I told them about my strawberry pink Sunbeam Alpine sports car back in Australia and how, with its hood down, the wind sailed over the windscreen as you zoomed along. And how my Russian mate, Dimitri, had a giant green American car with foot-high fins at the back. It left any other car standing in its rubber-smoked wake.

"Lots of Australians our age own cars," I said.

"We want to own these cars," said the ex-Italian. "But we cannot."

Fearing he might say something he would regret, I cupped one ear to the walls and Sergei shut up.

When they were about to leave, I noticed my crocodile skin belt was missing. Suspicious, I pulled up the jumper of the insolent one and found he was wearing not only my crocodile skin belt, but my dark green wool jumper as well.

I was mystified as to how he got them on, but made him take them off. Then Sergei got him to hand back my happiness cuff-links as well saying, with a shrug: "Here is Russia."

To rekindle our friendship, Sergei said I was his "tovarish", his comrade. He would take me on the underground train the next day to meet his girlfriend. But he said we should seek not to attract too much attention.

"This is why we try for to dress like tourists," he said. "So the authorities leave us alone." He suggested I leave my imitation sheep-skin jacket behind.

True to his word, Sergei and the others returned next morning. I expected it to be even more cold and dismal under the ground in Moscow but, instead, the stations were warm and bright and clean. No rubbish, or even rubbish bins, as far as I could see. Gold busts of great Communist leaders were indented in the gleaming white tile walls at eye level.

Sergei's girlfriend was a surprise. An eight stone Ukrainian blonde with eyes like green marbles, dark eyebrows and a pouting mouth. She didn't speak English.

"You might have to live under Communism, Sergei, but you are lucky to have such a beautiful girlfriend," I said.

"All these girls are mine," he said. "The Russians want big ones. But still I would leave."

"That's easy to say, Sergei," I said. "But once you left Moscow you would find you wished you were back with her." I told him about Jeanette back in Hong Kong, and how I already missed her.

Sergei suggested we have lunch and a cup of coffee, which surprised me. I said I thought Communists hated coffee-shop dwellers. But Sergei said that was a specialty of the Chinese Communists. On the way, we stopped at a special store where only foreigners could buy Russian Vodka, and at much cheaper prices than locals. I bought a one litre bottle for one US dollar, whereas just half a litre would have cost Sergei six roubles, or more than seven US dollars. For some reason, Sergei and his mate waited 50 yards away while only the angry student accompanied me into the shop.

The coffee shop was crowded. Large round heavy white cups and saucers covered every surface, mostly unwashed. These cups were badly chipped and cracked, and the table-cloths were stained with coffee. But it didn't matter. It was warm, and that was the main thing in Moscow.

We weren't served coffee. The boys were only after the opaque brittle coffee cups which they surreptitiously half filled with vodka from the bottle underneath the table.

Being a friend of Jim's, I had occasionally had a drink of straight vodka while still at school. I told them how I went on to skol vodka at journo parties in Brisbane, until the day a bookcase leapt up and just missed my face. My new friends were impressed that I could skol vodka straight, and, just to prove it, I downed the contents of my cup. They did the same. As we drank, I told them about the great life we led in Australia and how the only way they were ever going to get sports cars, cheap clothes, and gold cuff-links, was to get themselves a new government.

A non-Communist government.

The other English-speaking student pointed at Sergei and said: "He needed a Second Revolution."

Revolutions were something I knew a lot about, I told them. My speciality in all history exams was the causes and results of the French Revolution and Napoleon's "whiff of grapeshot". Hadn't I just come out of Red China which was now ruled by the victors of the 1949 Revolution? I told them of the failure of the miners at the Eureka Stockade in Australia. "To have a successful Second Revolution you need the army, not miners or students," I said, enjoying the warm glow of vodka. "The army should be your top priority."

Then, banging the coffee table for emphasis, I reiterated: "Without the army on side there will be no Second Revolution in Russia."

As Sergei's beautiful girlfriend left, I told them Chairman Mao got out of the caves and into government in China only because of his stated tenet: "All power grows out of the barrel of a gun."

I finished off the bottle.

The three Russians seemed transfixed by my knowledge of the world. So much so that they wanted to show me what they were up against — Secret Police Headquarters.

As in China, there were noticeboards in central Moscow for those who did not buy newspapers and, on our way, we passed one. I couldn't believe it: the Russians too had a kangaroo in the cartoon. This time it was hopping off to Vietnam carrying, for some reason I didn't understand, a briefcase marked "SEATO". Once again the kangaroo's pouch was packed with apprehensive Aussie soldiers. They must have copied it off the Chinese paper, I told Sergei and, being Australian, I began to hop down the street like a kangaroo — and so did all my tovarish-es.

We hopped to opposite a four-storey white building on a corner and Sergei said, holding out the palm of his right hand: "Here. What stops us: *Secret Police Headquarters*."

We were standing on the footpath across the street, and I was telling each of them that they needed a second identity, when two large men in heavy wool overcoats came walking purposefully towards us. Both had grey hair.

They obviously weren't interested in my three comrades, who were posing as tourists.

As soon as the two men spoke I knew they were English. They had the look of frustration borne by angry headmasters, and both seemed to speak at once, as far as I could tell. "Listen here," they said, "you're acting like a damn fool. There is an English school teacher, Gerald Brooke, in jail here right now for doing exactly what you're doing. They've locked him up for four years, and there's not a thing our government can do about it. Our advice to you is pipe down son. Pipe down."

They turned and left. That was what impressed me most. They didn't go on lecturing. They left because they didn't really care what happened to me. I sobered up immediately. I told my comrades I was late for an appointment in Paris.

The Second Revolution would have to start without me.

Early next morning I caught a second-class train bound for the Democratic Republic of East Germany, which seemed a misnomer if ever there was one. We travelled all day and into the night until after one o'clock the next morning when the train stopped at a railway station near the Polish border. Russian officials and armed soldiers boarded the train to check passports. I couldn't wait for them to move on so that I could sleep. But they ordered me off the train. None of them could speak English. The official just kept saying: "Not good. Not good".

A soldier marched me to a railway waiting lounge full of long smooth dark timber forms, like church pews with no backs. There were no other passengers, just a few tired Russian soldiers. My train left and, after an hour or so, I couldn't sit up on the backless pew anymore. So I stretched out for a sleep. I tried to work out what might have gone wrong. Nothing could be up with my visa, or I wouldn't have got in at Irkutsk. Did the Russkys know I had smuggled film out of China? Had my comrades been arrested and told on me? Did the Russians know I was leaving with more money than I came in with: all because I hadn't had time to buy a fur hat? Had Australia done something to upset the Russians in Vietnam? Or Indonesia?

A woman walked into the waiting room and shouted at the soldiers. They came over and lifted me up off the form by an elbow. When she left, I went to lie down again, but the soldiers stopped me saying *nyet, nyet*.

Not being allowed to sleep was torture, but the soldiers seemed friendly enough.

Soon after dawn a woman interpreter arrived and said "hello" without an accent. She was just a couple of years older than me, about 25, good looking and much better dressed than any woman I had seen outside the Hotel Ukraine: in a trim two-piece dress.

"What's going on?" I asked her.

"It is alright. Everything is in order," she said, motioning for me to pick up my typewriter, camera, lens, port, animal skin, National tape-recorder, and two bags of odds and ends.

She walked in front — a pleasant sight — for a long way down the platform in weak sun to the front of a train. Told me to climb on board, and then, as the train dragged off, passed up my passport with a smile.

"You are a very lucky man," she said.

I had no way of knowing why.

Presently we arrived at the border fence with Poland and the train stopped again, this time in an area surrounded by a high wire fence. Russian guards searched every compartment with torches and guns. I thought there would be freedom of movement within Communist Eastern Europe because there was no escaping to the West from Poland or East Germany either. But clearly there wasn't.

Were they scared of each other as well as the West?

The train pulled ever so slowly through a sub-machine gun guard of honour to a similar enclosure on the Polish side, where the train was again inspected by armed guards. Passports were again checked, and we set out for nearby Warsaw which I reckoned was more than 700 miles from Moscow. There was no canteen car on the train and, by the time we got to Warsaw, I was hungry — yet there were still nearly 400 miles to go to East Berlin.

Europe was much bigger than I thought.

Everyone else on the train, including the old lady in a scarf opposite, had brought food with them. I tried to concentrate on looking out the window. All of the countryside was cultivated, but there were no tractors. Farmers here still used horses and carts, and some of their carts still had solid wood wheels. It seemed as backward in this part of Europe as in China.

The old lady shared a few biscuits, but she couldn't speak English. She tried to communicate by pointing and using words like "kaput" as she read my left palm and, like Jeanette, traced with her forefinger the island in the middle of my lifeline. I couldn't understand what she was saying about it, but it was along Jeanette's lines. Something about me, and a relative of hers who was killed during World War II.

The train stopped for a couple of minutes at the major Polish town of Poznan. By now I was so hungry I could, as Olive used to say, eat a horse and chase the rider. On the platform a black moustached fat man stood behind a high wooden trolley loaded down with ugly fat sausages hanging on hooks all over the front. I was reluctant to leave the train, because I had no idea how long it would stay. But in desperation I dashed out, ran along the platform, and ordered a sausage.

When I went to pay with a handful of Russian roubles, the cart owner pulled the sausage savagely back so it was almost behind his back. He shook his head violently from side to side, and held out the palm of the other hand as if to push me away.

I was desperate for the huge sausage. Luckily I had some US dollars in another pocket. Even though the Chinese weren't supposed to be able to get US currency, I had no trouble changing all my Yuan back into dollars at Peking airport. Though the US notes were all old and crumpled. I pulled out the dollars and the moustached man almost leapt over his trolley at the sight of the almighty greenback. Faced with his greed for the Yankee dollar, I pulled it back behind my back, imitating him, and held the other hand out as if to push him away. Then I turned and ran back to the hissing train glowing with victory. I spent the next few hours wishing I'd bought the sausage.

Late that evening we reached East Berlin where a vastly over-weight officer in an ankle-length military overcoat and absurdly-peaked cap shouted English at the top of his voice.

He said there was no room in any hotel in the city. He seemed genuinely sorry for me. A German man spoke up saying, apparently, that I could share the room he had arranged in a private home. It was off Karl Marx Alley.

East Berlin looked like ruins. Street after street of half-bombed buildings, jagged broken brick walls, piles of rubble. The facade of every building in town was pitted with shrapnel and bullet strikes like a severe case of eczema.

We walked down Karl Marx Alley, me loaded down with luggage in the freezing cold, and turned into the entrance of what looked like a bombed-out and deserted six-storey derelict building. Naturally, there was no such thing as a light switch, so we made our way up an internal staircase which was now on the outside of what remained of the brick building. There was no rail to hold on to in the dark. I wondered whether or not to keep going, but there was nowhere else. I was aware that not only had lots of people been shot trying to escape from East Berlin to the West, but that Berlin was said to be full of "blackmarketeers, smugglers, and spies".

On the second floor, a door suddenly opened and light and family warmth spilled out, just as it used to at home when a couple of blow-ins arrived. It was the home of a middle-aged German lady who rented out a room to travellers. She was thrilled to have an "Americana" staying at her home. She quickly served me thick, hot potato soup and — using sign language and some words — said that when my fellow Americana, President Kennedy, was assassinated 18 months before, she and all her friends had cried and cried and cried.

I decided to remain an American for the night.

In the bedroom, five other men — including my German friend — got ready to sleep, each as if he were the only person in the room. Small individual beds, almost touching each other, covered the floor: each with a thick eiderdown inside an immaculate white sheet. I wore my moneybelt to bed, and had my warmest and best sleep since the Lantau Island Buddhist monastery.

The next day I saw that the city of East Berlin was not a complete wreck. There were trams here too, and a few small clapped-out cars. A couple of blocks in the centre of East Berlin had been completely re-built into an ultra-modern showpiece with skyscrapers, restaurants, nightclubs and shops. But the rest of the city had been left untouched. The Democratic Republic of East Germany looked a much poorer place than Russia.

That afternoon I returned to the station to go to Checkpoint Charlie and get a bus through the infamous Berlin Wall — the last barrier on my "two curtains and a wall" pilgrimage. But, instead, I was put on another train. After two stops towards West Berlin my papers were again checked by armed guards, and again I was ordered off.

Sitting on my luggage I surveyed the scene and started to feel I was actually in a James Bond film. To the left, standing above the tracks on a steel 20-foot high bridge, were three uniformed East German guards in knee-high leather boots, grey-green uniforms, and sub-machine guns held triumphantly across chests. Below on the bridge's clanging steel steps, in front of a railway tunnel, were two more. They all looked at me, because I was the only person there. And I looked at them, because the only way out was past them.

Half an hour later another train arrived. It stopped just before the bridge of guards.

This empty train too was searched. Using alsatians. Papers were again checked as I got on board. We passed over a small bridge, through a brick and barb-wire wall, and suddenly, I could tell by the cars, and the lights, and the heavy traffic, we were in West Berlin. Through the Wall!

Somehow I had completely missed Checkpoint Charlie. But I had not escaped yet. Soon the train was back inside East Germany. It turned out that Berlin — both East and West — was inside East Germany: like an island. For the first time I understood how the Communists had blockaded Berlin from the West a few years earlier, almost starting World War III.

After more than an hour we passed through a double-fence about 20 feet high guarded by watch-towers, to finally reach the West. For the first time in nearly nine months I wasn't in a Chinese or a Communist society.

Most of the passengers had to stand up all night: out in the aisles, or crushed between knees in seating compartments, because there weren't enough trains in Western Europe. But everyone was happy. They sang songs and laughed and drank and ate all the way to Paris.

Six days too late to meet Ken at the appointed time on the Champs Elysees: the French tennis championships were already entering the second week. After this, I was supposed to be going on to the German titles with Ken. But I had decided not to go: I had to get on to London and sell the Red China pictures and story.

I bought an *International Herald Tribune* and saw that Ken was in the last sixteen of the singles. He was to play the German champion, Ingo Buding, that day for the right to play in the quarter-finals.

Via the Paris Metro I reached Stade Roland Garros and, using my *Courier-Mail* Press Pass, got inside.

Monsieur Fletcher, they said, was already playing on Court Number One. He wasn't doing well. Fletch had won the first set, and led five-two in the second, but by then the French crowd had started to get on his goat. Already five Australians were into the quarter-finals: so the French wanted a European, any European, into the last eight. It was pretty obvious they were against Ken, and for the German. When Ken finally lost the second set, he threw his racquet high over the net to the other end of the red clay court and the crowd booed and jeered.

"I've got to go up that end anyway," Ken answered back. At which the people in the overflowing stands started whistling sarcastically: something I had never heard at a sports event before.

In the third set the mocking whistles and the constant cheering for the German finally got to Fletch. He stopped playing, walked to the side of the court, looked up at the lines of spectators above — hands on his hips — and, with sweat running like a waterfall down his nose, shouted out.

I was as surprised as the French spectators by what he said:

"The bloody Germans were goose-stepping up your Champs Elysees 20 years ago, and now you're cheering the buggers."

Then, suddenly, Fletch saw me on my haunches by the side of the court. He laughed, as if he'd been caught out. While the entire crowd whistled derisively, Ken walked over and leaned heavily on the fence.

"Bad days son, bad days," he said. "The whole world's changed sides: the Frogs are barracking for the Huns. But what took you so long? I thought the Commos had got you."

Postscript

SIDDIQ'S inaugural Pakistan Airlines flight crashed en route to Peking, the third worst air disaster in world history.

THE POSTCARD to Fred and Olive from Canton did reach Brisbane. But four of my five rolls of colour film disappeared between Paris and London.

EVE OF DESTRUCTION, sung by Barry McGuire, became the number one hit song around the world later that year: "*Think of all the hate there is in Red China … ah, you don't believe we're on the Eve of Destruction.*"

OLIVE was right to be worried. The next year, 1966, China's Cultural Revolution began: all universities shut; all Chinese with links to the West purged; traditional Peking Opera banned. The Red Guards — graduates from the dreaded Young Pioneers — stormed into Macau and forced the Portuguese Governor to bow; burned the British Embassy in Peking and assaulted the staff. Reuter correspondent Anthony Grey was held hostage for the next two years. The water supply to Hong Kong was cut. However, cricket matches in the Colony continued as normal.

AUSTRALIA belatedly recognised China after Gough Whitlam was elected Prime Minister in 1972. Six years later, in 1978, China opened its borders to tourists. The next time I saw Tranquility Boulevard and Gate of Heavenly Peace Square was in 1989: this time on TV broadcasts of the Tian an men Square massacre.

IN LONDON, every Fleet Street Editor asked to see my scrapbook: the one I had posted home from Hong Kong. But publication of "Through two Curtains and a Wall" helped me land the job I wanted with Reuters. They sent me to Vietnam as a War Correspondent and, during the Tet Offensive in 1968, I witnessed the invasion of Saigon by the Viet Cong. It turned out that Chen was right. The

Americans had no hope in Vietnam without the felicity of the people.

DAVID BONAVIA, the student of Chinese language looking for a flatmate in Hong Kong, became one of England's most famous journalists in the 1980s as *The Times* correspondent in both Peking and Moscow. He wrote acclaimed books on China and Russia.

THE KOWLOON CRICKET CLUB in the 1990s expanded the six-a-side competition into an International event. The Hong Kong Cricket Club site became the underground railway's Central Station, the world's busiest. Every Sunday, thousands of Filipino women meet above this station — where the cricket club once was — to sing and dance to ghetto-blasters. These Filipino women replaced the Chinese Amahs when the Colony boomed. Hong Kong's Gross Domestic Product per capita passed Great Britain's in the 1990s.

JIM moved overseas, and eventually left his heart in San Francisco.

KEN FLETCHER remained a Hong Kong tennis rebel and thus was never again selected for Australia. At Wimbledon in 1965 he won the Mixed Doubles with Margaret Smith, and reached the final of the Men's Doubles partnering fellow rebel Bob Hewitt. But Ken was beaten in the Singles by the eventual champion, Roy Emerson, in a nail-biting finish. In 1966, Fletch went within an inch of becoming the first person since Frank Sedgman to win all three Wimbledon titles. He won the Mixed with Margaret Smith; the Men's Doubles with John Newcombe; and served for the match at 5-4 in the fifth set against Manuel Santana of Spain in the quarter-finals. I closed my eyes as two Santana lobs swirled above the Centre Court only to land on the edge of the baseline. Santana won the singles final that year in straight sets against America's Denis Ralston.

IT WAS 15 years before I returned to Hong Kong. I lost contact with Victor Sun, Ken Archer, Ah Ping, and Max Schofield. And I never got back together with the lovely Jeanette Joyce Jones.

AND STEVE DUNLEAVY: One night while writing this book, I saw on TV a familiar face wrestling a grizzly bear. It was Steve dressed in a grey suit, hair perfectly groomed, as trim and tough as ever. Three decades after Hong Kong, Steve Dunleavy had become one of the biggest names on American TV: "one of the three or four most influential journalists in the US", where his haircut is described as "doo-wop". It is said that several characters in novels and films have been based on this former Bondi boy: including the TV host in Oliver Stone's *Natural Born Killers*. Before playing that role, Robert Downey Jnr spent three days at work with Steve as part of his research.

Steve's role just had to be played by an American: who was, of course, unable to manage our unique Australian accent.